THE Self-Propelled ADVANTAGE

THE
Self-Propelled
ADVANTAGE

*The Parent's Guide to Raising
Independent, Motivated Kids
Who Learn with Excellence*

Joanne Calderwood

NEW YORK

THE Self-Propelled ADVANTAGE

The Parent's Guide to Raising Independent,
Motivated Kids Who Learn with Excellence

ISBN 978-1-61448-296-3 paperback
ISBN 978-1-61448-297-0 eBook
Library of Congress Control Number: 2012945355

Morgan James Publishing
The Entrepreneurial Publisher
5 Penn Plaza, 23rd Floor,
New York City, New York 10001
(212) 655-5470 office • (516) 908-4496 fax
www.MorganJamesPublishing.com

Cover Design by:
Rachel Lopez
www.r2cdesign.com

Interior Design by:
Bonnie Bushman
bonnie@caboodlegraphics.com

In an effort to support local communities, raise awareness and funds, Morgan James Publishing donates a percentage of all book sales for the life of each book to Habitat for Humanity Peninsula and Greater Williamsburg.

Get involved today, visit
www.MorganJamesBuilds.com.

For Tim,
Nick, Lauren, Taylor, Franklin,
Olivia, Adrienne, Lydia, and Lilienne.

TABLE OF CONTENTS

PREFACE

I would like to take a moment to thank you for purchasing *The Self-Propelled Advantage*. Not only have I tried to make its contents as informative and helpful to you as I possibly can, but I've also provided an intimate and personal glimpse into the very structure of my family. You now have a front-row seat for the unveiling of one family's educational search-and-rescue mission.

We are just a normal family of ten. We have great days, and we have the occasional tell-me-why-I-got-out-of-bed-this-morning days. Either way, our lives have been simplified over the past fourteen of our eighteen home-educating years by choosing to educate our children with a revolutionary model of learning that has yielded amazing results for our family.

I can honestly say that as a home-educating mom of eight kids, the hardest part of my day is getting up in the morning. Because my children are self-teaching, self-motivated, and self-confident, they are able to do their schoolwork without me. I am free to run a home business and manage other aspects of our lives. I can't tell you the last time I washed dishes or cleaned up the house. I am responsible for my stuff, and I rely on my children to do their share of the housekeeping and chores around the house. For the most part, they work with excellence. (We all have a bad day here and there, right?) Excellence is the expectation; consequently, it is the norm.

It wasn't always this way. In fact, I wish I'd had the opportunity to read *Self-Propelled* before my first child was born. Had I known then what I know now, I would have enjoyed motherhood so much more because I would have had the confidence to give more educational responsibility to my children in their elementary school years. Instead, as a young mother I imposed on my children the classroom model of education where I was the teacher and they did what I said, when I said to do it. I corrected all of their work, testing and quizzing their little brains out. The classroom method is basically student micromanagement, and it yields very little in the way of joy in the journey for either parents or student. But I live and learn.

My children and young adults have benefitted enormously from the freedom to become self-propelled students and, in fact, self-propelled individuals. My family's journey into self-propulsion began accidentally, but your family's journey can begin on purpose.

The Power of a Parent

As a parent, you possess the amazing ability to mold and shape other human beings. It's amazing and just a little bit unsettling to think how our attitudes and actions influence our children, isn't it? I like to say that we are what we teach, and we teach what we are. Think about your own upbringing for just a minute. Can you see how—in your own life—you are a product of the very things your parents were passionate about? For example, my musician parents are passionate about music; consequently, I grew up studying music, playing instruments, and singing. I paid my way through college partly via music scholarships. As a result, almost all of my children are musical. If I go back another generation, I can see how my grandparents and their interests determined, in part, who my parents are today.

My husband, Tim, grew up with a focus on sports and athletic pursuits as a direct result of his family's passion for exercise and sports. All of my children enjoy sports and are very athletic, and I have definitely made strides in that direction myself due to my husband's influence, which is built upon *his* family's influence on him. My children are directly and indirectly affected by the attitudes and actions of their parents, their grandparents, their great-grandparents, and so on. Your children are also products of your attitudes and actions, those of your parents, those of your grandparents and your great-grandparents, and so on. It's fascinating to consider.

What things in your life are you passionate about? How have your kids picked up on those things and carried them into their own lives? Your interests and the things that you are passionate about will likely be passed down to your grandchildren in some form or other. Pretty cool, isn't it?

The same is true of our *attitudes:* we most definitely pass these on to our children. Our attitudes are influenced by the attitudes of our parents in some way. What were your parents' attitudes about your education? How does that affect your view of your children's education? Moreover, how does that affect your children's view of their education? If bad educational experiences are lurking in our backgrounds and affecting our thinking, a negative attitude toward school and education could be the outgrowth in our children. The opposite is also true. If we as parents are excited to learn new things, our children are likely to be inspired by learning as well.

Have you ever thought about how your attitudes about education are reflected in your children's attitudes about education? How can you influence their attitudes for the best and then channel those positive attitudes into behaviors that propel your children forward, with excellence, into an exciting and promising future? That is precisely what you will learn in the pages of this book.

The Greatest Choice You Will Ever Make

The fact that we as parents have the ability to influence our children in every facet of their lives is something I'm sure you don't take lightly. As a parent, you have the ultimate control over your child. You make decisions every day based upon your philosophy of how children should be raised. Your philosophy is reflected in the choices you make for your kids in areas such as diet and exercise, for example, and in the not-so-basic choices such as how children should be put to bed at night. One of the more complex choices you'll make for your child is education: you are the one who has the authority to decide how your child will be educated. *The educational model that you choose for your child will affect the course of his or her entire life.*

It is a fact that a child's formal education does not need to be separated from his home life. This runs contrary to the classroom model of education, where the child leaves the home for the majority of his childhood years and consequently is outside of his parents' sphere of influence for years and years. Excellence in education does not require a child to leave home. A parent does not need to give up control over a child's environment in order to educate him.

A parent doesn't need superpowers in order to home educate. I am a home-educating mom, but I don't have to know calculus. The self-propelled model of education doesn't require a parent to be a member of Mensa. If you have ever felt intimidated by the thought of home educating your child or children, may I assure you that you are already equipped by the fact that you know and love your child more than anyone else on the planet does? Teaching your child to read and write and perform the basic operations of mathematics is a privilege. You don't *have* to; home education means you *get* to.

In our society today, public and private schools are the primary vehicles used to deliver education to the populace. Both use the classroom model to teach groups of children together at one time. I'll be examining both the classroom model and the home-education model in the pages of this book, and I'll be providing parents of children in both the classroom and at home with strategies for raising their kids to be self-propelled. But I have a bias toward home education for a couple of reasons, one of the basic ones being that it is the method that currently provides the best environment for becoming self-propelled. Home education incubates the self-propelled student, whereas classroom education holds him back in comparison.

For Home Educators and Non-Home Educators Alike

Students who are self-motivated and purpose-driven are like the cream in a bucket of farm-fresh milk: they rise to the top. They can go wherever they choose to go in life. Self-motivated children thrive in the public, private, and home-education realms. Most often they are raised by loving, involved parents, although some children must fight against the grain to achieve their success because they lack parental support. *Loving, involved parents educate their children in public schools, in private schools, and in the home.* Each model of education contains parents who care deeply about their children and their children's educational processes; theirs are the children who will thrive anywhere.

Making sure your child is in the best learning environment possible is one of your primary jobs as a parent. While I will be discussing the merits of education at home, I do not believe that home education is the answer for every family. I do believe that in most cases, where there is the will to home educate, there is a way to home educate. But there simply is no one-size-fits-all way to educate children.

While not all parents want to home educate, parents (worth their salt) do want the very best for their children. If you don't think you want to go the home-education route, please hang in there with me. Parents *can* raise self-propelled children regardless of where the learning happens—be it in a classroom or in the home. In this book I present concrete ways for parents of private- and public-schooled children to work toward developing self-propelled learners. I leave you to make your own decision about what is best for your child. At the end of most chapters of this book, you will find a Parent's Corner containing things children can do in order to gain the self-propelled advantage while in a classroom environment. If your child is in such an environment, you can enhance and build on the education he is currently receiving by modifying your mindset, enabling your child to modify his, and plugging in the handful of strategies I'll be giving you.

The model of education that you choose for your child will hopefully be selected after much thought, soul-searching, and careful research. It is my hope that in the pages of this book, you will find valuable information to help you in making the all-important decision of which educational model to choose according to what best meets the needs of your family. May you have courage to make a change in your child's current educational environment should you deem it necessary.

I am excited about sharing with you the three-pronged secret that will propel your student down the road of self-discovery and ultimately into a world that will be blessed by his gifts and abilities. I hope you'll happily discover that you *can* raise lifelong learners who love to learn independently and who do so with passion and excellence as you begin to follow the simple steps to implement the strategies that we will explore together.

May your child become joyfully self-propelled: motivated, confident, and successful in whatever he or she pursues in life.

INTRODUCTION

When I speak about my passion, which is teaching parents how to raise self-propelled children, I inevitably get asked about the results that the Calderwood family has achieved—for good reason. Honestly, why would you care at all about what I have to share if I do not have out-of-the-ordinary results to back up my words?

For credibility's sake, I'd like to share with you some of the exceptional educational outcomes we have had in our home. Before I do, though, let me share my belief that all children are gifted, not just some. Although not all children are academically gifted, the vast majority of children do possess the ability to excel academically—but for one reason or another, they never reach their potential. Why? There are several reasons, but one of the biggest factors in the growth and maturity of the child is his parents. That is just a fact of nature. A child is born into a family, and the configuration of that particular family will mold and shape the child. Sometimes parents lack the skill, the knowledge, or (sadly) the inclination to help their children excel. After all, we weren't magically provided with user manuals when our kids were born, were we? It is a somewhat scary fact of life that we as parents determine, in large part, the success of our children. There is no denying that the home environment will have a profound effect on the educational outcome of each child within it. How is this so?

Think of an acorn: an ordinary, smallish seed packed with potential. If an acorn falls into the proper kind of soil and receives enough sunlight, water, and nutrients, it will grow into a spectacular tree over time. Children are akin to acorns in that within their young frames reside energy (which we parents wish we had), curiosity, and the potential for reaching the highest of heights. If nurtured in a caring environment, built up with praise and rewards, conditioned to understand right and wrong, and given the soil of a loving home, the child will put down strong roots that will uphold him throughout his life.

Your child comes to you packed with potential. How you nurture that child—how you guide, discipline, educate, love, and honor your child—will in large part determine who he becomes.

Two things I am sure of: your family is unique, and your children are gifted. The joy of parenting is discovering the specialness of each of our children. While your family's configuration is undoubtedly different from mine, our goals as parents are most likely very similar. We want to raise children who make wise decisions in all aspects of their lives, including, but not limited to, their health, friendships, education, relationships, vocations, and money.

My husband and I desire to train our children's hearts first and foremost, and then the educational pieces of the puzzle will fall into place. What do I mean by training our children's hearts? I simply mean training children in how to behave and how to relate as a family. These are primary skills that children need in order to live peaceably—in the family initially, and then with others in society at large. If you do not have your children's hearts, if they don't know how to behave to your standards or respect you and other family members, the educational aspects of life will most likely be burdensome and wearying to both you and your children.

While the goal of *Self-Propelled* is to enable you to confidently teach your children how to teach themselves, another perhaps more important goal is to highlight the all-important relationship between parent and child. It is the early behavior formation in the child that sets the stage for future self-teaching success. Then, armed with the ability to self-teach, kids will go further faster in the realm of education and in the realm of real life. They will have more self-confidence and will develop a yes-I-can mindset which is invaluable to the reaching of their potential.

I'd like to stress that my children are normal kids. They are not freakishly studious, and they are not perfect. Neither are their parents. But what my kids *have* had is the advantage of self-learning. Self-learners are privileged. They have been in the driver's seat of their education for years, and they do not do their work for their parents' sakes. They have been given the gift of trust coupled with expectations. They are working at their own pace for the purpose of their own education. Motivation, diligence, and a sense of responsibility are three of the major benefits to self-learning which have given my children an edge. They can do the same for your children.

How Our First Four Students Earned Free College Educations

I promised at the beginning of this not-very-brief introduction that I would highlight some of the more outstanding achievements of my kids as a little foretaste of the advantages that self-propelled students have. What I initially want to share with you begins with our oldest son, Nick, taking the ACT exam for fun as a high school freshman. When one takes a College Board exam, one has to wait for the results to come back, right? These results happened to come in the mail while Nick's grandparents (both teachers) were visiting. This was way back in 2003 before scores were posted online.

I will never forget that afternoon when Nick stood in the dining room with his test results, an unopened envelope, in his trembling hand. I watched him tear open the envelope and saw a puzzled look cross his face. His grandfather, a former teacher and guidance counselor, looked over Nick's shoulder as I sort of pushed my way in to glimpse the paper. I took a look at the composite score at the bottom of one of the columns and exclaimed, "You got 35 out of 36!"

I know I scared the poor boy, but a wide grin took over his usually self-controlled demeanor. I was proud that his grandparents were there to share in the celebration. Nick, on the other hand, was mad at himself for missing eight questions on the exam.

Obviously, this was the first College Board exam any of my children had ever taken, and the results were pretty good. But were they a fluke? Could Nick pull off more spectacular results? The answer is yes, he could, and he did. He is actually a perfect scorer on the SAT, scoring a perfect 1600 during his senior year.

Nick's other accolades during the high school years include being a National Merit Scholarship Finalist and being a finalist in the prestigious Presidential Scholar Award, which is presented by the U.S. Department of Education. I never knew there was such a thing as a Presidential Scholarship Award until we received an envelope from the Department of Education, which actually scared the fire out of me as a home-educating mom. Why were they sending anything to our house? What kind of trouble could we possibly be in with the U.S. Department of Education? Little did I know, it was quite an honor for Nick to be the recipient of this particular envelope!

Nick also graduated as valedictorian of his class of 1,044 seniors via our umbrella school. If you are new to the world of home education, an umbrella school is an entity in which a family can enroll and which requires attendance reports and semester grades to be turned in, among other things, by the parents in order to give a dimension of accountability. Being with an umbrella school gives us additional support, although the availability of and necessity for them varies from state to state.

Nick was recruited by Harvard, Yale, Princeton, and many other Ivy League schools and non-Ivy League schools. He was admitted to all colleges to which he applied, finally choosing Belmont University in Nashville, Tennessee, as his school of choice. He was awarded a hefty merit scholarship from Belmont along with several other merit scholarships and grants. In May of 2011, Nick graduated with honors and a degree in music business. He enjoyed a varied social life in college as well, in case you are wondering about socialization. (That was a joke.) He will be attending law school in the fall of 2012 and currently is going through the application process.

Let's move on to Lauren, child number two. Lauren was also a National Merit Scholarship Finalist, and she regularly scored in the ninety-ninth percentile on her College Board exams as well. She graduated from high school in May of 2008, tenth in her class of 1,049 students, and also had her choice of colleges to attend. She chose Lee University, where she is currently a senior majoring in English with a writing emphasis. It is interesting to note that Lauren receives several thousand dollars *cash back* each semester as a student at Lee as a result of her highest SAT test score, which was a 1450/1600. Her ACT score of 32 included a perfect 36 score on the writing section. Lauren is literally being paid to attend college, and she is very thankful for the opportunity. She received an Outstanding Freshman English Student award her very first semester and has been a tutor to her peers in numerous subjects including college algebra, a subject she didn't feel was her area of expertise in high school.

Taylor, child number three, is currently attending Lee University as a premed major. He is a sophomore, and he is very much enjoying the challenges of advanced math and science. He won the same academic scholarships that Lauren won, and he also *earns cash back* as a college student. He was a National Merit

Scholarship Commended Student in high school. After much test taking, Taylor scored an impressive 1530/1600 on his last SAT, assuring him of the all-important scholarships I mentioned previously. His score included a perfect score of 800 on the critical reading section. He was also the valedictorian of his high school class of 919 seniors.

My most recent student to reach high school graduation is Franklin. While Franklin is an outstanding student as well, his interests lie more in the realm of sports. I will share more about his college selection process in another chapter, as it was quite different from that of the first three kids. Franklin scored a 1280 on his SAT and a 28 on the ACT, good enough to be awarded the scholarship money he needs to attend the University of Tennessee in Knoxville. Franklin graduated in 2011, eighteenth in his senior class of 942 students.

Believe it or not, my husband and I have yet to fork over any money to a university for the education of our first four high school graduates other than the room deposit fees their freshman years, which aren't covered by scholarship money (darn). Yes, my high school graduates had to earn their respective scholarships, but to them it seemed pretty simple because they naturally utilized the three elements we will discuss in *Self-Propelled.*

Some folks may be appalled that I would freely share my kids' test scores. In my particular arena, however, it is necessary to divulge that kind of info as proof that being self-propelled bears good fruit all around. Please know that this information is carefully provided to you with no intent but to illustrate a point: self-propelled kids test well. Also, please note that high test scores are not the goal; they are simply the outgrowth of the system of education we have adopted. Winning scholarship money for college, however, is a goal that can be reached as a result of high test scores. I just thought you might like to know that self-teaching kids generally test well because they are used to thinking on their own each and every day.

So far, my four oldest self-learning students have made the college transition easily and with distinction. Self-learners are often better prepared than their peers to make that important educational transition from high school to college because they are not dependent upon their professors to spell everything out for them. They work well on their own, and they are motivated to not just do *well,* but to do their very *best.* They have the confidence to dissect a problem and to develop a solution on their own. How did they get that way? That is precisely what I will be sharing with you in the pages of this book.

Self-learning is a lifelong gift we give to our children: however, there are other, more important gifts we give to them. That's right: education is *not* the most important thing in my home. What could be more important than my children's education? The answer, as I will share, is actually the first—and most important—element of the self-propelled advantage.

Being a parent is the most important job I will ever do. I believe that with my whole heart. If you are a parent, you have no higher calling than to be a protector, teacher, and nurturer to your children. Their futures depend upon you, which can be a very unsettling thought, can't it? It is a beautiful and awe-inspiring thing to be a parent. Scary. Did I mention scary? It is scary as well. We are all afraid at one time or another that we are ruining our kids, aren't we? Although I cannot guarantee your results with your own children, I can say that if you are diligent in implementing the three core elements of the self-propelled advantage, your children will absolutely amaze you in how far they go, both in their learning and in reaching their post–high school goals. Of course, not all kids want or need to go on to college following high school graduation, but students will have the college option open to them—along with many other options—as a result of following the three elements you will be learning about in the pages of this book.

Read on to find out *what* these elements are, *why* you would want to use them in the first place, and *how* to get your kids on the road to self-motivation, self-confidence, self-learning, self-control, and ultimately, success in life.

CHAPTER 1

EXCELLENCE IN MOTION

Tell me and I forget. Teach me and I remember. Involve me and I learn.
—Ben Franklin

As you are undoubtedly aware, it is not perceived as normal to have children who work independently and with excellence. Why not, I ask? Why isn't excellence the norm? The answer to this question is multifaceted, to be sure. Today's youth are seen as a troubled lot who struggle with having even a basic desire for education, let alone excellence in learning. Ah, but that is the problem right there. Education and learning are two different things. Education is something one supposedly gets by attending school. Supposedly, by going through twelve or thirteen years of school, one becomes educated. Education is compulsory; learning is something one does willingly. You can lead a student to and through education, but you can't make him learn, as many a teacher can attest.

A student who desires to learn is obviously more likely to become educated than one who lacks the desire. But does having the desire to learn mean that one *will* learn? Not necessarily. I have had the desire to learn while still failing to do so, and I suspect I am not the only one. Other times, I have not had the desire to learn, but I've learned anyway (humanities classes in college come to mind) because I could see the big picture and how learning something I didn't really want to learn would benefit me in the long run. I think that is called *maturity*, something we don't all have when we are in our high school years. I'm still not sure how four semesters of humanities enriched my life, but I benefited because by successfully completing the classes, I was able to get my degree.

Sometimes we simply learn to jump through the hoops put in front of us, don't we? If you have a high school diploma, and especially if you hold any sort of degree, you know all about jumping through the educational hoops held out for you by The System! Our educational system in America is like a checklist: if you do this, this, and this, then you'll earn a diploma. You don't even have to know more than about 65 percent of what is placed before you in order to earn a degree. For example, what do you call a medical student who gets a D on his final exam? Doctor! Would you want to hire a doctor who only learned enough to get by in med school? I wouldn't either. I want to be seen by a doctor who is passionate about learning with excellence and passes on his expertise in the form of excellent care. I don't want a doctor or surgeon who barely made the grade.

Not everyone is cut out to be a doctor, just as not everyone is cut out to be a mechanic. Both have something in common, however. Both need a strong foundation in the basics: reading, writing, and math. The first grader who is able to master the basics with excellence will go on to second grade with confidence. At the same time, the first grader who fails a subject will carry that failure and the resulting educational gaps into second grade. If somehow there was a way to ensure that all children totally understood each concept that was presented to them each day in the classroom, success could be built upon success. Sure, we each have our own particular areas of interest, and generally our areas of interest are the subjects we find easiest to master. I loved English when I was in school. I loved reading. Math, however, was a challenge. I was just a young student when I began to experience failure in math, and failing to learn basic math concepts in elementary school still haunts me as an adult. I'll fill you in on that shortly.

There are definite reasons for failing to learn. Oftentimes students want to learn, but for one reason or another they fail to. A lot of times it is not the students' fault; it is the fault of our educational system. For example, I was educated in the public school system. I always thought that I had received a good education, until years later when I finally began to learn percentages, fractions, and decimals right along with my own elementary school children because I never learned these well when I was their age and in public school. Because of my embarrassing deficiency, I still use a calculator to do percentages, or I ask my husband or kids for aid in the event that a calculator isn't handy. Indeed, there was a huge gap in my mathematical education because I didn't really "get it" when fractions, decimals, and percentages were originally presented in my childhood years, but I was too scared to speak up back then. I suffered along in failure, embarrassed and ashamed. Teachers didn't have time back then to make sure every student in the class understood every concept to an A level before moving on to the next lesson. Come to think of it, they still don't have time. Bold kids may ask for help, but I was not a bold second grader.

The Startling Truth

As odd as it may sound, the job of teachers in schools is not to make sure that every child learns but that every child has the *opportunity to learn*. There is a huge difference. As a former teacher, I am well aware of the difference. Teachers lack the time to ensure that all students learn to an A level or even a B or C level. They present material as well as they can, throw it out there and hope it sticks, that students will absorb it. Some will and some won't. And the class moves on.

Sure, I had the *opportunity* to learn fractions, percentages, and decimals in elementary school, but I didn't receive the kind of tutoring that would enable me to learn them. Perhaps I just was not developmentally ready to learn that stuff at the time it was initially presented. Children don't all magically mature at the same time. This is a well-known fact. So why do we mass educate? "I'm sorry you didn't learn the material in the time allowed, but we have to move on now." Isn't that what a teacher intimates every time he or she goes on to a new lesson while knowing full well that there are kids in the classroom who haven't mastered the previous day's material yet? Time marches on.

That is precisely what happened to me in second grade. I was sick and missed a few days of school, and when I came back, all the kids in the class but me knew how to do fractions and decimals and percentages on a second-grade level. I was lost. Of course, I was still in the dark about fractions, decimals, and percentages in third grade and fourth grade. Middle school didn't get any easier, and neither did high school. My math failure haunted me, and I kept it hidden as much as possible. Because I had cracks in my foundation, so to speak, I just figured I was bad at math . . . and had been ever since second grade. Thus went my relationship with mathematics for the remainder of my school years.

Failure at such a young age can spoil you for life. Failure should not be part of a second grader's vocabulary! It wasn't that I was stupid or didn't have the ability to learn fractions and decimals, but I'd missed the boat, and the class had moved on without me.

Sometimes a student's failure to learn can be traced to a new concept not being presented to him in a way that he can understand. Other times, a young mind simply may not be ready to grasp certain complex or abstract concepts when the phonics book says he should. Young children especially need to be given time to grow into learning. While I may have floundered in math at times, I was a great reader. When you were in elementary school, were you and your classmates split up into reading groups? You know, the Aardvarks, the Beavers, and the Cubbies—or some other such groups designed to camouflage the fact that some kids were better readers than others? Come on, the Cubbies knew they were in the lowest group, and I guarantee it didn't help their confidence or love for reading to be in the bottom reading group. Why do we do that to kids? Well, teachers need some way to group children, don't they? Once again, children do not mature intellectually at the same rate and speed, yet we pack them into a classroom and hope for the best.

If teachers could be empowered to take any and all necessary time to work with those students who are struggling and to reteach the material as much as is required, or even to wait to present complex concepts to those children who are not intellectually ready to learn them just because the curriculum says they should be, failure to learn could be obliterated in the classroom. But teachers can't possibly take the time to do that day in and day out, even though they may want to. It just can't happen in the classroom model of education, so failure happens instead. Children fail, become unmotivated, and soon become labeled as this or that. Without intervention from his parents or a teacher who *does* have time to devote to his need for extra help, such a student is likely to develop a negative attitude about school along with a negative attitude about himself.

When you think about it, not much has changed in our educational system over the past seventy-five years or so. Something is broken and needs to be fixed. We all are aware of the problems, but nobody seems to be able to come up with a way to fix them. Sure, some students excel in a classroom setting, but even astute students end up with gaps in their education somewhere along the line. How can failure be obliterated and excellence become the norm? In the classroom, it is a challenge, and there is no one-size-fits-all solution. *However, with the self-propelled model of education, students cannot fail without the failure being turned into success, and excellence becomes a natural, unrushed progression.*

Educational success cannot be built upon unresolved failure. Success is built upon success.

Do you have gaps in your own learning from not completely understanding concepts in reading, language, writing, or math in the early years of your education? As you will see shortly, gaps are totally eliminated with the self-propelled model of education. If that's not exciting, I don't know what is!

Goals and Success

At this juncture, it may be wise to define what I mean when I use the word *success*. A student is successful when he reaches his goals. We all have goals, well-defined or not. Perhaps my goal is to keep from eating ice cream today, and another one is to clean the basement someday. Both are goals: one is short term, and the other is long term. The higher I set my expectations, the harder I have to work to satisfy them. If I'm going to finish cleaning the basement tomorrow night, I have to work harder than if my goal is to finish cleaning the basement by the end of next month. The higher the bar is set, the harder the work at hand, and the more determination required to meet the goal.

The thing about goals is they are oh-so-subjective. Think about the marathon runner who reaches the finish line first. Is he successful? That depends on what his actual goal was in running the race. If he is out to beat his personal best time, and he wins the race without doing so, he will not have reached his goal even though he won the race. The guy who finishes last does not necessarily look like a winner, does he? Yet, if his goal was simply to finish the race, then he was certainly successful. If his goal was to beat somebody, anybody, across the finish line, then he did not meet his goal. See what I mean about goals being utterly subjective?

Do I have to reach my goals in order to be successful? Not necessarily. You see, sometimes we have to revise our goals along the way. Sometimes we set them too high, and reality lets us know it. Lofty, unreachable goals are no fun. They result in major frustration. When setting goals, I reserve the right to adjust them as necessary in order for them to actually be reachable and not become stumbling blocks. Some folks never set goals out of fear that they will fail to reach them. I would much rather have to adjust my goals because I set them too high than not have any goals at all. I love a challenge, but I don't enjoy being challenged beyond reason. Do you set goals for yourself, even if they are just mental goals? We all have goals, whether we know it or not. Maybe your goal is not to have any goals (just to prove me wrong). It's still a goal. Goals can be very motivating things to put in place, and they can be very motivating for our children, especially when we allow them to set their own. We'll talk a lot more about goal setting and motivation as we go along.

What are some good goals when it comes to educating children? Here is a short list of the personal goals I had when I began home educating little Nicholas at age four:

1. Present new information in various forms: workbooks, readers, texts, etc.
2. Test when necessary to make sure information is learned to an A level.
3. Move on to the next thing, letting my child's readiness be the guide.

Because I had a degree in elementary education and had taught school before having my own children, it never dawned on me that children would enjoy learning if left to themselves. Isn't that a strange thing to say? But it's true. In the classroom, children had to be pushed and pulled along for the most part. In my experience as a mom who was home educating her child, however, I found that Nicholas moved very, very quickly through his lessons because he could go at his own speed. He didn't need to wait for the class to finish up; he *was* the class! Nor did he know that he should not be enjoying this thing called school. Ah! But that was the difference! It was *not* school; it was learning at home. We weren't up at the crack of dawn, gulping down breakfast, scrambling to find matching shoes, and running out the door to catch the school bus, separated from everything related to family.

Instead, learning was a natural thing done in the comfort of our own home along with family, on a schedule that worked well for us, not for an entire school system. What a cool thing it was to be able to tailor learning to my student! What an improvement over group learning! I wasn't just providing the *opportunity* for learning; I was there to ensure that learning took place, the learning of all the subject matter, not just 75 or 88 percent of it, but *all* of it. And then we moved on, directed solely by my son's desire to learn—a desire which was voracious.

Why would I want to send my child to a school when he could have such fun learning at home and could move at his own speed? I simply did not want to miss out on time spent with him either. If I put him on a school bus, that meant forty fewer hours per week I would have to spend with him, times thirty-six weeks in a year. That equals 1,440 hours apart per year. Multiply that times twelve years, not counting kindergarten, and that comes out to 17,280 hours—roughly three full years of his life spent elsewhere. Yikes! Why did I have a child only to entrust him to someone else to influence, mold, and shape? That didn't make any sense. I knew my son could learn better at home than he could anywhere else. For now, home education was for us. We'd worry about high school later.

Additionally, at age four, Nicky had been diagnosed with Type 1 diabetes. This was quite a shock, of course. And years ago, there was no way to accurately test blood sugar at home as there is now. Another reason we decided to keep Nicky at home was that we knew we could keep a better eye on his health challenges than any school nurse could. If your child has chronic health issues, learning at home is certainly a wonderful option to explore.

Thus began our home-education adventure.

How I Lost My Mind

While this book is not meant to be a treatise on home education, I want to encourage you, if you are at all interested in teaching your children at home, that it is not only possible to educate your children with excellence at home, but that you can actually teach them better than anyone else can if you have the desire to do so. How? By teaching them to teach themselves and to not be satisfied until they understand lessons to an A level. How did I discover this well-kept secret? Let's take a minute and revisit the winter of my discontent.

It was November. My fifth child, Olivia, turned two years old. Nicky was eight, and Lauren was seven. Taylor was five. Frankie was ready to start kindergarten at age four, and I was feeling rather overwhelmed. I should mention that I was also pregnant with my sixth baby, and I was lying on the couch most days feeling rather nauseous. At this point in time, I really didn't care if the children learned anything or not on any given school day ever again. It was Operation Survival at our house.

Up until this point, however, I was the quintessential teacher of my children. I mean, I followed the lesson plans in the teacher's editions of books, taught my children together in a group for history and science, and hosted Math Time at the kitchen table together first thing each day so I could look over all my children's shoulders and make sure they were progressing well. They all read out loud to me, individually, so that I could be sure they were progressing in their reading even though Nicky was in third grade but was reading on an eighth-grade level. I played teacher because that was all I knew to do. I really didn't ever think that a third grader might be capable of working independently. That is, until I discovered that I was just too sick to care.

You may chuckle, but it was true. I had reached maximum burnout. At that point, I instructed Nicky and Lauren just to do their work on their own and bring it to me to check. Then I began letting them check their own work and showing it to me when it was checked. I had them tell me what they had missed, if anything, and we would discuss it. They were quite happy with this newfound freedom to simply do their work, check their work, and then go outside to play. And I realized that because they were both good readers, they didn't need me to read directions to them and oversee everything they did.

As my children began to work independently out of necessity, I began to like it. My desire to oversee and control had been snuffed out by nausea and exhaustion, and when that happened, my two older children began to work ahead, accomplishing more than what I asked them to do because it was fun for them not to have to wait for me to go over things first before diving into their work.

Late in that school year, I decided to test Nicky and Lauren just to see if they were on grade level. I administered the 1970 California Achievement Test, a series of tests that were more advanced than other standardized tests at the time, and I mailed off the tests to wait for the results. The results blew me away.

Nicky, in fourth grade, scored at the eleventh-grade level in reading comprehension and in seventh grade in vocab. He scored at the ninth-grade level in math concepts and problems. In language, he scored in the thirteenth grade in usage and structure; eighth grade in mechanics, and sixth grade in spelling. (Incidentally, thirteenth grade is the equivalent of college freshman level.)

Lauren, who was in the third grade, scored in the sixth- and seventh-grade levels respectively in reading vocabulary and comprehension. In mathematics, she scored in mid–seventh grade; and in language, she was at the eighth-grade level in mechanics and the seventh-grade level in usage and structure, as well as in spelling.

Keep in mind that this was back in the late 1990s before computer games, cell phones, and Wii took the place of reading in many homes. We had spent a lot of time together at home, aside from going to the library regularly and attending some local playgroups. In fact, back then I tried to see how many days in a row I could stay at home. Wow! That seems so odd according to today's go-go-go standards. Consequently, the kids read a *lot*. They played outside together, and they found creative things to do on the dairy farm where we lived at the time. (We were not dairy farmers, incidentally, just renters, but I now have quite a lot of respect for dairy farmers.)

What I discovered was that my kids could do more without me than they could do when they had to wait for me to tell them what to do next in their schooling. Because Tim and I knew their hearts, we could trust them to do what they were supposed to be doing. But they surprised us by going even beyond what was expected because they enjoyed learning! At the same time, their independence gave me the time and presence of mind to care for the little ones who needed me full-time.

Soon I decided that I needed some sort of record-keeping system so that the kids could keep track of what they were learning. What resulted was something that we still produce to this day: *The Home School Student Planners.* These portfolios became my direct line to my students' accomplishments day in and day out. If I wanted to know what the older kids were learning, I would ask them for their planners, and I could then quiz them on what they recorded as having learned. They were in charge of recording what they did each day, not me. I put the burden of learning squarely on their shoulders at this point. The older children were trusted to record grades in certain subjects in their planners. I still needed to be sitting down with the younger children daily, helping them with their lessons, but that was manageable since the older children were now independent.

Days turned into years. Soon I was designing *The Essential High School Planners* so that I had a way of tracking progress throughout the high school years. I also hit on a system of short-term goal setting that involved the student in setting nine weeks' worth of goals for himself. I would look over the goal sheet contained in the planner with each child at the beginning of each quarter and then again at the end of each quarter, praising my students for the work they had accomplished. I orally asked for math scores at dinner every night. The kids were quick to let me know if they ever hit a wall in their work, and their dad or I would help them over the hump until they were confident they understood the lesson—but that happened rarely, even in the high school years.

Speaking of the high school years, I remember visiting a family with ten children one summer before my oldest student went into ninth grade. I was more than a little nervous about how I would be able to handle teaching high school at home. The mom of these ten children had graduated several of her kids at this point, and one was a nursing student. I remember asking her how she was able to teach her daughter biology at home. Did they do lab work? Did they dissect fetal pigs on their dining room table? Mom looked a little puzzled, and then she plainly stated, "I gave her the biology book." Oh. Okay. Here was another mom who expected her children to learn independently, and apparently self-learning worked well in high school. I was elated!

I discovered that with just a little oversight, the high school kids could work from a textbook with excellence, just as they had in middle school. High school was scary no more! I would look over their work from time to time, question them on material they had covered sometimes a month prior, and they would pass with flying colors. Why? Because they were expected to, number one. And secondly, learning was interesting when they were given the freedom to read and study on their own. I just let them go as long as they could answer my questions when I was checking their planners from time to time.

Keep in mind that I was working daily with my younger children up through grade three, allowing them more and more independence as their reading skills dictated until they gradually reached the point where they could work independently. This is certainly a process, and it is not the same for each child. All children grow and develop on their own timetables. Learning everything to an A level was just expected. I mean, why study something and not learn it well? That was my attitude, which translated to my children through the setting of expectations.

After we had been practicing self-teaching for a little while, it used to be that at the beginning of each and every school year, I would ask the kids if they would like to circle the wagons, so to speak, and study history or science together this year for a change. They would each politely decline my offer, insisting that they preferred to work on their own again this year. Now I've stopped asking. In fact, I still remember the feeling I had the day I realized that my kids really didn't need me in order to learn. It was a combination of euphoria coupled with gripping fear. Did they really not need me? Were they really learning without me? Was I ruining my kids by being as hands-off as I possibly could be in order to care for the younger children?

The answer to my question came the day that Nick received his ACT scores in the mail while his grandparents were visiting. The moment when Nick opened that envelope will forever live in my memory because self-teaching was vindicated that day. Yes, Nicholas could teach himself. No, I hadn't stunted his educational growth. What a sense of relief washed over me!

We were all amazed that Nick could do so well when he was tested in areas he had yet to study, such as chemistry and biology. (He had only had general science in ninth grade when he took that test.) Ah, but here is the very point of *Self-Propelled:* kids who are given the freedom to learn independently possess the ability to think, to problem solve. Nick had spent years reading directions, studying lessons, and figuring things out on his own with excellence. The ACT presented the same kinds of challenges that he faced every day in his schoolwork, so he was up to the task of problem solving and figuring out answers, making educated guesses if necessary.

Incidentally, I asked Nick how he could possibly do so well on the ACT without having taken higher math and science yet. His answer? "Mom, the answers are all right there for you." On a multiple choice test, the answers *are* all right there, aren't they? All you have to do is figure out which one is the correct one. Oh, that I had possessed that kind of confidence in my logic skills when I was taking my exams years ago!

Benefits Beyond Education

Self-teaching provided my high schoolers with the ability to get their work out of the way each day and still have plenty of time to pursue their interests. Nick started a website entitled *Sticker Avalanche.* He began teaching himself guitar, and he landed a part-time job locally. I remember that he also began playing games such as *Wheel of Fortune* on his cell phone at that time. Before you snicker, you should know that before he went off to college, he had won over two thousand dollars in cash and prizes! One may question whether that's a good use of time. I actually asked the same question, but Nick wasn't shirking any responsibilities while winning stuff; he would play at night. Isn't that crazy? A couple thousand dollars from a cell phone? He won everything from iTunes gift cards to a pair of mountain bikes to portable DVD players and random things like GPS systems. Some of what he won he sold on eBay for cash to put toward essential items, such as books for his freshman year in college.

Taylor also cashed in on the cell-phone games jackpot opportunity. Don't think this was an easy thing for them to do, either of them. They just had the persistence and the yes-I-can attitudes that didn't allow them to fail. Within about fifteen months, the company that offered the awesome prizes began offering wimpy ones instead, but not before Nick and Taylor used their skills to win a whole lot of cool stuff due to their determination and perseverance.

Lauren, in her free time, developed a penchant for selling wholesale jewelry-making supplies on eBay as her source of income. She now has an online company, BeadBoxBargains.com, where she buys wholesale and sells at a profit.

Her secret is volume selling, and she takes customer service seriously. She knows how to treat people kindly and with respect, which has won her loyal repeat customers. Recently she discovered a Facebook app which has widened her client base tremendously and rewarded her with orders and accolades. Lauren owns a growing small business as a college student, which is amazing to me. Free tip: choose a roommate who is supportive of having shipping supplies and product supplies sitting around the room!

Did my husband and I teach our children how to do this kind of stuff? Well, sort of. We started up two different online companies over the years. One company we sold, and we still own and operate URtheMOM.com. But the kids just came up with their own ideas according to their passions, did their research, discovered things on their own, and decided how to use what they had at their disposal to develop a network of successful ventures. I know this is directly linked to their self-propelled attitudes.

Today Olivia, at age fifteen, has an online Etsy site where she sells her hand-tatted items and handmade jewelry. Her work is beautiful, and she's discovered the fun of having her own business. So the trend continues. I'm certain that my last three daughters will come up with their own outlets for creativity as well.

Experience: The Best Teacher

Perhaps now you can see that what grew out of what I thought was failure turned into something magnificent! My failure as a "teacher" enabled my children to experience a freedom in learning that led to self-motivation, self-discovery, self-confidence, repeated excellence, and the feeling of a job well done.

I learned that the classroom model of education, which was all I had known up to that point in time, actually held kids back. Group learning fails to provide much, if any, freedom in learning. In a classroom setting, children aren't trusted to read freely; they are required to write out tedious answers to questions on stuff they have just finished reading. What a chore for students to continuously have to prove that they have indeed read and comprehended the material they were asked to read and comprehend!

I remember back in elementary school how much I hated classroom reading time. I may not have been a math whiz, but I was an "advanced" reader, and oral reading day frustrated the life out of me because I was slowed down by having to listen to others read out loud when I could read the material so much faster on my own. Some classmates, who couldn't read orally as well as others, hated classroom reading because everyone would suddenly be reminded of how poorly they read aloud. It was not a good thing for any of us. So why did we do it? Because the teacher needed to grade kids on their reading ability, which to this day I think is ridiculous. Why grade young children on whether or not they can read at the same level as everyone else? If they can't read well, giving them a poor grade is not going to inspire them to suddenly read better! All it does is bring shame and a sense of failure.

With home education, the young child is allowed to explore phonics with the parent, and he proceeds at his own speed. For some children, phonics and reading come easily, and they are off and running in kindergarten or even earlier! Other children require more time and patience in developing reading skills. Neither should be judged against the other. Eventually the student will grasp phonics, and when he does, if he does not feel any sense of failure, he will be off and running as well. In fact, he will eventually catch up with the student who was reading at a younger age. A sense of failure will definitely hold a student back, stealing his motivation.

There is no shame involved at all when children are treated as individuals, and this is precisely how education in the home works. I had a child who read at age three, and I had one who didn't read well until the end of second grade. Now that they are further down the road, there is no difference between them. Both enjoy reading now. They simply read when they were ready to read. There are just some things that cannot be rushed.

The Bicycle Analogy

Now that I have given you plenty of background on how I discovered the secrets to educational excellence, it's time to state my theories more succinctly. Actually, what were previously *theories* I held are now *facts* I've gathered and placed into book form. Over the past eight years I have done seminars, offered workshops, spoken to parents on the phone, and written countless answers to e-mails from parents who have either wanted to know how to implement self-teaching or have taken the plunge and found out for themselves that self-teaching works and have wanted to share their joy with me.

So how does a child become self-propelled? The answer is *gradually* and *steadily.*

Think about how you teach a child to ride a bike. Initially, you may take your baby or toddler for rides via a child-size seat on the back of your bike. But once the child is capable of learning to ride a bike independently, you offer him his own little bike as well as support in the form of training wheels. The child rides around the garage, around the driveway, and maybe even around the block with training wheels on his bicycle. Those training wheels are what support him, what keep him upright at that stage.

You also begin to teach him the rules of the road, right? You are going to make sure that the child understands the basics of bike riding. Learning safety rules is essential. We don't expect the child to learn those on his own; we make sure he is well versed in safety and cycling rules before he is allowed to proceed to the next step. Before long, the child is ready for the training wheels to come off (probably long before *you* are ready for the training wheels to come off!).

Once the training wheels are off, the child needs to develop his own sense of balance. He has had a small taste of balance with the training wheels on, but the ultimate test comes once they come off. When the parents and child feel he is ready, off they come. How exciting! However, before the child learns to totally balance on two wheels, Mom or Dad needs to hold onto the bike seat and walk (or run) beside the child as he learns to balance on his own.

Before long, though, he is ready for you to let go. You do. He wobbles a little, but off he goes on his own. There may be a fall in the near future, but hopefully not many. You trust that he will obey the rules of the road, and you watch to be sure that he does so when he is within sight. Once he is out of sight, you have to trust him.

You begin to allow him to ride further and further from home, as you are confident that he is able to ride safely. You will make sure he is out of high-traffic areas as he begins to ride independently. He will not have the endurance yet to ride for long periods of time or to ride up long hills that require focus and greater athletic ability than he possesses initially. All that will come later with time and experience. When you let go of that bicycle seat, your child becomes truly self-propelled.

Letting Go

For parents, letting go can be a very difficult thing to do. We want to be needed. Sometimes we get in our child's way because we don't trust him to be able to balance well on two wheels once those training wheels come off, and we end up hanging on to the bicycle much longer than necessary. In doing so, we hold him back. We don't allow him to become self-propelled because we think he is not capable of riding without our help.

The same is true educationally. Because we are conditioned to think that kids need a teacher as a mediator between knowledge and their young brains, we do not trust children to learn independently. In the realm of home education, many parents *never* let go of the bicycle once the child understands the fundamental rules of the road. Here I am referring to the child's ability to read, to do basic math, and to begin developing writing skills. Some parents constantly hover over the student, checking every bit of work the student produces, or ask questions following every chapter of everything the student reads without realizing that they are not allowing the student to learn to balance on his own without help.

Wouldn't it look silly to see a mom or dad running alongside of a teenager, holding on to the seat of the ten-speed bike the teen was riding (or rather, was *trying* to ride)? Of course it would! Letting go is a scary thing for some parents to do in the educational arena of life. I understand that all too well; however, by letting go we enable our children to go further, faster than they will go if we are micromanaging their time, their studies, and their progress in every little thing accomplished in a day. Micromanaged students lack motivation and don't need to take responsibility for themselves because they know that someone else will take responsibility for them.

As parents, we are conditioned to think along the lines of the classroom model of education, which cannot guarantee our students' success. It can, however, guarantee that the individual student will be led along on the same path that every other student in the class is led along, with no opportunity to stop and enjoy the journey if he wants to or revisit an area because he wants to spend more time there before moving on.

The classroom model can also guarantee that our students learn exactly the same thing at exactly the same time as everyone else, whether they are ready or not. Isn't that comforting? No, it certainly is not! Each child is unique and is embarking upon a unique journey in life. Yes, it is important to teach children the fundamentals of reading, writing, and mathematics. But once the child can handle the basics, it is time to trust him to learn to balance. This happens little by little for most children.

Why do we think that our children can't be raised to be independent at a young age? Probably because nobody does that anymore, so we don't have a model for independence in education. Until now, that is. I would like to introduce you to three elements that together have the power to motivate, to liberate, and to propel your student into the arena of lifelong learning.

The Three Elements of the Self-Propelled Advantage

Let's go back to our bicycle analogy. Picture a bicycle, if you will. There are two wheels on our bike, and a third element is also necessary: a cyclist. In the self-propelled model, there are three elements that work together to provide balance, not only in a student's education, but also in his life. Let's take a look at each of these elements, shall we?

Self-Learning

The first element is *self-learning* or *self-teaching*. They both mean the same thing, and I will use them interchangeably as we go along. Let's call the front wheel of our bike *self-learning*. Self-learning, like a wheel, is a tool. It is just one part of the vehicle, but it is an integral part. Just as the young child gradually moves from being totally dependent on his parents to feeding himself, dressing himself, and tying his own shoes, so the young student requires time to learn independence. Children prefer independence: "I can tie my shoes by myself. I can get dressed by myself. I can make my bed by myself." "By myself" is the refrain of childhood. So it can be educationally as well.

If your student is a self-learner, it doesn't mean that you are not involved in the educational process. It means that your role has changed. Once your child can read well, instead of being his primary teacher, you take on the role of coach. If he can read and understand the directions of a math lesson, he can simply read and do his math. Eventually he can read it, do it, and check his own work. With self-learning, we cut out the middleman, so to speak. Why? Because that role isn't necessary anymore.

We don't *force* our children to work independently; we structure their environment to *allow them* to venture into the realm of educational freedom. Consequently, self-teaching children begin to take responsibility for their education much sooner than do their classroom-educated counterparts, some of whom may never take that responsibility for themselves.

Self-learning enables a child to go at his own speed, although progress is utterly dependent upon the back wheel of the bicycle in order for him to move forward. Let's take a look at the back wheel, another element of the self-propelled model.

Mastery

What constitutes the back wheel of our bicycle? The back wheel is *mastery*. What is mastery? It is simply learning every lesson completely without skipping over anything. Mastery is absorbing a concept completely and not moving on until you have a full understanding of what you have just read or experienced. It is learning every lesson to an A level. A child should learn that he is not finished with a lesson until he understands *all* of it, not just 90 percent of it or 80 percent of it or 70 percent of it.

Mastery may take days or weeks to achieve, depending upon the age of the student, his readiness to learn a new concept, and the difficulty level of the material being presented. You simply cannot rush mastery. Mastery equals excellence.

If the classroom model of education were to incorporate mastery learning, students in the classroom would not move on to the next lesson until they learned today's lessons to an A level. However, a teacher in a classroom cannot juggle the educational needs of every student. She cannot wait around or reteach material until every single child in the classroom receives an A. It is expected that some children will fail. Why is that acceptable? It is acceptable because the child was given the opportunity to learn and did not. It is the child's fault. The teacher presented the material, but the child failed to learn it in the proper time frame.

Of course, I would argue that it is *not* a young child's fault if he has not learned something that has been "taught at" him. Some children need more time and explanation than others do for assorted reasons. There is always a reason why a child does not learn. In the realm of home education, a parent has the time to find out why a child isn't learning a particular concept, and the parent can tailor the child's lessons so that he doesn't move on before mastering the material, thus avoiding gaps in the child's foundational learning as well as bolstering his confidence in his ability to learn. A child who fails in a classroom can excel at home, especially when his readiness is a consideration in the educational process.

Today, in the realm of public education, teachers have become the scapegoats for the low test scores of their students. This should not be. It is a complicated system, to be sure, but I hold that it is the parents' responsibility to see that their children succeed in the arena of public school. Too many parents expect teachers to educate their children without doing what they can and should do as parents to set expectations and reinforce those expectations in the home. What can parents do to foster mastery learning when their children are in the public school system? I'll provide some strategies in chapter 5.

If your young child is not excelling in the public or private school system, I'd be willing to bet that if he were given adequate time to absorb lessons at his own speed, and if you could be sure that he is ready to grasp a concept when it is presented, he would begin succeeding. It is very important to build success upon success, and mastery learning guarantees that the student will fully understand a lesson before he is moved along to the next one.

If you notice, I am talking about young students at the moment. There is always a reason why a student fails to learn a new concept or perform well in the classroom. The reasons that older students fail in a classroom may be different from the reasons a young child fails. Young children are more pliable, and their attitudes about learning have not had as much opportunity to be sullied in the younger years. By the time a student is in middle school and/or high school, his attitudes and thought processes have been formed much more permanently. It takes more effort to correct an older student's attitudes and behavior than it does a young student's. If we can incorporate self-teaching and mastery learning when children are young, they will enter the middle school and high school years with a yes-I-can attitude which will serve them well the rest of their lives.

Let's talk about *attitudes* here, because both behavior and attitudes are of vital importance to a student's approach to his education. Whoever said "Attitude is everything" was right on. Our attitudes shape our actions each minute of each day. While a student balances on the wheels of self-learning and mastery, he doesn't get anywhere just sitting there. In fact, it takes energy to become self-propelled. When a student expends energy to learn independently to a mastery level, he gets somewhere. He moves forward! He moves forward at his own rate of speed, well-balanced and self-propelled.

How quickly he moves along is in direct proportion to the amount of energy expended on his part, which is a reflection of his attitude about learning. If he doesn't throw himself into his work fully, he will not be balanced, and the bike is likely to simply fall over. He gets nowhere without being fully engaged. But if he is fully engaged, he can go wherever he would like to go, as fast as he would like to go.

A human being is comprised of body, mind, and spirit. We cannot separate ourselves from any of these three parts. For example, if the body is not healthy, then the mind and spirit are likely to suffer as well. Our minds—how we think—form our attitudes, which in turn form our actions. Having a healthy outlook on life, a healthy attitude toward learning, and a strong body makes for the likelihood of maximum success. Certainly we all have to work with what we've been given. There are lots of different varieties of bicycles out there: different sizes, different makes, different colors, and different models. What do they all have in common? Each possesses two wheels, which is what makes it a bicycle in the first place. The bike, however, is just a vehicle for travel. Without a rider, it stays where it was last put. We can give our students an educational vehicle comprised of the wheels of self-learning and mastery, but if their attitudes smack of indifference toward their education, they will not get anywhere. You can lead a bike to the road, but you can't make it go without a rider! Attitude is truly everything. A yes-I-can attitude is what motivates and energizes.

Quick quiz: What are two elements of the self-propelled model of education? Answer: The front wheel of the bicycle is self-learning, and the back wheel is mastery. Easy enough, right? If you missed either of these, you have not mastered the material, and you should go back and study a little more. Just kidding. Didn't you hate quizzes in school that were comprised of just one or two questions because if you missed one, you definitely weren't going to get a passing grade? Ah, the memories.

Self-learning and mastery make up the framework for educational success: together, they represent potential. They are simply tools that the motivated learner can leverage.

A skilled cyclist can travel on his bike to amazing places, but he doesn't become skilled overnight. Not only must the rider learn how to operate a bicycle, but he must also develop his own physical prowess, which is hard work. Riding a bike takes strength and balance. A serious cyclist eats well and trains for the long haul. There is discipline involved. Discipline? Sure, I can hop on my bike without the discipline of a serious cyclist, but before long I will become tired, winded, and crippled by my loudly shrieking muscles. It does take discipline to become an able cyclist. If I intend to travel very far on my bike, I will need to build both mental and physical endurance.

That leads us to another element a self-propelled student needs in order to progress, and it is a little more complicated than the other two elements. We know that a student's "bike" is made up of two major parts: self-learning and mastery. But how can a student get anywhere using just self-learning and mastery? What else does he need to have in order to get going on the educational highway that stretches out in front of him?

Self-Mastery

Perhaps the most important element of the self-propelled model of education is *self-mastery*. Defining self-mastery is pretty simple. Self-mastery is mastering one's self. Simply stated, self-mastery means controlling yourself. Self-mastery is pretty darn tough to do, isn't it? In fact, it is a lifelong process of overcoming ourselves in various areas of weakness.

Have you ever played the arcade game called Whack-A-Mole, where you have a really big, puffy, padded mallet, and in front of you are a bunch of mole holes? The object of the game is to react to the moles that intermittently pop up at you by whacking them on their little heads with the mallet before they disappear back into their holes. The problem is they sort of all pop up at you at once, sometimes out of your reach, and they tend to disappear before you can pop 'em on their little mole heads. There is no way to get them all at once.

So it goes with self-mastery at times. You think you have one area of yourself under control, and then a weak area pops up, and you address that issue, and then another area pops up, so you address that issue. Self-mastery is a lifelong process for sure, and often we must work on one area at a time, master that, and then move on to the next area. If self-mastery is hard for us as adults, how much harder is it for our children?

Ah, but here is the interesting thing: If a child grows up with good habits, he is likely to stay in that vein as an adult. It is much harder for adults to change their ways. It's the old-dog-new-trick thing. Having the expectation that our young children will do what we want them to do and govern themselves well is the secret. We cannot wait until children are teenagers to start setting expectations. It has to happen when they are young if we are to reap the fruit of good behavior, respect for others, and strong morals in the teen years.

I firmly believe it is the parents' job to teach their children lessons in self-mastery. As a matter of definition, self-mastery has to do with controlling one's self, and that means adhering to moral standards first of all. Lying, cheating, and stealing are wrong. Hurting others is wrong. It is important to raise children to respect their parents and all other authorities over them. *Having high expectations for behavior is one way we teach self-mastery.* When a student exercises self-control, self-discipline, and self-motivation, he demonstrates self-mastery. In order for a child to learn self-mastery, his parents must train his heart. I will sometimes be referring to self-mastery as *heart training* for this reason.

Self-mastery arises from one's own attitudes and expectations. If you have the attitude that you are going to get in shape no matter what, the behavior you adopt will reflect that attitude. Once that behavior becomes repetitive and you continue exercising regularly and adjusting your food intake, you *will* get in shape. Being in shape reflects an attitude, just as *not* being in shape reflects an attitude. Self-mastery occurs when you meet your expectation, your goal of being in shape. You have mastered something very difficult—a facet of yourself!

Attitudes are to behavior as expectations are to success. If you don't expect yourself to be in shape, you probably won't be. (I merely use getting in shape as one example that most of us can relate to, and one that I struggle with myself.)

Parents cannot simply talk about self-mastery; they must live it. While we have authority over our children by virtue of the fact that we are the parents, we must earn their trust and respect by having self-mastery ourselves. If we are lazy, our children will learn laziness. If telling the truth isn't important to us, it won't be important to our children. If our favorite pastime is sitting in front of a screen, guess what our children will like to do! The cool thing is that if we enjoy being outdoors, our children most likely will as well. If we like to sit and read, our children most likely will too. If we speak kindly to our spouses and children, they most likely will speak kindly to others as well. Modeling the behaviors we want to see exhibited in our children is extremely important to teaching self-mastery.

Recognizing the effect our actions have on our children is the first step towards self-improvement and self-mastery. I know that my children inspire me to do things that I should do, such as take care of my health, obey the speed limit, and return the empty grocery cart, plus other things I could confess right here if I wanted to. If I didn't have kids, I might not care as much about some things. Of course, there are seasons in life where we work on different areas of our own lives. I just want to encourage you to be teaching your children self-mastery by modeling the attitudes and behaviors that you want them to have.

Let's go back to our bicycle analogy. What is the front wheel of our bike? It is self-learning. The back wheel? Mastery. *Self-mastery* is what gives the cyclist the want-to, especially when he doesn't want to. Learning is work, isn't it? Children must learn that work can be fun and profitable, but it may not *always* be fun. Teaching them to work diligently at a task—even when they don't particularly want to be working diligently—is vital to their success in life. We'll talk at length about motivation as we go along.

Now, if a student is in a traditional classroom environment, the teacher is the one who assists with the pedaling of the bike as well as the steering of the bike. The teacher often gets in the way of forward motion, and the student can't see around the teacher. The student can only go as fast as the teacher will allow. Nor can he choose his direction. However, if the teacher or parent acts as a coach and stands out of the way while the student propels the bike, progress is once again made.

A self-propelled student ultimately will be successful in reaching the destination of his choosing. We as parents coach him along the way. Think about it: how many people hop on a bike without a destination in mind, or at least a general idea of where they are headed? Most of us don't get on a bike without knowing where we are going. So students need to know where they are headed. When we as parents help our children navigate to a specific destination, we are setting them up for success.

Our students may be learning independently, mastering their lessons as they go, but they still need our guidance. As a self-propelled student matures, the parent's role morphs from teacher to coach to mentor to—ultimately—friend and confidant in the child's adult years. A sweet fruit of our labor as parents is friendship with our grown children.

The Most Important Thing

Earlier, I stated that education is not the most important thing in my home. What could be more important than raising children who do well in their schooling? I can honestly tell you that training my children's hearts is more important to me than anything. As parents, we have the responsibility and privilege of forming in our kids the attitudes, beliefs, and morals that they will carry for years to come, perhaps for the rest of their lives. That is an enormous responsibility, is it not?

A child's home environment is the garden soil where he will put down roots. I am the gardener of the young plants that have been entrusted into my care, and I will reap what I sow. My tender plants require food and water, weeding, the right amount of sunlight and shade, fertilizer, and above all, the wisdom of a seasoned gardener in order to grow to their full potential. I may be raising various kinds of plants who will serve various purposes upon reaching maturity, but they all need the right balance of love and care. A plant can't weed itself, can it? I am charged with the job of making sure the plants have room to grow without interference from pesky weeds or insects. Fertilizing sure is a stinky job, but somebody's got to do it. Gardens are rewarding, but it sure does take a lot of time, energy, and work to raise vigorous plants.

I don't want to raise ordinary plants, do you? I don't want to raise young adults who meet ordinary standards, the status quo, if you will. My husband and I desire to raise kids whose pursuit of excellence goes beyond mere education. We want them to be self-propelled in all areas of their lives, following their God-given dreams and ambitions. Their years of formal education are not just preparation for a job; rather, these years provide opportunity to develop self-learning and mastery skills which will not only benefit them today but will give them an edge in life once they've jumped through the hoops of formal schooling. May self-mastery be a lifelong pursuit for each of us!

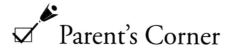

Parent's Corner

Here are some questions to stimulate thought and discussion:

1. Is excellence the norm in your home? Do your children pretty much work to the best of their ability whether they are doing chores or doing school work?

2. How are you preparing your children to be extraordinary individuals? How are you giving them an edge?

3. Do you believe that your child should be given time to learn each of his lessons to an A level before moving on to the next lesson? Is mastery really THAT important?

4. Do you want your children to be able to work independently? Do you believe it is possible for them to learn without a teacher's help?

5. What long-term goals do you have for your children?

6. What would your kids say *your* attitude is towards school and learning? (Ask them just for fun to see if you are right.)

7. How do you model self-mastery to your kids?

8. Do you believe that your children will mirror the values of those with whom they spend the most time? Who spends the most time with your kids?

9. Is it hard for you to let go of your children and let them try new things by themselves? Are there areas where you should be more hands-on with them?

10. Are your children primarily cheerful, obedient, and respectful to you and your spouse? To siblings?

CHAPTER 2

OPERATION MOTIVATION

*People who are unable to motivate themselves must be content
with mediocrity, no matter how impressive their other talents.*
—Andrew Carnegie

I love to learn; however, I don't love to learn about everything. Some things interest me, and other things do not and never will interest me. One example of the latter is chemistry. Call me shallow, but I don't care about molecules and things that I cannot see. What about you? What sort of thing would be torture for you to do or study? Do you know why you dislike it so much? I know precisely why I am not interested in chemistry to this day: chemistry and I had a bad relationship in high school. I'll reveal why later in this chapter.

What do you enjoy learning and studying as an adult? What was your passion when you were school-aged? Are they similar? How did you become interested in your current pursuits? What motivated you to want to learn about them? Perhaps you adopted the interests of your parents, as we talked about earlier. Perhaps a teacher inspired you. Perhaps you can't answer that question. That's okay.

Certainly, it is much easier to learn about some things than others due to our individual likes and dislikes. We won't debate whether one's love for gardening or architecture is a result of nature or nurture, but by looking at what *we* enjoy and studying the reasons *why* we enjoy those particular things, we can understand more easily how our children are motivated to learn. I recommend taking some time and thinking about the questions asked in the above paragraph in order to pinpoint for yourself how you acquired a taste for the things you enjoy as an adult. By examining the *how*, you will understand what motivated you to go in the directions you've gone.

Sources of Motivation

Attitude Is Everything

Motivation is literally whatever causes us to do something. Everything we do has some sort of motivation behind it, even the things we do without thinking about them. For example, what motivated you to get out of bed this morning? Most likely you got up because that's just what parents do, but *why* did you get up at the time you chose to get up? Did you have to take your children somewhere, or did you go off to work? Did you sleep in because it is Saturday, and you want to start the weekend rested? Did you get up early to do something in particular? What does your rising-and-shining-time say about you, just as an example? There are no right or wrong answers here.

Nowadays, I regularly get up at six o'clock to get walking time in before my kids wake up. But *why* do I go walking? I go because I know it lowers my blood pressure, gives me time to think, strengthens me physically, and invigorates me for the day. Now that I am older, I realize the importance of exercise, and my motivation is that of sanity preservation as well as health maintenance. I didn't always have a good attitude about exercise, however. Motivation to exercise has certainly evolved for me. I've always understood the science behind good health, but because I was young and relatively slim, I just wasn't motivated to work out with any regularity. I felt just fine without exercise, thank you very much.

Time changes everything, as the saying goes, and eight babies later, I woke up and realized that I didn't feel as well as I used to feel. I was tired all the time, and I had gained some unwanted pounds. My back hurt, and headaches plagued me. I began to see a reason to exercise! I still didn't want to. There were several obstacles in my way, but I knew nothing would change if my attitude didn't change. I had to take charge of my health, and I began to see that this was possible if only I focused on removing the obstacles and took action. Consequently, my attitude towards my own health and mental well-being is what now motivates me to get up early, get myself out to the lake, and put in my five miles. Attitudes are definitely behavior-shapers! Now I have a yes-I-can attitude about being healthy, and the cool thing is that I actually enjoy my walking time and miss it on days when I am unable to go.

Just as surely as we have reasons for the things we do, so our children have reasons for everything they do. As a parent, you have the opportunity to motivate your children in positive ways. One of the most effective ways we motivate our children is through *our* attitudes. Our attitudes shape our children's attitudes. Our attitudes have a huge impact on our children, so much so that our children will reflect them. Don't agree? Take a look at the children you know from outside your family. How are they like their parents? Chances are they are a reflection of their parents in major ways—for good or for not so good. Attitude truly is everything.

So why is attitude everything? Attitude is everything because our attitudes shape our behavior. Does it follow that our attitudes shape our children's behavior? Absolutely! Our babies come to us as blank slates, if you will, and we have the responsibility to train their hearts and instill in them the kinds of attitudes that will motivate them to display appropriate behaviors when they are young and as they grow.

Sadly, some parents lack the motivation to follow through with the training of their children. Instead, they expect others to do it for them. Contrary to modern thought, it does *not* take a village to raise a child; it takes committed parents who are motivated by a sense of responsibility for their children's hearts, attitudes, and behaviors. It only takes a village to raise a child when parents don't accept the responsibility, or when they are (for some very valid reasons) unable to do so. Sometimes others do need to step in, but those cases should be few and far between, rather than the societal norm.

Think about it: Many a classroom teacher would have a more manageable job if parents were motivated to shoulder the responsibility for their children's education instead of leaving this job completely to a teacher. How can something as important as the formation of a child's attitudes and resulting behaviors be left up to teachers? It takes positive parental involvement in a child's life to provide a foundation for education, whether in the classroom or at home. If you are reading these words, you obviously already understand your vital role in the healthy development of your child—physically, emotionally, mentally, and spiritually—and you are open to learning. You want to give your child every advantage possible, and I sincerely applaud you. There need to be more parents like you in this world!

I truly believe that the answer to America's education crisis today is to *motivate parents to take responsibility for their children's attitudes and behaviors*. In order to do that, the whole it-takes-a-village attitude must change to an *it-takes-the-parents* attitude. How to motivate parents is the trillion-dollar question. When the government has taken away the need for parents to be involved in education, it is very difficult to motivate them again.

I have a friend who is a teacher. Recently, one of her young students was not picked up after school, so my friend called the child's mother, who said it was the grandfather's job to get the child that day. My friend called the grandfather, who said that he wasn't going to do it because he was fifty miles away, so the mother was again called. She refused to come pick up her child and said, "Isn't it the school's job to get my kid home?" The teacher said no, not when the parent could pick up the child herself but she just didn't want to do it that day! Do you know that the principal called the police because the mother would not pick up her child, and this little third-grade boy was driven home in the back of a police car? When a parent's attitude is one of "my child is not my problem," what chance does the child have of developing the kind of attitude that will motivate him to do well in school?

It is true that good attitudes yield good behavior and increase the likelihood of good educational outcomes. Excellent attitudes yield excellent behavior and the likelihood of excellent educational outcomes. Poor attitudes yield poor behavior and the likelihood of poor educational outcomes…unless someone or something intervenes to motivate the student and change his attitude. All too often that job— changing attitudes— is left up to the classroom teacher.

Can you see how attitude is the source of motivation? Or does motivation beget attitude? In the case of a child's attitude toward his own education, his motivation is most affected by his parents' attitudes. A parent's *attitude* toward the child's education will dictate how *motivated* the parent is to ensure that the child makes the most of educational opportunities. Parents who place a high priority on excellence in education are a teacher's delight.

Ownership

Let's talk about *ownership*. The parent who thinks it is the school's responsibility to make a good student and a good citizen out of his son or daughter is deliberately taking himself out of the responsibility loop. Furthermore, if the *parent* is not taking ownership of his child's education, how likely will the child be to take ownership of it himself? The child's attitude is likely to reflect the parent's attitude of "It's the teacher's job, not mine."

Parents must be accountable and hold up their end of the educational bargain even if they send their kids to school. "I'll send my well-behaved and respectful kids to you to be educated, and you teach them the things they need to know in order to get through high school." Wouldn't that at least be better than the attitude of most parents these days, many of whom are just too busy, too stressed, and too immersed in their own lives to take on the responsibility of making sure their children are learning in the classroom?

But there is hope: more and more parents today are taking ownership. Many parents are pulling their children out of the public and private school systems because they want to have the opportunity to influence their children's attitudes and behaviors instead of their children being influenced by their peers, who lack the attitudes that lead to excellence. These parents see that their children are becoming victims of a system that does not value creativity, individuality, or excellence in education. Rather, the system prefers to teach material that students will be asked to regurgitate at the end of the year on standardized tests so that teachers and schools in the system look good, allowing the school districts to gain the all-important federal funding. If we as citizens are not aware that teaching to tests instead of imparting knowledge is the MO of public (and many private) schools today, we are out of the loop, under a rock, or in an alternate state of reality.

This is the reality: some superintendents, principals, and teachers are under such pressure to raise their schools' collective test scores that they have chosen to lie and cheat in order to meet standards. This is outrageous! In the spring of 2011, schools in Atlanta, Georgia, were embroiled in just such a scandal, as were schools in Philadelphia, Pennsylvania, just to name two districts where cheating by adults was rampant. Teachers literally went in and erased answers on their students' individual score sheets and then filled in the correct little answer bubbles! What was their motivation to cheat, lie, and deceive? Federal funding, state funding, school reputation, and perhaps some form of personal accolade or monetary incentives. How far we have fallen from moral and educational excellence in the hallowed halls of our *alma maters!*

I wonder about the students who attend schools in Atlanta and Philadelphia. Do they feel cheated? What is their motivation to learn now that they are aware that many of their teachers and principals willingly doctored their test scores because the scores weren't good enough? If I knew that my teacher had taken my achievement test, scored it, erased my answers, and penciled in the correct answers to make herself look like a more effective teacher, I would be thoroughly disgusted—and probably demotivated.

While in the case of Atlanta and Philadelphia, teachers have been held accountable for their actions, the fact is that teachers today have little authority in their own classrooms as far as what can be taught and how. If attitude is everything—and it is—a teacher is hamstrung by the attitudes that her students walk into the classroom with every year—attitudes formed by parents, many of whom hold the teacher accountable for whether their kids learn or not. This is entirely backwards. I've been there as a teacher in a classroom; I know how frustrating it is to have no recourse when, for example, kids don't do their homework because they just don't care. Parents won't come to parent-teacher conferences for one reason or another, and they don't answer notes sent home. What is a teacher to do when he or she is not respected by parents *or* students?

Good teachers do not like to see their students fail! But teachers cannot win the attitude game when their opponents are their students' parents, who have little control over their own offspring. If the system doesn't change, if the emphasis remains on test scores, and if a high percentage of parents continue to have a "stop, drop, and roll" mentality—they stop what they are doing just long enough to drop their kids off at school and then roll on with their own business— then something else must change in order for educational excellence to have a chance in this century and beyond. Our nation's future is at stake! Mediocrity does not provide an edge.

What If?

What if there was a way to put the ownership of education squarely on the shoulders of the students, empowering them to learn for the sake of gaining knowledge; with the feeling of a job well done as their reward! Of course, that would also require parents to take ownership of their child's education in the early years because kindergarteners need instruction in the basics of reading, writing, and arithmetic. What if parents were to define expectations and educational standards for their students while giving them the opportunity to set their own goals and earn the trust necessary to work independently? What if parents helped their children find a reason to learn and even provided an opportunity to focus on their strengths in the high school years? What if students were allowed to take ownership of their own learning adventure? Would a student be more motivated to learn in an environment over which he had a measure of control? You bet! Welcome to the wonderful world of the self-propelled student.

This is not just a challenge for those whose kids go to school. Parents who decide to home educate are definitely taking on the responsibility of educating their children. However, in many instances even home-educating parents do not get the desired cooperation from their children in the course of a school day. Many a home-educating mom has been frustrated because her kids don't want to do their work, and she doesn't know how to motivate her kids to help around the house, let alone take their education seriously. Just because a student learns at home doesn't mean he will be motivated to study without a parent standing over him. So how do you motivate kids, anyway?

Types of Motivation

Let's dive into a little psychology here. There are two simple types of motivation: that which comes from the inside or the outside. That was easy, wasn't it? Okay, well, that was the simplified version. Let's go deeper. The type of motivation that comes from things or forces outside of you is called *extrinsic motivation.* The other type of motivation is a little more complex, and it comes from inside of you: *intrinsic motivation.*

If you are intrinsically motivated, you do something for the sheer pleasure of doing it. For example, some people enjoy working on cars in their spare time, and they do it for the sense of pleasure derived from messing with cars. Many of us are intrinsically motivated to pursue hobbies, which are a perfect example of doing something for an intrinsic reward: the feeling of a job well done.

What kinds of things do you do for the sheer joy of being involved in the pursuit? I've heard of some women who are intrinsically motivated to clean their homes; they do so out of the sheer joy of having a clean house while, others need to be bribed with something delicious in order to get the job even started. I was intrinsically motivated to clean the little one-bedroom apartment where my husband and I lived right after we were married. I couldn't sleep if there was anything that needed to be ironed. I would stay up until everything in our little love nest was perfect according to my high standards. Motivation shifts and changes over time, however. Now I need a healthy dose of extrinsic motivation to get me to clean and straighten because I am old and tired. I will usually think of a way to reward myself when the work is done, and then I'm more motivated to get busy working.

Obviously, extrinsic motivation is the opposite of intrinsic. It is motivation that comes in the form of something concrete, such as a paycheck or a handful of gummy bears. A car mechanic may be motivated to go to work only because he receives a paycheck at the end of the week, not because he loves fixing cars. Originally, he might have gone into the field of auto mechanics out of intrinsic motivation; perhaps fixing cars was a hobby. As I said, motivation waxes and wanes. That's why it is not always a good idea to turn a hobby into a job. Something that was fun may suddenly not be fun anymore because now it is work. On the other hand, some people don't perceive their jobs to be work at all because they enjoy what they do so much that they would do it even if they weren't being paid to do it. That's a wonderful situation to be in. That's intrinsic motivation at its best!

What is a hobby? Generally, a hobby is something one does for fun or adventure during one's free time. Is there any reason why studying and learning can't be perceived as a hobby? I mean, when I presented my first child with little phonics and math workbooks when he was four years old, he was thrilled! For some reason, I did not need to bribe him to spend time learning. Learning was fun!

Babies are born, and they are immediately interested in the world around them. They are curious little things, aren't they? Curious and sleepy and hungry. They spend their days eating, sleeping, and learning. A toddler is a little Energizer Bunny, always on the go, always wanting to taste, see, touch, feel, and experience. We can't wait to teach our toddlers how to do things by themselves, such as feeding, dressing, and going potty. Tying shoes is a triumph for a child. So why do we stop teaching them how to do things by themselves? Sure, they need instruction in the basic building blocks of written and verbal communication, but then they can be off and running on their own! Why can't seniors in high school see pursuing their interests as a hobby? Why isn't this the norm? It truly *can be* when a student has the self-propelled advantage!

Extrinsic motivation is not necessary to get my kids to dive into their school work each day. They just do it. Why? They know that they have to, first of all, because it is expected. No, they don't bound out of bed in the morning, simply dying to get into their school work. It is still work. But they do enjoy learning independently. It's kind of like this: if we have to work, don't we want to work the way we want to work, when we want to work, and how we want to work? Isn't that what is so attractive about being self-employed? With self-learning, we give students the tools that they need, and then we let them work how they want to work, where they want to work, and the way they want to work. In other words, we give the gift of ownership.

It would be unrealistic to expect that our students will want to deep-dive into every subject, just as you and I aren't wild about studying some things either, but when it comes down to it, education should not be something we shove down children's throats. We should not have to offer extrinsic rewards, such as money or candy or what-have-you, in exchange for our students getting "good grades." The student who is intrinsically motivated will work for the sense of a job well done. He will desire to work with excellence because he is working for himself, not for a parent or a teacher.

Drive

The "discovery" of intrinsic motivation occurred about fifty years ago in the middle of the twentieth century. Since then, scientists have been experimenting with the causes and effects of this type of motivation, and what they have learned is fascinating. Daniel H. Pink recently wrote a book about motivation entitled simply, *Drive: The Surprising Truth About What Motivates Us*. If you are interested in doing your own research on motivation, Pink's book is a must-read. I was floored as I turned page after page and saw that his research concerning motivation and the business world closely matched my own research concerning motivation and the business of education. He primarily discusses the flaws in our reward-and-punishment system in business, but his findings most certainly apply to the traditional reward-and-punishment system found in education as well.

One of the basic tenets of *Drive* is the fact that external-control systems, for the most part, don't work. Scientific research has clearly demonstrated this, yet businesses and organizations still use the "carrots-and-sticks" method of motivation and "if-then" rewards. "Carrots and sticks" refers to dangling carrots as motivation and beating with sticks as punishment, not literally of course. If-then rewards are various kinds of bonuses that are given when performance goals are met. *Drive* discusses these kinds of extrinsic rewards in great detail, concluding that rewards and punishments are less than effective in the twenty-first-century business world where creativity and thinking outside the box are becoming essential.[1]

On the other hand, *Drive* talks a lot about the types of rewards that are effective when used appropriately. In the realm of education, there are appropriate types of rewards for various ages and stages. The younger the child, the more extrinsic the

---

1   Daniel H. Pink, Drive, p.17.

motivation will be. It is okay to offer gummy bears to my second grader if she gets all of her math page correct the first time around. She is learning basic skills. She will benefit from a little motivation to get her checking her work. However, my high school freshman should not be working extra hard on her algebra in order to get gummy bears. At this point, she should be intrinsically motivated.

Is extrinsic motivation a good thing? Pink has much more to say on this subject, but for our purposes here, we'll conclude that extrinsic rewards can be a good thing if used in appropriate circumstances with the *young* child. Intrinsic rewards should gradually take the place of extrinsic ones as a child matures. Feedback is the one type of extrinsic motivation that should remain: all students, no matter their ages, will benefit from positive, heartfelt feedback that is very specific. Young children should be offered plenty of praise as a reward for their hard work, and older students definitely need to see that we appreciate the way they do their work with excellence. Telling our children what exactly they just did to make us proud or happy or satisfied is completely necessary. Positive feedback is a reward that costs us nothing except time, but it is invaluable to our children's emotional well-being.

What About Grades?

Grades are a controversial subject. Is our whole educational grading system out of whack? Should we suspend grading students' work altogether? Of course not. We need a system to evaluate how much a student has learned so that he can be given feedback, hopefully positive. That said, I don't think taking grades is necessary in every subject every day. Grades fall into the extrinsic motivation category. Some students are very motivated to work for an A. If parents set the expectation for their young student that he will learn his lessons to an A level, and if the student has the tools necessary to learn to an A level, the student should be able to meet that expectation. When we praise the student for his achievements, motivation to continue working hard is the result. However, we can't set expectations that are not attainable for our children. Frustration will be the result in such a situation.

In the realm of home education, we have the opportunity to break tasks down into manageable pieces or skip over material the young student isn't yet ready for and wait until he is developmentally ready to tackle it. Contrast that with the first-grade classroom where a student's readiness to learn phonics or tell time is not taken into account. If the textbook says it's time to tell time, and he is not ready to tell time, he will receive a poor grade which will in turn lower his self-esteem. Receiving a bad grade is one of those "sticks" that Dan Pink talks about, while the promise of an A is a "carrot." This is a common situation. Yet psychological research has shown that students do not respond well when they are bribed with carrots or threatened with sticks. In fact, the result is they tend to lose interest.[2]

In addition, comparing students to other students via grades is hardly fair, in the classroom especially. It is common knowledge that children do not all learn at the same rate, so why lump them all together and grade them according to how they compare to the other students in the class? In the home-education environment, children move at their own speed (which is generally faster than the speed of a thirty-student classroom). Children are not corrected in front of other children, which is important to self-esteem. If a young child does not completely grasp a concept, the parent-teacher will catch it right away and can correct the situation early on, before the student is labeled a "slow reader" or "not a math whiz."

Grades are not always useful metrics, and I don't advocate their usage as anything besides a yardstick against which a child can measure *his own progress*. While I certainly want my children mastering their material daily, sometimes they have to work harder to achieve mastery than they do at other times. Understanding becomes the goal, not simply getting an A. Self-propelled kids understand that yes, they can do well independently, and they don't want to lose that freedom by neglecting to reach mastery. Self-teaching is a freedom, but it is an earned freedom. If my students are not showing mastery, I will be looking over their shoulders to find out why. They don't like being restrained in this manner. Grades are not the ultimate goal for self-propelled students; freedom to work independently is.

Some kids read better than others, and as a result, they are able to progress quickly. Some kids may read well but be less gifted in logic. All kids have strengths and weaknesses. All kids have subjects they like more than others. The secret to motivating our children to learn is not to teach them that the goal is an A. We must go further than that and help them see the big picture: self-effort is rewarding. If you work harder, you'll get further, faster. Making progress becomes an extrinsic reward.

Grades are a necessary evil in the classroom because a teacher lacks the time to teach everything to each student's level of mastery. Unfortunately, some students become accustomed to failing which over time causes them to resist learning altogether. Then there are the higher-achieving students who barely need to break a sweat in order to make all A's. Remember those "smart kids" in high school who didn't even have to study? They might not have it so good after all. When

---

2   Daniel H. Pink, *Drive*, p. 37.

they are faced with a challenge that does require their utmost concentration and effort, they may actually taste failure because they haven't been conditioned to put out more than a minimum of effort. I've seen this happen time and time again. College is often a rude awakening. The motivation to work hard was never developed in these students because everything came easily, so when they actually need to pour on the effort, they can't dig down deep and find the resolve to truly work for the sake of learning. That is unfamiliar territory. Giving kids material that is challenging—not too easy or too difficult—is the key to full engagement in high school and beyond.

Time for Change

Mr. Pink makes the point that business needs have changed over the past century. During the Industrial Revolution, our country needed workers who could perform rote, manual, repetitive work quickly. Gradually, machines began to take over functions that before had belonged to humans. Because many jobs were void of creativity, companies used the "carrots-and-sticks" method of extrinsic rewards. Today, however, our economy has shifted to where a lot of industries require innovation and creativity to stay competitive. The carrots and sticks don't work so well in this type of environment, so a shift must take place in the business world to create a new kind of motivation that goes beyond the external rewards so effective not long ago.

Job satisfaction really wasn't to be expected in the past. Work was work, and people worked for a paycheck. (Many country music songs reflect this, don't they?) Not so anymore. Mr. Pink gives many examples of companies who are changing their structure and policies to reflect a concern for employees and their needs. Business owners are beginning to get it that certain things motivate more than others. Micromanaging is on the way out. I want to share with you the three components that Pink believes will revolutionize businesses upon implementation, but first I want to say that these three components are precisely what can also revolutionize *education* in America. Keep that in mind as you read over the following needs that employees (and students) have:

1. Autonomy. Pink states that "our 'default setting' is to be autonomous and self-directed." People should have control over "task (what they do), time (when they do it), team (who they do it with), and technique (how they do it)."

2. Mastery. Pink's definition of mastery is "becoming better at something that matters." Businesses who want to be on the leading edge should give employees responsibilities and tasks that are not too hard and not too easy so their work will be suited to their abilities and just challenging enough to promote steady, personal growth. [3]

3. Purpose. Believe it or not, some companies are actually looking beyond the bottom line and are seeking to make contributions to others on the planet. In the past, purpose was seen as "ornamental" to many companies, meaning it wasn't the goal, but if it turned out to be a byproduct, that was a bonus. New policies that allow employees to pursue purpose will motivate folks because "humans, by their nature, seek purpose—to make a contribution and to be a part of a cause greater and more enduring than themselves." [4]

Just as Dan Pink dares business owners and companies to rethink their outdated methodologies of managing employees in order to maximize human potential, creativity, and overall purpose in their lives, so I challenge educators and parents alike to rethink their outdated methodologies of micromanaging children in order to maximize the human potential for creativity, genius, and purpose in their lives.

The Marshmallow Study

Many moons ago, in 1972, a landmark study was done by Walter Mischel of Stanford University using marshmallows to assess the ability of preschool children, ages four to six, to delay gratification. Children were placed in a room by a researcher, and each was given a marshmallow. They were told that if they could wait until the researcher came back into the room before eating their marshmallow, they would be rewarded with a second marshmallow. Then the researcher would leave the room for fifteen long minutes. (Remember how long fifteen minutes seemed to you when you were a preschooler?)

The results? Some of the children resisted eating the marshmallow—others didn't. Out of the roughly six hundred children who participated in the study, only one-third were able to resist the call of the marshmallow and receive a second one as a reward.

---

3   Daniel H. Pink, Drive, p. 222.
4   Daniel H. Pink, Drive, p. 223.

While the original purpose of this study was to confirm a hypothesis about delayed gratification and age, this experiment has been repeated many, many times to prove or disprove various other hypotheses. In fact, Mischel performed a similar experiment on the island of Trinidad using chocolate bars in order to see if ethnicity had any effect on delayed gratification. He found that while ethnicity did not, social and economic status did. Isn't that fascinating? But what fascinates me even more is a follow-up study that Mischel did on a group of the original "marshmallow children." Researchers interviewed them years later and discovered that those who were motivated to hold out for the second marshmallow, exhibiting self-control at a young age, had become more successful as adults than their counterparts who had given into temptation.

What does this study say about intrinsic and extrinsic motivation? The kids who waited those fifteen long minutes weren't thinking intrinsically, were they? I mean, they weren't focused on the good feeling they were going to get from successfully waiting out the researcher. No, they were *looking to the end goal* which was two delicious treats instead of just one. They were able to see the big picture which enabled them to demonstrate self-control. They definitely liked marshmallows, right? It wasn't that one-third of the children hated marshmallows. We can say they were motivated extrinsically—but one marshmallow wasn't enough. One marshmallow just didn't make sense when they could have two. This study reveals that some children aren't satisfied with what just anyone can have; they want more, and they will do what it takes to get more of what they want—in this case, marshmallows. They weren't trying to make anyone happy by their choice. They were just doing what came naturally: "Well, if I can have two, why settle for one? This is easy! All I have to do is wait."

The other, larger group of children apparently couldn't see the big picture. They could only see what was before them: a fat, squishy, deliciously-tantalizing marshmallow, and the motivation to get twice as much out of the deal just wasn't there. They gobbled up the first marshmallow (although some of the children played around with their marshmallow first, licking it a bit and holding it in their hands before giving in), and their reward was only one marshmallow. From this study, it was concluded that those who had the ability to wait for gratification became more successful adults, and I am assuming that by "successful," the study means better jobs and all the trappings that go along with that.

If you are interested in the application of the Marshmallow Study, as it's been dubbed, to success in business and in your personal life, I recommend a book entitled, *Don't Eat the Marshmallow...Yet! The Secret to Sweet Success in Work and Life* by Joachim de Posada and Ellen Singer. This gem of a book looks at why intelligence and hard work don't necessarily equal success, and how you can utilize delayed gratification in your daily life to reach your own goals. Common sense dictates that if you are smart and work hard, you will be successful. Not necessarily, according to *Don't Eat the Marshmallow...Yet.*

After reading de Posada's book, it became apparent to me that the real secret to success is seeing the big picture, which is an incredibly motivating thing to do. When we only see the little, individual marshmallow instead of the benefits of waiting to eat it—doubling our reward—we miss out on half of the benefits. We lose opportunity as a result of our impatience and shortsightedness. It takes foresight and vision to hold out for the rewards that are ours when we keep our eyes on the big picture and finally reach our ultimate goals. Incidentally, *Don't Eat the Marshmallow...Yet!* offers a "Five-Step Marshmallow Plan." Following this simple plan really helped me focus and see what I needed to change and do in order to begin reaching my goals via delayed gratification.

Seeing the Big Picture

What motivates a student who thinks that he is at the mercy of his teachers and that he must do whatever those teachers tell him to do? Very little motivates him when he has no control over his environment. A home-educated student is also unlikely to be motivated day after day when he doesn't see the big picture, when he doesn't see a purpose in the work he is doing. A big part of motivation is understanding the *why* behind what we are doing. I will be much more intrinsically motivated when I see how what I am doing right now will benefit me in the long run. How will what I do today or what I am asked to do by my employer or by my teacher be moving me towards my goals?

If we have no goals at all except to get through the day, chances are good that we will be unhappy. The human spirit thrives on challenge and success. Motivation, both extrinsic and intrinsic, is necessary for a well-balanced life. I admit that I have worked simply for a paycheck before. Perhaps you have too. Because I could see the big picture—putting food on the table—I was willing to work for that extrinsic reward. Eventually, my situation changed. Remember me saying that motivation changes? It sure does. Now I am self-employed, and I'm very intrinsically motivated to work for the sake of helping others and not for monetary reward. In fact, I hate taking people's money. If I could, I would give all of my products away. (Of course, there is still that putting-food-on-the-table thing, so thank you for buying this book!)

The self-propelled student is motivated intrinsically by seeing the big picture, setting simple goals, and then moving closer and closer to those goals. By teaching our children to see the big picture, teaching them how to set goals, and helping to remove any obstacles that would prevent them from reaching those goals, we are giving them an edge. We are giving them the tools with which to master themselves, and as a result, they will hang in there not for immediate gratification, but for the purpose of reaching their goals. That is delayed gratification at its best.

Interestingly, another follow-up to the original Marshmallow Study was done in 1990, and it found a correlation between the ability to delay gratification and higher SAT scores. Those who did not eat the marshmallow scored higher on the SAT than those who gobbled up their marshmallows. Isn't that fascinating? I think so.

The Perfect Score Study

Speaking of high SAT scores, I'd like to relay a little of my own experience in tandem with a study done by Tom Fischgrund, PhD. While browsing a local bookstore a couple of years ago, I came across a book, entitled *SAT Perfect Score: 7 Secrets to Raise Your Score*. What interested me about this book was the fact that the author, with the blessing of the SAT Board, did a study of one-hundred-sixty college-bound high school seniors who had achieved perfect 800s on both the verbal and the math portions of the SAT in the year 2000. His goal? Find out what makes these kids tick. What do they have in common? Who are they? How do they think? What do they aspire to? What are their academic habits? He also did a study of average-scoring kids, and this group served as a control group. No study like this had been done before.

Since I have a perfect SAT scorer and a near-perfect SAT scorer in my home, I was more than a little interested to see what this study revealed and how my sons, Nick and Taylor, compared to the kids Dr. Fischgrund interviewed for his book. Unfortunately, *SAT Perfect Score* is out of print, but you can find copies on Amazon and other used book outlets. I highly recommend this book for anyone who is a student of motivational theory. You'll see why as I share some juicy tidbits of information that relate to motivation from my well-worn copy of the *7 Secrets*.

First, here is what the author says about his work: "I have to admit that I was surprised by many of the findings of the Perfect Score Study. As a professional educator and a high-level recruiter, I have studied the best and the brightest for twenty years. When I looked at the information I had gathered in the Perfect Score Study and shared the results with knowledgeable professionals in the education field, we all agreed that we were amazed by the common trends that exist among perfect score students. The brightest of the bright students have common personality traits and lifestyle habits that made it possible for them to score a 1600. I call these the 7 Secrets of Perfect Score Students."[5]

Keep in mind that this particular study involved the interview of one-hundred-sixty high school seniors, plus about fifty average students from a control group. Parents of the perfect score students were also contacted in order to corroborate what their kids said, as well as provide input on how self-motivated they thought their students were. I will not reveal the seven secrets here because I think everyone should get the book and read it for themselves, but I will share a few surprising statistics from the study. Here we go.

Who do you think studied more, the perfect score students or the control group of students? Surprisingly, they both averaged ten hours a week of study time. About 80 percent of perfect score students attended public high schools, and there was not a higher incidence of perfect scorers from private schools with smaller class sizes. The average class size was twenty-three students, which is close to the national average.

"Only 1 percent of perfect score students are homeschooled, which is even less than the national average." And only one perfect score student in the study was home educated. In fact, Dr. Fischgrund states, "The *7 Secrets* will reveal that homeschooling doesn't offer an advantage—and may even be a disadvantage when it comes to doing well on the SAT."[6] We will definitely take a closer look at home education and scoring well on the SAT.

Here is a startling statistic: "90 percent of perfect score students come from intact as opposed to divorced families, compared with 66 percent of all U.S. high school students who come from intact families."[7] Just so you truly get this, let me put it this way: The vast majority of perfect SAT scorers came from public schools *and* from homes that had been untouched by divorce. Fascinating, don't you think? It makes sense that homes where there is relative peace will spawn children who can be more single-minded in their pursuits.

---

5   Tom Fischgrund, PhD, SAT Perfect Score; 7 Secrets to Raise Your Score, p. 53; hereafter cited as 7 Secrets.
6   Tom Fischgrund, PhD, 7 Secrets, p. 44.
7   Tom Fischgrund, PhD, 7 Secrets, p. 19.

One other statistic I am compelled to share: "Perfect score students are just as athletic as other high school students."[8] Some people may find that surprising.

Are Perfect Scorers Weird?

What does a perfect scorer look like? First of all, it is important to know that perfect SAT scorers from this study saw their scores as simply a means to an end and not as the end itself. They had a well-rounded view of life in addition to a core set of values. They were always looking for a challenge, and they were multi-faceted individuals. Most were avid readers who read for enjoyment and learned for enjoyment. They were not motivated by external rewards; they possessed an intrinsic motivation system that drove them to do their best and to be self-motivated. And believe it or not, these kids were not classified as geeks. They were very likeable kids who were not likely to broadcast their perfect scores because they were quite humble about their achievements.[9] That pretty much sums up my sons, Nick and Taylor. They don't discuss their test scores because they are not defined by a test score. They are both humble, athletic, fun-loving guys who throw themselves into every project they undertake.

Alas, my other six children are oddly motivated to succeed as well. They all have a desire to excel at whatever they undertake. While my kids may not all have perfect SAT scores, they all sport the same drive and determination to succeed. They each have one or two core passions that drive them, and they have parents, siblings, and friends who support them in their daily lives. I don't care whether or not any of my kids ever score perfectly on any test. What is important is that they possess attitudes that fuel their motivation about learning and that they pursue their passions.

Perfect Score Kids and Motivation

So what did the Perfect Score Study reveal about kids and motivation? The study found that these students set high standards for themselves. Notice: they set them for *themselves*. Their parents didn't set the standards for them. Dr. Fischgrund found that "they're rarely satisfied that they've accomplished enough, and they see their education as a path of discovery as opposed to a destination."[10] It is so important that our children realize that education is more than a desk, textbooks, and a teacher.

---

8   Tom Fischgrund, PhD, 7 Secrets, p. 49.
9   Tom Fischgrund, PhD, 7 Secrets, p. 163
10   Tom Fischgrund, PhD, 7 Secrets, pp. 64-65.

I love the "path of discovery" thought because that is exactly what happens when the self-propelled student is allowed to explore his interests. He takes the road less traveled and meanders here and there, not controlled by linear thought. He doesn't have to go from Point A to Point B because it is the most expedient way to learn. He'll master a concept and go on to the next thing; however, if he wants to take a side trip and explore something more deeply, he is going to do that on his own. He will chase his thoughts wherever they may take him.

The X Factor

All this talk about achieving mastery and setting standards may make you wonder which comes first, achieving mastery or setting standards. The Perfect Score Study "couldn't answer this question, but it did find that, almost without exception, perfect score students are incredibly motivated to succeed—not just in academics, but also in life. Motivation is the key to high academic achievement and a perfect SAT score. It's the spark that drives students through their high school years, college, and beyond. It's the dividing line that separates successful people from those who aren't."[11]

A person may be a talented athlete, an amazing musician or artist, but if he lacks motivation to pursue that in which he is gifted, he will not taste success. In order to have success in any area, one must possess motivation. As a teacher, I've seen kids who had above-average ability in various areas, but the only ones who became truly successful were those who were motivated to pursue their passions. Young adults who are encouraged to stay on track and pursue their dreams will be much more motivated than those who lack a support system. However, there are those who make it despite the odds because they still possess motivation. Those who lack motivation don't get anywhere, no matter how strong a support system they have. Perhaps they will become motivated in time, but if they lack motivation, they just won't make progress.

Dr. Fischgrund says, "The missing *x* factor really is *motivation*. Perfect score students are incredibly self-motivated, but they also have parents who expected them to achieve from the start. By believing in their children, these parents infused their kids with a belief in themselves which led to strong self-esteem. This self-esteem enabled perfect score students to become their own motivators in high school and beyond."[12]

---

11   Tom Fischgrund, PhD, 7 Secrets, p. 65.
12   Tom Fischgrund, PhD, 7 Secrets, pp. 65-66.

I think it's incredibly important to note that when perfect scorers were asked who they credited with motivating them, a whopping 90 percent said they *motivated themselves*. Only 69 percent of the control group of average students said they motivated themselves. One perfect score student said, "I'm a self-motivated person. I understand that I determine my own future." Another said, "I just approach every class with the desire to do my best. I have high standards and am driven."[13] Amen and amen.

What About the Parents of Perfect Scorers?

Dr. Fischgrund, in his chapter on self-motivation, writes, "Perfect score students learned to become self-motivated by watching their parents giving the right amount of assistance, enough but not too much—during their grade school years. These students said they relied strongly on their parents to motivate them in elementary and junior high, but that their parents stepped back from this role when their children entered high school and became self-reliant."[14]

This parental pattern of being more hands-on when children are in elementary and middle school and then stepping back in the high school years is 100-percent consistent with what I propose for raising self-propelled students. I would add that parents must trust their instincts in supporting young children as they begin their educational journey in the early, formative years; however, it is just as important that parents understand that to everything there is a season. There is definitely a season for letting go of the bicycle seat. Holding on to it prevents autonomy which will wreak havoc on the student's motivation.

Home-Educated Students and the SAT

Remember Dr. Fischgrund's statement about home education not being an advantage in SAT performance? Then there was the statistic which stated that less than 1 percent of perfect score students are home educated. Those were the only two sentences on home education in the entire book. Of course these sentences ate at me.

Well, I vowed not to sleep until I got an explanation from the author about his outrageous comment. Okay, maybe I didn't literally lose sleep over it, but I definitely couldn't accept his statement without an explanation, so I did a search on the Internet for the author. I ended up contacting Dr. Fischgrund by e-mail and

13   Tom Fischgrund, PhD, 7 Secrets, p. 66.
14   Tom Fischgrund, PhD, 7 Secrets, p. 67.

asking if he had time to go over some material from his book with me. I told him up front that I am a home-educating parent, formerly a professional educator. That didn't seem to scare him, so he gave me his phone number, and we set up a time to talk. Talk we did! It was an interesting hour-long exchange of ideas and thoughts, and I was very grateful that he took the time to discuss not only his book, but also educational theory with me.

In our discussion, I found out why it is that Dr. Fischgrund feels that home education is a stumbling block to raising high achievers who score brilliantly on the SAT—and I strongly concur with his explanation. Would you like to know the reason why home education may actually be a hindrance to raising perfect scorers? Hint: he used the words "helicopter parents" in his explanation. His experience with home-educating parents has indicated to him that home-educating moms, especially, tend to hover over their students, helping them way too much and not forcing them to work hard and get out of their comfort zones. Sound familiar? He and I talked about the micromanagement factor and how harmful it can be to the motivation of middle and high school kids.

Our conversation turned to the fact that 90 percent of perfect scorers came from intact families. I asked the obvious, wondering aloud why having a mom and dad who had not been through divorce was so pivotal to these students' achievements. Dr. Fischgrund discussed the importance of having a two-parent family where Mom plays a specific role and Dad plays a specific role in the children's lives. You can probably see how you and your spouse contribute very different yet equally important components to the family unit. The stress and upheaval of divorce drastically alters the support structure of the family, the very structure which is designed to provide the stability that enables children to function normally. Remove that supportive, secure environment, and children are distracted at best.

If you have been or are divorced, I don't mean to discourage you. Remember, there are exceptions to every rule. Understanding your children's need for your time and attention, as well as for a strong sense of security, is the first step in repairing the breech in the family foundation. Peace in the home is extremely important to children's growth and development.

A Word on Parenting

Let's take our thoughts back to our role as parents. Dr. Fischgrund writes, "Because these perfect score parents planted the seeds for self-sufficiency when their child was younger, they were able to sit back and serve as a support system during their child's high school years. Yes, some children may be born more internally driven than others, but all of us have the potential to be self-starters."[15]

Your role in the early years of your child's life is to teach and to guide educationally and morally. But once that foundation has been laid, your role moves to a more hands-off approach. You become a coach on the sidelines watching your now-skilled young adult further develop his skills—independently. You provide support and at times help remove obstacles, but you should not be out there on the court playing your child's game for him. We actually become obstacles to our kids by getting in their way and not trusting them to progress without us.

It is important to note that the parents of high achievers did not expect their kids to score perfectly on the SAT. It is important not to set goals and expectations *for* our high school students, even though expectation setting is key in the earlier years. We can still be involved with them in the process. We must trust our young adults to enjoy meeting challenges of their own making. When I think about my sons' SAT-taking days, I now see that they went into the test determined to beat it as best they could. They knew from taking practice tests that they could do well, and they wanted to rise to the challenge and succeed. I certainly never asked them if they thought they could get a perfect score. They just knew that it was possible. My hope was simply that they would be able to do their best, as there are so many variables on test day. Had my husband and I raised our kids to doubt themselves at a young age by not allowing them to set their own goals and reach as high as they wanted to reach, their attitudes would have been different going into the test room on SAT day.

Finally, this is very cool: a whopping 75 percent of perfect score students listed either their mom or dad or both parents as the most influential people in their lives. The study also revealed that parents had the most impact on the top performers, but teachers had the most impact on average performers. So do parents of high achievers have more influence on their children's lives? Are they more involved in their children's education? Do schools better serve average kids than super bright kids? Or, as Dr. Fischgrund put it, "Which comes first, the perfect score students or the perfect score parent?" He goes on to answer this question by saying he doesn't know that the study can answer it, but "Certainly, perfect score students do rely more on their parents than on teachers for input and guidance in their schoolwork."[16] If that is true, then why don't home-educating students score more

---

15 Tom Fischgrund, PhD, 7 Secrets, p. 66.
16 Tom Fischgrund, PhD, 7 Secrets, p. 68.

highly on the SAT since they presumably spend more time with their parents? Again, I believe the answer lies in autonomy. Self-confidence comes from a feeling of control. The Perfect Score Study concurs completely.

Self-Esteem

In several of the interviews done with perfect score students themselves, it was found that high achievers' parents respected and encouraged their kids. "Perfect score students don't operate in a vacuum. They can't tap into their inner motivation without first having high self-esteem. They need to believe that they can succeed before they develop the drive to succeed. Parents, of course, can build or tear down their children's self-esteem. Starting at the youngest age, children get cues from their parents about how high their expectations are. If children know that their parents expect great things that are realistically achievable, then they will be motivated to achieve those things."[17]

Some would scoff at the whole concept of self-esteem and believe-in-yourself psychology. To them I can only say there *is* such a thing as self-esteem or self-worth. It is very real, and a child either has low, average, or high self-esteem. While self-esteem is internal, it is formed by external factors or cues from parents, siblings, friends, and other relationships. A young child's parents and close family members have control over his self-esteem, and children raised in a loving home will have higher self-esteem than those raised in a home where they do not feel important or valued.

Parents need to instill in their children the belief that they have the ability to succeed. That is not to say that failure isn't going to occur. Failure is a part of life, and teaching our children that sometimes things will not turn out the way we want them to is vital. Learning how to deal with failure was a real challenge for my children. Because they tend to throw their whole selves into a project or activity, they take failure personally when it does come. But there are always important lessons to be learned through failure, and my husband and I don't discourage our children from trying a new activity out of a fear of failure. It's not easy to watch our children fail, is it? No, it never is, but we recognize that struggle is part of what brings out the beauty of the butterfly as it breaks the restraints of its cocoon. Freedom requires struggle.

As a tenth-grade chemistry student, I quietly fought against failure. Because I was an honors student, failure was especially humiliating, and I hid it from my

---

17 Tom Fischgrund, PhD, 7 Secrets, p. 69.

parents until my first semester grade report arrived. I don't remember my parents saying much at all. They knew I was a "good student" who always tried to do my best. In reality, there was something unapproachable about the chemistry teacher; he didn't talk much. His classroom was always eerily quiet. I still remember the way he would look at me and my lab partner during labs when we didn't know the answer to a question. He would look at us with a sort of grin on his face as if to say, "What do you mean you don't know? You're kidding, right?" So I stopped asking questions, and so did my lab partner. I ended the year with a solid D. Looking back now, I cannot believe my questions were not taken seriously. The teacher was not gifted in teaching at a high school level, and I was not a self-learner. Consequently, the last thing I would want to study as an adult is chemistry because I still don't think I can. "No-I-can't" is what I hear in my head when I flirt with the idea of studying my high schoolers' Apologia chemistry book.

Academically, a student who is self-teaching is going to find out that yes, he can do things on his own with excellence. Parents who require mastery learning are setting their kids up for success because mastery ensures that a student is constantly moving on but not before he is ready to do so. That yes-I-can attitude is what translates into positive self-esteem. Setting realistic goals is very important to building self-esteem. In order to set goals that are challenging as well as realistic, the student has to understand that he can do it, but it's going to take a lot of work. Is the student willing to do what it takes to achieve his goal? Does he understand how hard he is going to have to work to achieve it? While a student may work hard to achieve a goal, he is naturally going to work harder if he has set the goal himself than if a parent has set the goal for him. The "realistic" part comes into play when the student sees just how much effort is required to meet the goal. Is it an amount of effort that he is willing to give? In the long run, achieving a goal will depend upon the student's personal motivation.

How to Demotivate

Let's say my eleventh-grade son wants to be on a debate team. If he has an interest in debate, then by all means, I will look into the possibility of getting him involved. He and I do some research and find a local team, and I step back and allow my son to set his goals from there. I won't harass him with how I think he should do things. I may give some guidance if asked, but for the most part, I'm letting experience be the best teacher. A self-teaching student who has a yes-I-can attitude will head into the activity wanting to be the best. Why do something if you aren't going to do your best? That is the attitude I find that my children naturally have. I have not taught them to be competitive—I don't have to push them; they just feel that anything worth doing is worth doing full-out. There is no halfway. They are intrinsically motivated to do their best, and when they are pitted against other debaters who feel the same way, the results are going to be quite interesting.

However, if I as the parent decide that I want my son to participate in a debate team apart from his own choosing, he is not going to be enthused, and I don't blame him. As parents, we need to give our young adults support when they choose an area of interest. I may tell my son 24/7 that he could be a wonderful debater if he would just try, but if he lacks the interest, I am wasting my time. Sure, I can insist that he do it, but what will that yield? Frustration and discouragement—on both our parts. I am just creating a battle scene.

Here is a third scenario. My son comes to me and expresses an interest in being a part of a debate team. I ask him, "Is that something you really think you can do? I mean, you've never been good in front of people, and logic isn't your strong suit. Don't you think you should try something else?" Wow, I have just totally motivated my son to never ask me to help him in the future! Parenting self-propelled children means encouraging them to spread their wings and fly, to branch out and try new things. In this last scenario, I caused my son to go from yes-I-can to maybe-I-can't. I shot a hole in his self-esteem. Maybe logic isn't his strength at the moment, but if he has the desire to hone that skill, then I surely can help him find opportunities in which to develop it. It is a joy to help children find opportunities to engage and develop their skills. However, it is never acceptable for me to decide what I want my young adults to excel at and then push them, micromanaging their lives so that my dream for them comes true. May it never be! *Our job as parents is to equip our children to become the people they are created to be.*

Final Thoughts on the Perfect Score Study

To conclude our section on the Perfect Score Study, I'd like to point out that the students who were the subject of the study did not revel in their perfect scores. Sure, they were happy, but they didn't define who they were by test scores. As Dr. Fischgrund found, "Perfect score students would probably never have been able to succeed if their parents never took the giant leap of letting their kids have some control over their academic lives."[18] Letting go and allowing our children to have a measure of control academically is vitally important.

---

18   Tom Fischgrund, PhD, 7 Secrets, p. 74.

Yes, I was very, very encouraged by the way the Perfect Score Study results echoed the results my family has had. The similarities were almost eerie. It should not surprise me that strong family values are so important to academic success because apparently the Moms and Dads in this study set expectations when their children were young and didn't allow them to slack off at home. They were able to motivate their young children, and as the children matured, the parents were able to take a more hands-off approach to their young teens' learning. Once the teens became high school seniors, they had a sense of purpose as a result of developing one or two core passions before graduation. They had a direction to pursue after high school. They could see the bigger picture.

Parents, we have not only the responsibility but also the privilege of having the greatest influence on our children. Would your children say that you and your spouse are the primary influences in their lives? This is what I get from the Perfect Score Study: kids succeed with support in the home. I'm not talking about simply success on the SAT; I am talking about success in life!

Scoring well on the SAT or ACT is not a goal in my home-educating family. I want that to be perfectly clear. What I am laying out for you in *The Self-Propelled Advantage* is the fact that young adults who have been given the opportunity to be independent learners, who master each day's work before moving on to the next day's lesson, will be equipped to score well on the College Board exams. Does that mean I think these exams are good things? No, not necessarily. I hate that so much hinges on them, and I guarantee they are not predictors of success in college or beyond. They are hoops through which our young people must jump if they want to head to college, and especially if they want to earn scholarship money for college. Self-learning and mastery learning will absolutely give your children an advantage in scholarship competitions. Beyond that, a firm family foundation will give your children an advantage that goes way beyond that type of success. There is nothing that can replace the value of family.

Purpose

If you recall, Dan Pink from *Drive* mentioned purpose as one of the three elements of his new business motivation model. I also list purpose as a motivating factor for students, but I am referring to a reason to learn, a purpose for learning, instead of the giving-back kind of purpose Dan talks about in his business model. But both speak to our need to be a part of something outside of ourselves. Students will be motivated if they can see the big picture, have a plan, and know where they are headed. How is what they are studying relevant to where they hope to be five years from now? Ten years from now?

Students need a reason to pursue a subject or an activity. We as parents can help students see how things make sense in the big picture. Sometimes the answer to the sense question has everything to do with, "Because you have to learn this before you can move on and learn that." But at least that is a reason to learn. Avoid using the words "because I said so" when dealing with your older children and young adults. Autonomous people need to see the why and know where things fit into the big picture. Remember the Marshmallow Study? Seeing the big picture is a great motivator for success.

However, keep in mind that while coaching our children to future success, we can't forget about the present. Understanding how what you are doing today benefits you today and not just somewhere down the road is an essential part of personal motivation. Sometimes seeing the big picture isn't enough; in fact, the big picture can sometimes be overwhelming. For example, when writing the manuscript for this book, I spent many a morning procrastinating because I could only see the big picture. The big picture overwhelmed me! The ability to break a goal down into manageable pieces is important to motivation. When I saw that if I only did *some* work every day, I would eventually reach my goal of finishing an enormous project, I was motivated to do a little bit every day. I began to enjoy the journey of writing when I saw how writing every day benefitted me today and not just at some time in the future. In that sense, be careful using the big picture as motivation.

As we move through the chapters of this book, we will apply what we've learned about motivation to each of the three elements of the self-propelled advantage. I hope that in this chapter you have gained some insight into the minds of students and what motivates or demotivates them. We will be building on this knowledge going forward.

Bonus Tip: Four Little Magic Words

I have a pet peeve, and it is whining and complaining. Was that an abrupt transition? There is nothing that annoys me more than a whiner and complainer. (Usually someone who whines is complaining, which is why I lump those two into the same category.) I don't know if your children ever whine or complain. While my husband and I don't like whining or complaining from our kids, that doesn't mean it never happens. It is rare, but it happens. We are strong proponents of discussion, and we want our children to feel free to discuss anything with us as long as it is done in a proper tone of voice. I do my best not to whine and complain in return. It's hard not to whine and complain sometimes, isn't it?

Just in case you have occasional whiners and complainers in your family, I will share with you my four little magic words that are (almost) guaranteed to eradicate whining and sling the complainer into motivation mode. It's true! I use these four words regularly to motivate myself to walk five miles on days I would rather stay in bed. They are mindset changers when used appropriately.

The next time one of your kids says to you in that whining kind of voice, "Awwwww, do I have to?" your four-word response should be, "No, you *get* to." You don't have to, you get to! For instance, if one of my daughters is complaining about (this is hard because they really don't complain very often), say, volleyball practice, I will say, "No, you don't have to go to practice; you get to." When your kids see the negative and vocalize it, just turn it around and make it a positive you-are-blessed-to-be-healthy-enough-to-play-volleyball kind of statement. It works like magic.

Seriously, I say this to myself daily, depending on what kind of mood I am in and what is on the to-do list. "Do I have to be the mom who drives the entire team to the game two hours away just because I have a fifteen-passenger van? No, I *get* to be that mom." Seeing the positive is a habit I've had to nurture, as I am a glass-half-empty sort. I see things much differently when I put this kind of "I'm blessed" spin on it.

The next time you hear a complaint from one of your dear children, make the next words out of your mouth, "No, you get to," and see what happens. E-mail me and let me know, okay?

I don't recommend using this on your spouse. It has a tendency to backfire.

An Inner Drive to Succeed

Think about the young children you know, or think back to when your children were young—age five or six. Don't young children *want* to learn? Don't they want to do things by themselves? Why then do we assume that kids will not like school? Why do we tend to think that we must bribe children to learn with extrinsic rewards? Why is it that kindergarteners love to learn, yet by the time they've got another couple of years of school under their proverbial belts, they have a negative attitude toward learning? Teachers put a lot of effort into making lessons full of razzle-dazzle, fun, sparkle, and color. Children become accustomed to such hoopla and will soon require such promotional material in order to learn. They become accustomed to being entertained. Children who are taught to learn this way spend hours upon hours each weekday in a setting devoid of autonomy or self-paced learning. The teacher is not accustomed to trusting children to learn information on their own, and she lacks the time to check up on every child individually and make sure each is doing what he or she is supposed to do in six, seven, eight, or more subjects every day.

Because middle school and high school students often lack the self-mastery to work independently and with excellence, the rest of schooldom is punished by requiring information to be spoon fed to all. I could have functioned perfectly well and quite happily working on my own in the classroom with the teacher occasionally checking in on me to approve my work. Consequently, I didn't love to learn. I was bored. I remember graduating from college and thinking, "Whew! I'm finally done learning!" I was incredibly sick of being told what I had to know. I had learned enough useless information to last me a lifetime. It took years before I ventured into a library or bookstore to read for the sheer joy of reading. Isn't that sad? I don't want that for my children.

Will you choose to immerse your children in a love-to-learn environment where they become intrinsically motivated to work with excellence and mastery, confident because they have the time to build success upon success, and competent because they have accepted ownership of the learning process? The self-propelled advantage is motivation!

Coming up in the next chapter, we will examine the models of education available to children in American society today. There may be more options than you think! As we look at these options, I'll give you a heads-up on which is most conducive to raising self-propelled kids.

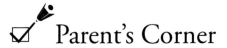

☑ Parent's Corner

If you have students in a classroom environment, what kind of motivation techniques can you use to help them love to learn?

1. Help your children see the big picture of why they are studying each subject. What will mastering each subject do for them? Give them a reason to learn.

2. Give kids as much control over their homework as possible: where they work, when they work, when they take breaks, etc. Ensure that they understand this is a freedom you are giving them as long as they work with excellence. Praise them for work well done.

3. Facilitate the setting of goals for each grading period in each subject: "Understand everything I get wrong" or "Relearn anything I miss in math" or "Tell Mom if I don't understand something in one of my classes." Some kids are reluctant to ask for help.

4. Be involved in your children's daily learning as much as possible. Trust your instincts and find a way to connect with each child daily, passing on your enthusiasm over their progress. Inquire, don't demand to know.

5. Consider your home environment: is it conducive more to extrinsic motivation or intrinsic? Do you offer extrinsic rewards that should be phased out and more intrinsic motivation brought in? Do you verbally praise your children with sincerity, as often as possible?

6. Be careful not to allow so many extracurricular activities that your student has little time for study and reading for pleasure. If you have to, curtail screen time in favor of reading opportunities.

If you have students in a home-education environment, what kind of motivation techniques can you use to help them love to learn?

1. Help your children see the big picture of why they are studying each subject. What will mastering each subject do for them? Give them a reason to learn.

2. Give kids as much control over their work as possible: where they work, when they work, when they take breaks, etc. Ensure that they understand this is a freedom you are giving them as long as they work with excellence. Praise them for work well done.

3. Facilitate the setting of goals for each grading period in each subject. (We'll discuss this in much more detail later.)

4. Trust your instincts and find a way to connect with each child daily, passing on your enthusiasm over their progress. Avoid micromanaging them.

5. Consider your home environment: is it more conducive to extrinsic motivation or intrinsic? Do you offer extrinsic rewards that should be

phased out and more intrinsic motivation brought in? Do you verbally praise with sincerity, as often as possible?

6. Be careful not to allow so many extracurricular activities that your student has little time for study and reading for pleasure. If you have to, curtail screen time in favor of reading opportunities.

In case you didn't notice, these two lists are very similar. But that doesn't mean that classroom and home-education environments are alike. As you go on to the next chapter, you'll be able to easily compare and contrast the various methods of education in existence today and see if your child needs an educational makeover.

CHAPTER 3

EDUCATIONAL OPTIONS

If you are going to achieve excellence in big things, you develop the habit in little matters. Excellence is not an exception, it is a prevailing attitude.
—Colin Powell

As parents, we pass our values on to our young children whether we realize it or not. Hopefully we are passing on good stuff. Having children has helped me realize what my values are through the choices I make for them. How we choose to educate our children is a major reflection of our values. If you are in the process of evaluating what kind of education is best for your child, I hope that your choice will reflect your values and not those of a friend, family member, or group of people who are seeking to pressure you into their way of thinking. Trust your instincts when making this decision.

In chapter 1, I introduced the three elements that constitute the self-propelled advantage: self-mastery, mastery, and self-learning. The most important element, if you recall, is self-mastery. Why? Because morals and values beget behavior. When a child has been raised to have proper attitudes and behaviors, he is on the road to self-mastery. When a child is respectful, obedient to parents, able to control his words and actions, and possessing a yes-I-can approach to challenges, education is going to be a positive experience for him. Contrast this child with one who is out of control, doesn't respect his parent's authority, and won't do anything that's not of his own volition. Clean up his toys when asked? Mom doesn't even ask anymore; it's too much of a struggle to make him do it, so Mom cleans up for him. The only peace in the house is when this child is finally asleep at night. Have you met kids like this? Mom and Dad have given up trying to control this strong-willed child. Pity the classroom teacher who gets to work with this kindergartener if Mom and Dad can't control him!

The longer parents wait to teach their children self-mastery, the harder the job will be. If your four-year-old daughter doesn't respect your authority now, she will not suddenly do so when she is fourteen. Why do I place such an emphasis on self-mastery in a chapter on educational choice? I want to stress that in order to develop a healthy relationship with your children, you must actively mold and shape their attitudes and behaviors. You do that best by being with them, correcting and nurturing them day by day. Consider carefully the educational choice you make in the early years when your child is most influenced by those around him.

Young children are vulnerable and easily persuaded. Because of this fact, my husband and I decided that we wanted to be the most important influence in our young children's lives. We wanted to be the ones who most influenced our young children instead of allowing the primary influence in their lives to be people we didn't even know. That is one reason that we chose home education for our family. Is it by chance that my husband and I have thus far raised four mature young adults who have left the nest without ever once challenging our authority? Is it by chance that we have great relationships with all four of our adult kids?

Don't believe the conventional wisdom that seeks to prepare you for "those awful teen years." The teen years can be absolutely wonderful! We have had six teens in our family so far, and never once have we heard words such as "I hate you! You are ruining my life!" coming from any of our teens, or even anything that resembles such sentiments. You see, by the time our children become teens, they already have major control over their learning and activities each and every day. They are not dependent upon us to tell them what to do. They prefer to get to work and do so independently and to a mastery level. We respect our kids and don't hesitate to thank them for their help and praise them for work well done.

We don't just love our kids; we like them too! But we got to this point by teaching them, at a very young age, to obey cheerfully and to adhere to a simple code of conduct. As they began to master their behavior, they received more responsibility and freedom. This spread into the realm of education where once they learned the basics of reading, they took off at a sprint and kept going until high school graduation. Were there bumps in the road? Of course, but not major ones. While we've had to make some attitude adjustments along the way, so far we've successfully navigated the wild waters of child rearing by taking ownership of our children's behavior *and* their education.

In the high school years, our teens have branched out into their unique areas of interest, aided by their parents as needed. Our children have been allowed to grow and mature in a safe place. They have adopted the standards of behavior and the attitudes of their parents as they've moved along a continuum of shouldering more and more independence so that they've earned our respect and trust. My fifteen-year-old daughter, Olivia, just got a job at a local coffee house this week. She can't wait to get to work and earn her own money, which she intends to put toward training for what she hopes will be her future career in music. She will need to structure her time well to work the hours at the coffee shop while keeping up with her studies. Her dad and I have no doubt that she is ready to branch out into the adult world. Olivia knows that to get where she wants to be will require time, commitment, and money. Step one? Make money. Check.

As we examine the educational options available to our families at the beginning of the twenty-first century, I hope that you will read over them carefully with a heart open to understanding which option will provide the biggest advantage to your child both now and in the years to come. After looking at what each option offers students, you'll see an Advantage Score which reflects how likely your child is to receive the self-propelled advantage in that particular educational arrangement. You'll be able to assess how likely your child is to learn self-mastery, work to a mastery level, and become self-learning in each environment via the Advantage score. Let's see what's out there.

Public Schools

First, let's look at the most common option, the public school system, which has been in place for several generations and which we know is having major issues across the country. Perhaps your local school district does not have any monetary or staffing issues; perhaps test scores on average are good. If you have children who are currently attending a public school, I hope that is the case. Some states struggle more with performance issues than others. I know that my state, Tennessee, is near the bottom of the barrel. Metropolitan Nashville Public Schools recently announced that only 46 percent of third graders had average or above-average achievement test scores in mathematics in 2011. That means that 54 percent of third graders were below average in mathematics! Apparently mastery is not the standard.

The public school system, in most cases, offers a classroom model of education. A teacher is given control of a self-contained classroom with any number of students. In the 2007–2008 school year, the average American public school classroom had 20.3 students, reports the U.S. Department of Education, National Center for Education Statistics (2009). As budgets have been cut over the past few years, class sizes have increased.

Why might parents choose public schools?

1. Parents choose public schools for their children for many reasons, but often the choice is made by default. Parents were raised in public school, as were their parents before them and their parents before them. In many people's minds, there is no other option.

2. Public school is a less expensive option than some of the other educational options. Because of this, many parents feel they have no choice but to use the public school system, regardless of how they would like to educate their children.

3. Parents make the choice to use the public school system because it meets the needs of their family.

4. Some parents choose to send their children to a public school due to the wide variety of extracurricular activities available. High school sports are extremely popular for athletically inclined students, and college athletic scholarships often favor student-athletes from public high schools. Band and choral activities, and drama and service clubs are examples of other activities parents favor for their children.

Other schools within the public sector include:

- *Vo-Tech schools:* Public high schools may offer part-time vocational-technical training to students. Programs often include business, construction, culinary arts, agriculture, technology, mechanics, healthcare, and human services, just to name a few. Students attend their high school for half the school day and then are bused to the area vo-tech school for the remainder of the day. These sorts of schools focus on career preparation which can place students on the fast track to post-secondary employment.

- *Charter schools* are a type of public school; however, they are a school of choice, meaning that teachers and students choose to be a part of them. Charter schools typically are not as regulated as regular public schools, and because of that, they offer more freedom in exchange for the expectation that academic results will be better than those of the general public school system.

- *Virtual schools* are a fast-emerging school choice. Some virtual schools are actually schools which is why I list them here. In a virtual school, a student is enrolled online, and a portion of the coursework is done online by the student at home. In my area, Metro Nashville Public Schools has recently introduced the option of a virtual school to a limited number of qualified students. These students work independently at home with public school curriculum. They generally check in with a teacher either through video chat or by telephone at least once a week.

Another example of a virtual academy is K^{12}, which I have examined closely. K^{12} is a private company that offers several types of virtual education. One type is free to students in selected areas and features some online work along with hard-copy curriculum which has been approved by the local state or county-level public school system. (Currently K^{12} is not available in all fifty states.)

K^{12} is an online public school, but it also has an online private school through its K^{12} International Academy. K^{12} is worth investigating for parents who are interested in teaching their children at home but don't want the responsibility of record keeping or choosing curriculum for their children. The program currently requires students to check in with a teacher by phone weekly or more often if needed. Students are required to master lessons to an 80 percent level.

One drawback is the program's inability to allow students to work ahead beyond a few days. In other words, if a student loves math, he cannot do as much math as he wants to do. He can only do the math that is assigned for the current week. I do, however, recommend looking into this program by visiting www.k12.com. It is a good program to use to transition from a classroom approach to more individualized home instruction.

Public Schools and the Self-Propelled Advantage

How well do public schools offer their students the self-propelled advantage? Let's break it down:

- Mastery: 10/33

The public school classroom is a place where mastery *potentially* can take place, at least for vocal students who aren't afraid to ask questions, or for students whose parents keep a close eye on their grades to ensure that they are mastering material to an A level. It's important to keep in mind that mastery will seldom be the standard in public school. A student blessed with parents who help him set high educational standards for himself can utilize mastery learning on his own. But in the public school classroom, there are few times when the classroom teacher will award *all* students an A average in any given class.

- Self-Learning: 10/33

Except in unusual circumstances, the public school classroom is *not* going to promote self-learning. Teachers are in the classroom to teach, and most classes are teacher-led. Sometimes a student may have the opportunity to learn independently, but that is not generally the case. Students who have the ability and desire to work independently may become bored and frustrated in the classroom. I did award a few points here because of homework assignments, research papers, or lab work where students occasionally do work on their own.

- Self-Mastery: 15/33

I simply cannot award many points to the public school classroom environment for being conducive to the development of self-mastery in children. Children will become like those with whom they spend the most time. Parents cannot oversee their children's behavior while they are separated from them, and a classroom teacher has his or her own standards of behavior which may or may not match those of the parents. Another consideration is one's faith. The public schools are designed to be neutral on faith issues, so if your faith is pivotal to your value system, don't expect those values to be reinforced, let alone taught in the public school system.

Children will begin to assimilate the attitudes and behaviors of those around them, so if their school friends are kind, loving, obedient, respectful, honest, trustworthy, and a delight to be around, you are in luck! If not, and if you would like to raise children who are kind, loving, obedient, respectful, honest, trustworthy, and a delight to be around, I recommend becoming the primary influence in your child's life for the duration of his childhood. Peers *will* have an influence on your child. There is no escaping that fact. Not all of that influence will be negative, but I urge you to consider the risks in twenty-first-century America, especially if you are a family of faith upholding strong moral values.

A student can definitely excel educationally in the public school system—and kids do this every day. However, the question is how far that motivated student might have been able to go if he had been allowed to follow the self-propelled model of education. Attending public school can definitely slow down a self-propelled student. The student is—quite simply—limited by the structure of the day where a certain amount of time is allotted for each subject in the classroom. A student is not free to move quickly through the bulk of his work in the morning, for example, in order to immerse himself in his particular passion in the afternoon. The mere structure of a public school day calls for the student to bend to the rule of fifty-five minutes for this subject, fifty-five minutes for that subject until the school day is over.

Remove those constraints, and the student is free to spend his afternoons pursuing his passion: shadowing a professional in a field of interest, beginning an online business from scratch, or being involved in other far-reaching projects that will give him a jump-start early in life.

I also must point out that although a student may excel educationally or perhaps in athletics or music in the public school, at what cost does he excel? What attitudes and behaviors will influence that student along the way? Is a student's relationship with his parents encouraged and enhanced via his peers? These are important questions to consider for those parents who want to maintain a vibrant parent-child relationship during the child's formative years and into adulthood.

The Advantage score for public schools: 35/99

Private and Parochial Schools

Private and parochial schools are the choice of many parents for their children. These types of schools generally come with a hefty price tag, although sometimes they offer scholarships. The primary learning arrangement is the classroom and a teacher, just like the public school.

Why might parents choose a private or parochial school?

1. Having taught in a private parochial school, I know that children are often given a private school education because parents feel that the instruction their child receives will be better due to a smaller student-teacher ratio than is found in the public schools.

2. Parents may choose a parochial school because they want their children to be raised in an environment that reflects their own religious or other values. This may or may not be the reality because the actual teachers the children receive will influence them the most, and not all teachers in a parochial school hold the same values the school holds. In those cases, the discrepancy is bound to come across to the students in some form or other during the course of a year. On the other hand, being taught by a teacher who shares a similar worldview ups the odds that a child will be influenced positively by that teacher.

3. Some parents, when faced with their child's expulsion from a public school, will enroll their child in a private school as a last resort.

4. Private schools often have higher standards of student behavior. Since parents elect to enroll their children in this type of school, the institution can require that students adhere to a strict and enforceable code of conduct.

5. Curriculum at a private school often matches the worldview held by the institution itself. For example, when I taught at a private Christian school, we used A Beka curriculum which is written from a Christian worldview. I had never been exposed to faith-based curriculum before, having grown up in the public school system. I can see why parents would choose a school whose curriculum supports their worldview. It is a nice option to have. However, during my year of teaching in this Christian school, the headmaster was caught having an affair with one of his two secretaries. (The other secretary was his wife.) This became common knowledge among students and parents. If actions speak louder than words, what did the students hear the headmaster saying that year? I decided not to go back and teach there the following year.

6. Sometimes parents place their children in a private school due to the elite status of the school itself. Attending certain private schools can give one a perceived edge in society. Those students who graduate from elite private high schools may be more desirable to elite colleges and universities. Notice

I said *may*. I doubt this is written on paper anywhere, but I guarantee that graduating from an elite, name-brand high school is a positive in the mind of an elite, name-brand university admissions representative.

Examples of schools within the private sector:

- *Montessori schools:* Montessori schools use a philosophy of education that emphasizes teaching children in a homelike setting. Maria Montessori designed a child-centered classroom where children are self-paced and given large blocks of time in which to learn. Montessori is a whole child approach to education that isn't centered around teaching facts, but allows children to learn by experiencing their environment. This process fosters knowledge, independence, and self-esteem.
- *Waldorf schools* are similar in some ways to Montessori schools. However, Waldorf schools promote fantasy and toys in the child's early years, whereas Montessori does not. Both strive to liberate children from rote learning while engaging them on many levels, especially through the arts. Waldorf education promotes more group activity with a higher level of structure for young children, stressing that children need structure and design. It is interesting to note that Waldorf education is humanistic and seeks to teach lessons about the soul, but not from any specific religious viewpoint. Educators in this vein feel that religion is a matter for the family to teach. They seek to raise independent thinkers who grow into self-directed adults.
- *Virtual schools* may also exist in the private sector. K^{12} is one example of a company offering a private virtual school experience. Students learn right in their home environment using a combination of textbooks and online learning, followed up by contact with a real-time teacher.

Private Schools and the Self-Propelled Advantage

How well do private schools offer their students the self-propelled advantage? Here's the breakdown:

- Mastery: 16/33

The private school classroom gets a 16/33 for being a place where mastery can *potentially* take place. But this is a good time to point out that the normal private school classroom is still a classroom learning environment, which by its very design is not set up to accommodate the time it takes to teach every student to a mastery level. I'm awarding more points here for mastery than I did for public schools because there is a greater likelihood that mastery will occur in a setting with fewer pupils per teacher.

While the private school classroom size may be slightly smaller than that of its public school counterparts, there is still the likelihood teachers will proceed to new lessons before every class member has learned the previous lesson to an A level. The expectation of A-level mastery by all students is most likely absent. Why? That is a very good question to ask your child's classroom teacher. Why aren't children given the time and tutoring necessary to learn everything to an A level? Moving on before a student understands what has been presented today means a gap in his learning that may or may not be filled in later.

- Self-Learning: 17/33

There is a greater likelihood that students will be given opportunities for self-learning in a private school setting. However, this was not true when I taught in a private school. My classroom resembled that of a public school except that the children I taught were better behaved—on average—and my class had at least ten fewer students than did the average public school classrooms at the time.

I did not actively promote self-learning in my classrooms years and years ago when I taught school. Why not? Probably because I was not trained to do so while in college. It just didn't feel right if my students were not all on the same page. I didn't want some students working ahead independently and some lagging behind. I wanted everyone to learn at the same rate. Of course, the reality is that this will not happen because children are not robots. So what actually happened is that I inadvertently held the more advanced learners back and gave them extra credit work to do while I worked to pull the rest of the class along. That is life in the classroom, be it private or public. I am willing to bet that most classroom teachers have a similar story to tell.

- Self-Mastery: 20/33

The private school classroom may be more conducive to the development of self-mastery in children than its public school counterpart by virtue of the fact that private schools often have higher standards of behavior. If your child attends a faith-based school, the population of students will, we hope, be kinder and gentler than the average public school population. Whether or not that is true will depend upon the school leadership and the expectations they set forth for their students.

Keep in mind, though, that having a strict code of ethics and firm behavior policies does not guarantee that students will not bully or harass other students. It just means that this behavior will be less overt. The likelihood of students being disciplined for such behavior is greater in a private school because once again, students attend by choice, and they agree to uphold school policies when they enroll. Private schools have leverage to remove students with poor behavior.

Parents have no control over their children during the day when they send them away to a school building in another part of town. It is a fact. There is a whole lot of trust involved in dropping a young child off at a school building. I confess that it doesn't make sense to me why people do it. In this era of violence and perversion, I cannot think of a place that is truly safe for young children besides the home. (For many children, their homes are not safe places to be—I realize that. Talk about a tragedy. But many children are still much safer at home than anywhere else.) It is a much different world than the world you and I grew up in.

I think it is interesting that Montessori schools attempt to create a homelike environment. That is ironic, isn't it? Remove a child from the home and educate him in a homelike environment. And the point of that is…?

The Advantage score for private schools: 53/99

Home Education

Home education is a relatively new option for parents to consider, brought to the forefront in the 1980s. When my family began its home-education adventure in 1991, home education was still barely accepted as a legitimate form of education.

Pardon me for going on a tangent here, but I'd like to relate how I learned about home education. I was born, raised, and educated in Pennsylvania, and I had never even heard of home education or homeschooling until my husband and I moved to Nashville, Tennessee, in the summer of 1988. I will never forget when a woman I met—who had two strikingly well-behaved boys—told me that she homeschooled her sons. My response was an indignant, "That's legal here?"

As a degree-toting teacher, my feathers were ruffled to think that a parent would dare think she was qualified to teach her own children! Then my new friend told me that she had been an elementary teacher before she had children. I felt a little better about home education then—at least this woman had a degree. In my defense, I should mention that I didn't even have children of my own yet. Once

I had my first, second, third, and fourth babies all within five years, I learned a lot about what parents actually know about their kids. Ha! I learned more about children and how they learn once I became a parent than I had ever learned in all four years of my college experience! And that is not an exaggeration.

I have to tell you that what initially drew me to home education was the behavior of the two young boys I told you about. They were probably ages eight and ten, and they had a respect for their parents that I had never seen in my classroom-teacher years. That is how striking and stark the difference was in these boys' attitudes. My friend's family was a cohesive unit, and I enjoyed being around them. After teaching other people's children, I was turned off by the crummy attitudes that many children possessed, and I honestly didn't want to have children of my own. But when my husband and I discovered a family whose children were delightful to be around as a result of the parents taking responsibility for their education, my heart changed. I had hope that we could train our future children to be as respectful and loving toward each other as these boys were.

So I went crazy having children. Yes, I did.

When we began home educating our children, we knew only a small handful of parents who did the same. Today, that statistic has changed, with good reason. The results are in, and many home-educated children are not "normal." Who wants to raise normal kids? If it is not the norm to raise children who are self-controlled, respectful, motivated, independent learners who learn with alacrity and passion, then I don't want normal kids, thank you very much.

Parents choose home education for various reasons:

1. Some parents simply want to be the major influence in their children's lives.
2. Parents are concerned with the quality of education (or lack thereof) their children receive in public schools.
3. Parents are concerned for their children's safety due the bullying factor and the outbreak of random, violent attacks in schools.
4. Some parents recognize that their child has special needs that will not be adequately addressed in a classroom situation.
5. More and more parents are choosing home education as they witness firsthand the results: home-educated high school and college graduates who are often more prepared and mature than their peers.

6. The growth of distance-learning opportunities, online programs designed for students to enroll in and complete from home, is advancing the popularity of home education. Virtual schoolwork can be completed at home, so why go to a school building?

7. Students can study college-level materials while in high school and receive both high school and college credit for the same course, effectively killing two birds with one stone (which is called dual enrollment).

8. Parents are gaining confidence that yes, they *can* educate their children at home and do a much better job of catering education to their children's interests and abilities than any public or private school.

9. Children have more time to develop their individual skills such as music or art. Heck, children have more time to spend on everything when they are learning at home. School subjects are not clock-driven but understanding-driven. Sometimes a math lesson takes ten minutes for a child to complete, and sometimes it takes longer. Every day is different, as it should be.

10. Flexibility in scheduling is another reason some parents opt to home educate their kids. Many don't like having to follow a school's schedule. Instead, they set their own schedule—one that fits their family's needs. This works especially well for families who travel frequently.

Examples of schools/approaches within home education:

- There are many and varied *approaches* to home education. We've already mentioned the Montessori and the Waldorf methods (although I don't personally know anyone who home educates in this manner). There's the Charlotte Mason approach, the Trivium approach, a Thomas Jefferson Education, and more. The list of curriculum and approaches is practically endless since home education by its very definition allows for individualized approaches to education according to the needs of the student and the desires of the parents. Just be aware that home education is not one-size-fits-all. Finding what is right for your individual child can be a little daunting at first. (Refer to chapter 9 for curriculum help.)

- *Homeschool co-ops* are often parent-organized groups that meet once a week for the purpose of pooling resources and teaching specific courses based on the needs of the group and the gifts and abilities of the parents.

This is small-group learning, for the most part. Sometimes students teach other students.

- *Homeschool tutorials* are similar to co-ops except that parents hire teachers or tutors to come in and teach specific subjects instead of teaching the classes themselves. This is similar to learning in a private school environment.

- *Unschooling* is a branch of home education that does not use curriculum or tests. Parents may use different degrees of unschooling in the home, but the tenet most hold is that children learn most naturally when they are allowed to learn only what interests them on any given day.

- *Virtual schools:* Some virtual schools cater to home educators as well. There is a lot of discussion currently in the home-education realm about whether or not virtual schools qualify as homeschools since there is still a reliance on hoop jumping and public-school-approved curriculum. I choose not to enter the fray, at least with both feet, but if I had to tiptoe around a bit, I would say that indeed, virtual schools are homeschools if the learning takes place at home.

- *Umbrella schools* are interesting critters. My family registers with an umbrella school each and every year. In some states, parents do not have to report to the local school district if they enroll with an umbrella school. The umbrella school, which may be online or may have a brick-and-mortar location, requires parents to turn in attendance records, grades, and curriculum lists, usually on a per-semester schedule.

    The umbrella school usually deals with high school transcripts, diplomas, and all of the necessary record-keeping stuff for college application purposes but retains the parents as teachers. Technically, according to current Tennessee state law, my children attend a private school. Of course, we are a private school in name only. Laws are silly sometimes.

Home Education and the Self-Propelled Advantage

How well does home education offer students the self-propelled advantage? Here is the breakdown:

- Mastery: 33/33

No other environment that I am aware of allows for mastery every day, in every subject, as effectively as home education does. The point of education is to learn, so why not learn well? It may take a little time to absorb some lessons to an A level; it might require going back and relearning a lesson here and there. Sometimes we must do some shuffling around if a student is not developmentally ready to learn a concept at the time the curriculum calls for it, but mastery is the standard and the expectation. (See how this is fleshed out in chapter 4.)

- Self-Learning: 33/33

Self-learning is not only possible in the home school, but in most cases, it should be the goal. Not every subject needs to be self-teaching, especially in the later elementary school years and into middle school. But a student should have the capability to read instructions, follow directions, read a book or text, and digest the material presented. Sometimes a student may hit a wall, so to speak, but with some adult guidance and advice, he should be able to get right back on track. Most students prefer getting at their books themselves without having to stop and be quizzed on every little thing by Mom or Dad. As parents in home education, we should be trusting our students to maturely digest their work and truly learn the material.

- Self-Mastery: 33/33

Who is more aware of your child's strengths and weaknesses than you? Who cares more for your children than you do? Who sets the standards of behavior in the home? You and your spouse, right? Setting forth expectations for behavior is our primary job as parents. Our children get their cues about what behaviors are in or out of bounds from us. Sometimes parents have blind spots where their children's behavior is concerned, but for the most part, parents are pretty dead-on when it comes to understanding their kids and what makes them tick. No one is better suited to train your child in proper attitudes and behaviors than you are. If you don't do it, who will?

Self-mastery *is* home education. Not too many parents these days seem to understand that if they can't stand being around their own kids, chances are good that nobody else can either. And no one else has the authority and opportunity to train their children as they do. If all parents took seriously their responsibility to mold and shape their children's hearts, the world would be a much different place for all of us. Home education presents the best opportunity for parents to teach their children self-control, kindness, obedience, respect for others, honesty, integrity, and all the many other things that a child needs to know to be successful.

The Advantage score for home education: 99/99

Why NOT Choose Home Education?

Not long ago, I posted a question on my Facebook page and on my blog. I asked my non-home-educating friends why they did not choose home education for their children. The results?

1. The results overwhelmingly indicated that most often, parents simply don't know *how* to home educate their children. They don't know where to start. I certainly understand that! Each state has its own rules and regulations regarding home education, for starters, and then there is the whole subject of curriculum. There is help, however! Lack of information and information overwhelm *can* be overcome.
2. Parents often do not home educate because both parents have full-time jobs. They don't see how they can teach their children at home while working full-time.
3. One friend entered motherhood later in life, and she indicated that she didn't have the patience to deal with her son 24/7. Many parents share that feeling of dread when faced with the possibility of spending all day, every day with their children. They just don't think they can handle that, and isn't that why they pay taxes? So that someone else can take over that job? (I'm not being flippant here. This is all stuff that was told to me by parents who do not home educate.)

Which Type of Education Is the Best?

We've looked at the main genres of education and some of the reasons why parents choose or do not choose them for their children. But which one is best for children? I can confidently say that the best type of education for your child is completely and utterly subjective. Remember our discussion on goals and how subjective they are? Your family's goals and values will dictate which type of education you choose for your children. I would encourage you, however, to do everything in your power to educate your children according to your values. Don't let anything stand in the way of seeking out the best education for your children. Remember, however, that education is not all about book learning. It is also about character development and preparation for real life.

I want to take a minute here and make a very important statement. I am convinced that no education can give a student the ability to become self-propelled as well as home education can. In fact, the other types of schools don't even offer self-teaching and mastery as options within their systems!

If you choose to home educate, it is an easy thing to incorporate group learning into your child's education by becoming involved with an educational co-op or participating in enrichment activities with other home-educating families. However, if your child is in the public or private school system, it is *not* an easy thing to incorporate self-teaching or mastery. These concepts go against the very nature of the system itself. Be warned! Incorporating them may actually be impossible. Group learning is king in these systems. Sure, there may be some opportunities here and there for self-study, but the teacher will almost always stand between your student and the material to be learned.

I advocate home education for those parents who desire to raise their children to become independent thinkers who learn with excellence in all aspects of their lives. You as the parent, with just a little know-how, can send your child on a lifelong journey that will bring joy and satisfaction to both you and your student. Parent-child relationships are enhanced via home education in a way that's impossible to replicate when a child spends all day, every day with a teacher and a classroom full of children.

Sure, it is possible to raise smart, hard-working kids who attend public or private schools. Some students thrive under the watchful eyes of teachers and prefer group environments. I get that, and I agree that home education is not the right choice for all students or their parents. However, kids who have the maturity to do well in public school most likely have the maturity to branch out and really fly in a self-learning environment where they can go full speed ahead, as fast as they want to go. The fun part as a parent is finding outlets for each child's special abilities and passions. I love helping my kids develop their talents, and home education provides the necessary time for them to devote to interests that go way beyond book work.

Many parents do an excellent job of teaching their children life skills and doing the necessary heart training at home, all while sending their children away from home and into a classroom for their education. I know parents have good reasons for choosing the classroom method of education for their children. It is their right to do so, and I rejoice that there are parents in this world who love their children just as much as I love mine even though we make different choices for our kids. What I am putting forth in this chapter is food for thought. I want to challenge parents to think beyond their children's academic learning and consider the bottom line of home education—that your children can go further, faster in a tailored setting that puts them in control of their education.

Once kids see the big picture, experience the delicious taste of freedom that self-learning gives, and are actually entrusted with the responsibility of their own education, nothing holds them back! It is education á *la carte,* suited to the gifts and abilities of each individual soul. And you get to teach your young children the joy of reading! No, you don't have to—you get to. You get to see your baby grow into a reader, a writer, and a mathematician, all under your initial tutelage. It's the most satisfying thing in the world! It beats the heck out of meeting the school bus at 6:30 a.m., five days a week, and all the while missing out on the biggest achievements of your child's life thus far.

Parents may think they lack the patience necessary to teach their offspring, but in reality, relationship building with my children is the most valuable part of home education to me. Sure, as a family we all get on each other's nerves from time to time, but it happens a lot less often than I remember it happening in my family when I was growing up.

My brothers and I never got along, it seems, and even now we are a bit estranged. I hate that. I don't want my children to dislike each other. I want them to learn how to have successful relationships with family and with others. I want them to be close both now and when I am no longer on this earth. A family is something very special, and its bonds are not broken even by death.

Do your children like each other? Do they respect each other? If not, I implore you to not rest until there is peace in your home. It's *that* important.

What If Both My Spouse and I Work Full-Time?

While I was blessed in my early child-rearing days to be a stay-at-home mom, I began a home business with my husband when I was pregnant with our seventh child. Because my older children, ages eight and nine, were primarily self-teaching at that young age, I was free to help with the business. Not long after we began our first online company, I began creating and selling *The Home*

School Student Planners to others due to the fact that the planners had solved every problem in my life as a home-educating mom! I knew that if I couldn't live without them, most likely they would really, really help others maintain their sanity too. I was right.

When my eighth child was two years old, we sold our original online company, and my husband and I went back into the workforce full-time. That's right, both of us worked full-time for a company located forty-five minutes from our home. Our hours generally didn't overlap, so one of us was home most of the time. When I was home, I was running my online company and overseeing a household of ten. My oldest was a high school sophomore in the fall of 2003, when I went back to work, so my kids were ages fourteen, thirteen, twelve, eleven, nine, seven, five, and two. Of course, my co-workers were incredulous when they learned that we home educated our children. I was constantly asked how that was even possible, and my reply always was, "Self-teaching and mastery learning. It's pretty simple."

During those years, my children helped run the household, and they helped each other with anything necessary. I will explain in later chapters exactly how I was able to home educate and work full-time. For our purposes here, I just want you to know that self-teaching made it possible. Your situation will look different than mine did when I worked full-time, but where there is a will, there is certainly a way. I just encourage you to look at all of your options before deciding against home education because you are working parents.

Single parents home educate their children every single day. It is totally a sacrifice on the part of the parent in one way, but in another way, his or her life is easier because the children are not out in the wild and crazy realm of the world doing who-knows-what with who-knows-who. If you are a single parent, with a small support system you can orchestrate home education and raise self-propelled children who are independent both now and in the future. Independent children are such a blessing to their parents in so many ways!

A friend of mine, Mary Jo Tate, lives in the single-parent realm, and I invite you to head over to her blog to find some especially encouraging and uplifting messages for single parents. Her blog is entitled *Single Parents at Home*. Here's a link to a beefy article on home educating as a single parent. Type this into your browser, hit enter, and read away: http://singleparentsathome. com/blog/2009/06/10/homeschooling-as-a-single-parent-how-you-can-make-it-work/

If You Don't Know Where to Start

If you are interested in offering the self-propelled advantage to your students, but you don't know where to start, simply continue reading. We will be discussing this very thing as we flow from the next chapter into the next chapter. One of the goals of *The Self-Propelled Advantage* is to give you the tools you need to begin implementing self-teaching, mastery, and self-mastery immediately with your children.

One of the important prerequisites to this type of learning is the necessity training your child's heart in proper attitudes and behavior. Actually, this part of parenting is absolutely vital no matter what educational venture your child embarks upon! In fact, instruction in self-mastery begins long before a child reaches school age. If you want to enable your child to have paramount success in life, heart training—self-mastery— must come first.

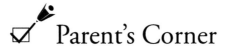 Parent's Corner

If you have young to very young children and are looking ahead to how you would like to educate them when the time comes, here are some questions just for you:

1. How am I already teaching my children? What do they know already because of me?
2. What values do I want my children to learn? What kind of people do I hope they will be?
3. Am I capable of teaching my children the basics they would learn in kindergarten?
4. Do I want to be separated from my kids five days a week?
5. Will I need to work outside my home when my kids reach school age? Does that mean I have to send my child away from home to be educated? Is there anything I can do to prevent this if I want to home educate?
6. How can I best give my kids an edge in their education?

If you already have school-aged children who attend school outside the home, here are some questions just for you:

1. Are my children respectful to me? Am I happy with my relationships with my children? Is there peace in my home?

2. Am I convinced that my kids are getting the best education possible? Do they have a good attitude about school?

3. Do my kids strive to learn to the very best of their ability? Are they A students? If not, do I believe they are capable of becoming A students? Is mastery important in the scheme of things?

4. Do my kids have friends whose values, behaviors, and attitudes I don't like? Who spends the most time with my children? Does something need to change here?

5. Am I willing to do what it takes to help my children get more out of their education? To help them understand all of their lessons to an A level? To check their homework to ensure that they are truly doing their best work?

6. If I know that my kids are not enjoying their school years, am I willing to make a change in how they are educated so that they can have the self-propelled advantage?

7. How am I currently giving my kids an edge or advantage via their education?

If you already home educate your children, don't feel left out. Here are some questions just for you:

1. Do my children get along pretty well most days? Do I like how they talk to each other? Are there behaviors that I need to work on with them?

2. Do my children older than age nine need me to help them with their school work daily? Is this really necessary? Would I like them to be more self-motivated?

3. Do my children get an A average each semester in their individual subjects? Is it okay to just understand 80 percent of a lesson and move on to the next one? Is mastery really important?

4. Do I believe it is possible for my kids to wake up each school day and do their work independently and cheerfully? Am I willing to do what it takes to help them get to this point?

5. How am I currently giving my kids an educational advantage?

CHAPTER 4

ELEMENT 1: SELF-MASTERY

The most important part of education is proper training in the nursery.
—**Plato**

The minute your baby enters the world, you become his teacher, and he begins learning from you. You get to teach him the foundational things he will be doing for the rest of his life, such as walking, talking, feeding himself, dressing himself, bathing, using the potty, and the list goes on. You begin to teach him self-mastery in the most physical sense, and most of this training occurs within the first twenty-four months of his life. Self-mastery begins during the initial phase of parenting; therefore, it is the first element of the self-propelled advantage.

After the first year or so of rapid growth, a toddler possesses self-awareness. He realizes that he can't do just what he wants to do, when he wants to do it. He learns that there are rules to his world. Some of these rules are designed to protect him. (No, you may not put your fingers into an electrical outlet.) Other rules are in place to begin teaching him respect for others. (No, you may not take your baby sister's toys from her.) Thus, character training begins in earnest.

Perhaps you're familiar with Robert Fulghum's book, *All I Need to Know I Learned in Kindergarten*. The first essay in this powerful little book traces the roots of all personal and social knowledge back to the typical American kindergarten classroom. The author touches on learning to be kind, cleaning up after yourself, sharing, balancing work and play, and my all-time favorite—taking an afternoon nap, just to name a few. I am a fan of Mr. Fulghum's work; however, I think that these lessons, attributed to the kindergarten teacher, should be credited to Mom and Dad. Shouldn't parents be teaching all of these things in the home long before kindergarten pulls the child off into a classroom somewhere?

These days, many infants go directly to daycare once Mom's maternity leave is up, where they essentially are raised by babysitters before being sent on to kindergarten. Many homes have simply become a place for breakfast before daycare; for supper, bath, and bedtime after daycare. Who is teaching these children the self-mastery skills that well-behaved children possess? How does character training occur if Mom and Dad are too busy to attend to the children?

The U.S. Department of Health and Human Services reports that in 2006, 53 percent of infants up to age one were in daycare centers, as were 60 percent of toddlers, ages one up to just under three. Finally, 66 percent of children ages three to six were being cared for in daycare centers.[19] These are jaw-dropping statistics, don't you think? Well over half the children in America were in daycare centers in 2006! So who was doing the character training for over half the children in America that year?

The sad truth is that frequently, character training—of sorts—happens in daycares across America instead of in homes via loving, caring, invested Moms and Dads. Daycare character training often yields children starving for attention, who are willing to do just about anything to get that attention. I understand that in a tough economy, parents do the best they can. Sacrifices must be made; however, too often children are the ones sacrificed in our society.

The youth of our culture are very often disconnected from their parents. More are disconnected than are connected, especially in the high school years. Instead of primarily growing up with their parents and siblings, as young people did before the advent of the mandatory government-funded school system, the youth of today grow up with their peers, apart from their parents and siblings for the majority of their waking hours. Is society the better for this, truly?

Families were designed to be character training grounds. Blessed indeed are the children who are taught their earliest life lessons by their parents and not by

---

19   Office of Childcare. 2006 "Table 13. Childcare and Development Fund. Average Monthly Percentage of Children in Childcare by Age Category," Administration for Children & Families. http://www.acf.hhs.gov/programs/occ/data/ccdf_data/06acf800/table13.htm [December 21, 2011].

their peers or sitters. The best way to teach a child acceptable behavior is to model acceptable behavior. Children will model the behavior of those around them. That is how they learn; they watch and do. Parents who live their lives with character are apt to make a more positive, indelible impact on their children than those who talk about having character, yet don't live it.

A Parent's Incredible Impact

As parents, we have an incredible amount of say in how our children turn out. I believe this with all of my heart. There are certain variables in the equation, of course. The power we have to shape our children, for better or for worse, is a very scary thing, and I do not say this lightly. Look at how your own mom's and dad's influence (or the lack thereof) has made you who you are today.

Imperfect parents are a given, and we can't place all the blame on parents when their children go astray, but parents have a responsibility to raise their children to lovingly respect them as the parents, and they also have the responsibility to raise children worthy of the respect of others. I believe that the lack of *loving* discipline from parents, and the lack of effective consequences for a child's behavior, beginning when he is young, are responsible for much of the heartache in our society. Children who never learn self-mastery are apt to not fare well inside or outside of the home.

The classroom teacher can learn a surprising amount about a student's parents by observing the student himself. A child's behavior is a direct reflection of parenting style. If a student is neat, organized, gets to school on time, and has her homework done every day, the teacher knows that education is valued in the home. If a student is lazy and careless in the classroom, falls asleep in class, and seldom presents completed homework, the teacher will make the assumption that there is a lack of educational support in the home. I've learned that there is invariably some sort of back story that explains why a child behaves irresponsibly at school, and it usually stems to an issue in the home. The teacher is the one who must deal with the fallout of parents who don't take it upon themselves to teach their children self-mastery.

Children *are* a reflection of their parents. How well children do in their school work is—in large part—a reflection of the expectations parents set and the support they give to their children.

Public Displays

We've all been in a public place and have seen a young child act up and defiantly rebel against parental authority. I immediately think of the mom standing in the check-out aisle at the grocery store, buying a bag of candy for her two-year-old darling because she knows if she doesn't, he will scream his head off. Giving in cannot become a way of life. Putting one's head in the sand as a parent and ignoring or giving in to behavior that you know is crying out for correction is a bad habit to get into and bears crummy fruit. Giving in is a form of rewarding the unwelcome behavior, which only serves to reinforce it and invite it back. We all know that, right? Yet it is hard for some parents to say no to their children's demands.

I like to say yes to my kids as often as I possibly can, but when I say no, they know there is a good reason for it. I tell them the reason for my decision, discuss it if necessary, and then I expect them to abide by that decision. Say yes as often as possible, but don't reward demanding behavior by doing so.

Controlling, manipulative behavior will only worsen as a child grows older. It is not just a stage, I assure you. Undesirable behavior must be nipped in the bud, or you can bet the teen years *will* be horrendous. I mentioned earlier that the teen years are wonderful years of building the parent-young adult relationship, but that is only if self-mastery was taught way back in the early years. Teaching a teen self-mastery once bad habits are locked in is difficult, but it can be done. There is hope. We'll talk about teens and self-mastery in the latter part of this chapter.

When Tim and I only had four children, we frequented a local Chinese restaurant. We were kind of celebrities when we went in because the staff couldn't believe how sweet and respectful our children were. At that time, the children would have been ages six, five, four, and two. The Chinese waiters would stare at us and then praise our children as if having sweet, respectful children was an unusual thing. To us it was not.

We expect our children to be sweet and respectful and obedient. Do children just come that way from the hospital? Uh, no. It takes a lot of attention to child training to raise children who behave well in public as well as at home. As parents, we certainly reap what we sow. We do not do our children any favors if we fail to teach them good manners, coupled with self-control. Well-behaved children reflect well on their parents. The good news is that poor behavior can be changed into good behavior!

Parents who have their children's respect, respect their children. I truly respect and value my children; however, I recognize that I am in authority over them and not the other way around. I must diligently train my children's hearts in obedience, respect, and right attitudes. It is a daily process in the early years with no respite except for naptime and bedtime. Self-mastery training is of primary importance and occurs way before the formal schooling years begin.

How Do You Teach Self-Mastery?

What if there was a formula for raising cheerful, obedient, respectful, trustworthy, fun, smart, overachieving kids? Would you be interested in knowing the formula? Is it even possible to turn lazy, underachieving, misbehaving, disrespectful kids into well-behaved, motivated self-learners who work with excellence because they want to, not because they have to? Yes! It is possible, and in this chapter, I am going to reveal the very formula that my husband and I have used for twenty-two years to raise self-propelled young adults. This formula is called the five steps to self-mastery.

Are our kids perfect? Are we perfect parents? Uh, no—a thousand times, no—to both questions! I have had my share of missteps, and I have regrets from my parent-past. I've learned some important lessons as a mom, that's for sure.

What Tim and I have done, however, is to take full responsibility for how our children turn out. We're molding, shaping, disciplining, loving, praying, laughing, and cheering for them all along the way. I should probably add crying to that list. Having children taxes the nerves, zaps mental and physical energy, disrupts sleep, and may even cause one to hear voices.

I've done my share of throwing my hands up in frustration at times, sobbing into the phone to my husband when he'd venture to call home on lunch breaks; yet the time spent disciplining and training our children's hearts has been the most important thing we could possibly have done for them in this life. Because we love them, we train them.

My kids are surrounded by love each and every day. It is a delight to nurture them, to pour out my life for them. I know that you would give your life for your children. Wait, if you are pouring your energy and your faculties into your family, you *are* giving your life for them. By being the best mom or dad you can be, you are laying down your life for their sakes.

If you did not have children right now, what would you be doing? The answer to that question tells you a bit about what you are sacrificing for your kids. The time you invest in training and teaching your babies will come back to you a thousand fold. A strong parent-child bond develops naturally as we love and take delight in our children. But we cannot neglect to mold and shape our kids as well. Neglecting to teach self-mastery yields children who are not delightful to be around.

The Five Steps to Self-Mastery

How does a parent teach a child to have good attitudes and behavior? Where does one even begin? Training children involves identifying and snuffing out behaviors that need to go, and rewarding behaviors that need to stay. It's that simple. While sharing the time-tested secrets to self-mastery, I am not going to hold anything back. I don't want to step on toes, but I don't want to neutralize the message either. Parents who want to utilize the five steps to self-mastery should honestly and completely read this section and honestly assess the current state of their children's hearts.

These five steps are logical and sequential. Following them will make it possible for a parents to lovingly get a grip on their children's hearts. Before we get to step one, however, I need to ask a question.

Who Runs Your Home?

Let's just get this question out of the way. May I ask you who runs your home: you and your spouse, or your children? If you are wondering how to tell if you run your home or not, take a look at the list below, and check off the behaviors you deal with—if any—on a regular basis.

We are not in control if our children repeatedly:

- yell or scream
- do not obey the first time they're asked to do something
whine or complain
- fight with siblings
- slam doors out of anger
- throw things out of anger
- lie
- talk back to parents or others
- ignore parents or others
- regularly do things they know are not allowed

If your children do any of the above with regularity, then your children run your household. Why do I say this? All of the behaviors I've listed above are behaviors that reflect a lack of respect for parents. Parents—by virtue of their status as parents—have authority in the home unless they abdicate that authority and allow children to usurp it. Children have authority when their misbehavior and bad attitudes run wild and unchecked.

In essence, when children disobey, they are saying, "I've decided not to follow your rules today, and here's proof."

Think about a police officer. An officer has authority by virtue of the fact that he has a badge and has been imbued with that authority. While he doesn't make the rules, he is there to enforce rules and protect citizens in the process. What are the consequences if I decide not to obey the No Parking rule? I will pay a fine and may even have to go find my car because it's been towed.

We live in a world of rules as adults, and our children must learn to do so as well. Children who do not obey their parents' authority will become adults who have issues with authority.

Certainly we are not police officers in our homes, but we must have rules. We set the rules. Isn't that a dream come true? Don't you just love that now *you* are the parent and get to make the rules? Lest all of this authority go to your head, remember what your mama said to you when you were a teen? "Just wait until you're a parent, and your son or daughter decides to do what you just did!" I remember my mom telling me something like that.

Parenting should not be a power struggle. You are the parent; you have the power to set the rules and expectations for behavior together with your spouse. The onus is on you to do so. Setting expectations is actually step one of the five steps to self-mastery. Let's take a closer look.

Step 1: Set House Rules and Expectations

Ideally, a parent begins to set boundaries when a child is old enough to comprehend right and wrong. You have to trust your instincts on this one because there is no set age at which children begin to understand what you want them to do. I guarantee that they understand us long before we give them credit for doing so.

Expectations and the Very Young Child

Toddlers can be quite willful, can't they? Begin to set expectations for behavior, such as—for example—not allowing the toddler to swipe toys from his baby sister. The first time he takes something from her, a parent must explain to the toddler that he may not do that, and if he does, he will receive a light smack on the top of the hand (or whatever consequence you deem to be equal to the crime).

He should understand now that it is not acceptable for him to take the baby's toys from her. Does this take care of the problem? Probably not. The toddler is probably going to put you to the test because taking the baby's toys is quite alluring. It's almost like a game. Take toys, see baby sister cry. But now you have set the expectation that taking toys from the baby will cause something slightly unpleasant to happen.

What do you do when the toddler once again takes a toy from the baby? Be diligent in issuing the consequence, just as you said you would. Sometimes the undesired behavior will stop for an hour or just for a day; it might start up again the very next day. Toddlers can be quite willful and stubborn, so you have to be diligent. Be very diligent. Don't give up teaching and training, and you'll reap the benefit eventually.

With young children, setting rules as you go along is fine. You don't need to have a powwow with your spouse and map out every if-then scenario your little one will need to know before he graduates and leaves home. That's just silly. Address misbehavior—even innocent misbehavior—by explaining to the young child what it is that he just did that isn't going to be tolerated, making sure he understands the action as well as its consequence. If that particular behavior arises again, follow through with the consequence.

The flip side of consequences for misbehavior is rewarding good behavior. Catching your toddler making a good decision is a time for celebration! If you see your 18-month-old child carefully handing the baby a toy, hug him and tell him how proud you are! Reinforce good behavior every chance you get. Young children love to please their parents, and they often do things simply to please you. (Savor those moments.)

Being diligent with our little children is imperative. We should know where they are and what they are doing at all times. Because this age requires such vigilance, we have many opportunities to diligently train and reward them daily. Children under the age of two are rapidly learning what is okay to do and what is not okay to do. Your job is not so much setting expectations as it is shaping the behavior you observe, minute by minute. Toddler training is spontaneous and intense. But the more diligent we are in training at this stage, the easier things will be for them and for us down the road.

Hopefully, you have been faithfully setting expectations for your child's behavior since he was very young. If you have not been, and you have a ten-year-old child who has never really been disciplined for his behavior issues, deciding to start now is going to be tough. By all means, start! Just understand that the longer you wait to set expectations, the harder it will be to get compliance.

Now let's take a look at how to set expectations for children over the age of two.

Expectations and Older Children

Expectations for behavior in the home are subjective. Perhaps your best friend has a higher tolerance for noise than you do. That is fine. But set *your* house rules according to the behaviors and attitudes you and your spouse want to encourage in your home, and stamp out the behaviors and attitudes that are not welcome therein.

Here are some expectations we've set for our children:

- Be kind to siblings and others.
- No yelling, screaming, hollering, or fighting.
- Do chores with excellence.
- Obey the first time asked.
- Be cheerful.*
- Do not whine.
- Work to the best of your ability.
- When in doubt, get permission.
- Lying will get you in serious trouble.
- Don't be sneaky or dishonest.
- Share whenever possible.
- Respect the property of others.
- Extreme silliness gets on Mom's nerves—be warned.
- Ask before eating between meals.
- Don't drink Dad's Diet Code Red Mountain Dew.

I think that pretty much sums up House Rules 101 in our household. I encourage you to make a list of the kinds of behaviors and attitudes you want to see reflected in your children, and a list of what you don't want to see. Putting it all down on paper is a good exercise that helps parents think about what they really want to foster in their children, and what behaviors they really dislike. Remember, you are the authority in your home. (Hang on to your list because you'll need it for the next section.)

If you noticed, I put an asterisk beside the "Be cheerful" rule in my list above. Tim and I don't allow our kids to walk around for days on end with a sullen expression. If there is a problem, we will, of course, be concerned and talk with the child and see what is up. Being sullen for the sake of being sullen can be done in one's bedroom, away from everyone else.

When siblings get upset with each other, as siblings tend to do at times, we will all talk together and work out the problem until all is well once again. Sometimes Tim and I send the siblings off to a room together to work out their differences, but the problem has to be resolved and isn't allowed to fester.

It is also important to note that our kids are not allowed to walk around mad at their parents. Communication is extremely important in relationships, and we always want to know what our children are thinking and feeling. If I think one of my children is upset with me over something, I will investigate and find out what is going on in his head. I want to listen. I want to understand his viewpoint. If I have inadvertently offended him, I certainly will apologize and ask for forgiveness.

Self-mastery truly is a lifelong process, and perfection is not the goal for us or for our children. Perhaps I should say that again: *perfection is not the goal*. As we are helping our children develop self-mastery, we must realize that everyone has crummy days, and there will be times when things don't go exactly the way we would like them to go. That's okay. Sometimes we just have to remember that tomorrow is another day, and we walk on.

Keys to Expectation Setting

Some important things to know about the process of setting expectations:

- *Begin setting expectations when your child is young.* Begin as early as possible to instill in your child the behaviors and attitudes you want to see. You do this best by correcting undesired behavior as it arises. Toddlers often do not mean to misbehave; they are merely being curious. But our job as parents is to protect them from themselves during those curious phases. For example, a toddler who crawls out of bed should be told not to crawl out of bed, but immediately the parent needs to take steps to ensure that the toddler cannot hurt himself when he tries to crawl out of bed again, because chances are he will try again.

Be prepared for your young child to test out his environment and keep him safe first and foremost, but also be prepared to issue a consequence when the child disobeys in order to teach him that it is better not to crawl out of bed in the first place.

- *Set expectations with your spouse.* It takes the two of you working together, and both parents must take an active role in expectation setting. When you are starting out with a young child, you can address issues as they arise. If you have older children, and you are just now beginning to clarify expectations for them, make a list.

- *You get what you expect and reinforce, so have high expectations.* Do not make excuses for your children's misbehavior. "Oh, she is just cranky because she missed her nap today." With all due respect, we get what we allow. If my child is whiny, it is because I allow it. If my daughter cheats on her school work, I have to do something about it and not ignore it. If my son doesn't do his work cheerfully and does not act respectfully to me, his mother, then I need to solve the problem immediately. It will not solve itself.

Story time. When my first seven children were ages one through ten, my husband was working a night-shift job. He was gone from 7 p.m. until 7 a.m., and he would come home in the morning and go right to bed. This kind of shift is incredibly taxing for both parents; we had very little family time together.

One morning when Tim came in from work, he found me crying in our bedroom. I had had a difficult time the previous day with the children not doing what they were supposed to do. I don't remember all that had transpired, but I had had to discipline a couple of them more than once. I was worn out and didn't want to face another day like that one, I sobbed to Tim.

Tim immediately asked all the children to come into the dining room, and they sat down on the floor along the wall, which was odd, but I still remember all the kids sitting Indian-style on the carpet. He proceeded to tell them—breaking down into tears—that he loved their mama, and he hated to see her so upset. He had heard about how difficult they had been the day before, and he wanted them to know that he wasn't going to allow them to treat their mom this way.

This was all the children needed to hear, because when they realized how their behavior affected their mom and their dad—when they saw how sad Tim and I were—they immediately were tearfully repentant. They weren't trying to make life miserable for me personally, but it took their daddy revealing his heart to them to make them see how their behavior affected both of their parents.

They all sincerely apologized, and I happily and tearfully hugged 'em right back. (I think there might have also been a group hug in there as well.) Tim proceeded to tell them that if I had to discipline any of them more than once during the day, they would be disciplined by him again when he got home. Yikes.

My point in sharing this story is to illustrate one way that Dad backs up Mom. He does so by letting the children know that Mom deserves respect, and respect equals obedience. Furthermore, he will not allow them to show disrespect to her without consequences from him. Moms need that. Children need that. My life was much easier from that day forward.

- *Model the behaviors and attitudes you want to see in your children.* It isn't fair for me to expect my children to have good table manners if I don't have good table manners, for example. Have you ever listened to your child and thought, "Wow, there's a lousy attitude that has to go"? We all have encountered crummy attitudes in our children at times, right? Sometimes, though, the reason a child has a bad attitude is that he has been modeling the attitudes of those around him. Sometimes he is even modeling the less-than-cheerful attitude that Mom herself woke up with. Yep, that happens in my house sometimes.

The realization that Mom's attitude affects everything is quite foundational to family life, and I am still learning and growing by understanding the effect my attitude has on those around me. Even our cats can tell when I am in a bad mood. They look up into my eyes, wait for me to say something, and when I just stare back at them, they cower, then scurry off in the opposite direction.

Have you ever thought about the fact that *how* we wake up our children in the morning has an effect on them for pretty much the rest of the day? If I stand at the base of the staircase and yell, "Alright everybody; it is past nine o'clock! Why isn't anyone at the breakfast table? Let's get moving!"

then I will have children that come to the breakfast table feeling grumbly, downcast, and definitely on edge. Who wants to wake up to that?

However, if I go into each of their rooms and greet each child with a simple, "Good morning! It's time to do the rise-and-shine thing. Breakfast is ready for you, so please come on downstairs," I am much more likely to be surrounded by sleepy but cheerful children at breakfast.

How you greet your children first thing in the morning has an impact on them for the rest of the day. What kind of mom were you first thing this morning? I frequently ask myself this question as well.

Attitudes are formed by the choices we make. Initially, we have to choose to be cheerful. Every morning we make a choice which will affect us and everyone else for the day. Once the day gets going, it is tough to turn around our negative attitudes.

Think of a train poised on the track at the tippy-top of a mountainside. That train represents you at the beginning of your day. Once the train gets started down the mountainside, it will pick up speed and will be virtually unstoppable until it comes to rest in the valley many miles later. When you wake up in the morning, picture that train in your mind. Picture yourself at the top of the mountain, poised to set out on your journey for the day. Realize that changing direction once you start down the hill takes a miracle, so it is best to start the day cheerfully.

Controlling *our* attitudes is a huge part of our own self-mastery as parents. Being polite to the clerk in the check-out aisle at the grocery store—who is more interested in gossiping than in working quickly, causing me to wait forever in her line—is pretty darn hard to do. If I have kids with me, they are watching me to see how I will respond. Am I polite, or sarcastic and rude in return? Ouch.

What if you wake up and don't *feel* cheerful? What if you have a headache or feel lousy or just don't want to get out of bed? I believe that is where we have to choose to put on a different attitude, just as you put on your clothes in the morning. You make the choice. It is really, really hard sometimes to choose cheerfulness, but it *is* your choice. Your children will be picking up on your attitude immediately and will be keying off of you. What attitude would you like your children to have today? If we want cheerfulness, then we need to be examples of cheerfulness. It takes an enormous amount of self-control some mornings, that's for sure.

I imposed a rule upon myself when my first four children were young. I told myself I was not going to yell or holler simply to get their attention. That meant that I would get up off the couch and go find whomever I wanted or needed at the moment. For example, instead of yelling, "Taaaaaylorrrrrrr!" when I needed him, I would actually look out the window for him or jog up the stairs to see if he was in his room. It was a lot more work than just bellowing, but in my book it was worth the effort.

Then I had four more children. I became older and more tired. Yep, I started to get lazy and would call for the kids when I needed them. I lowered my standards little by little without even realizing it. One day I heard my children yelling for each other and thought, "What is up with *that*? How annoying!"

So what did I do? I yelled, "Come see me right now!" Ahem. Then the irony of the situation hit me, and I remembered, "Oh, yeah. I never used to yell. What happened?" Guess where their yelling came from.

Here's some homework. Try it for a day to see how conditioned you are to yelling for your children. (We are not even talking about yelling *at* them. I don't recommend yelling at children for any non-life-threatening reason.) Try not yelling at all for anything for just one day. At the end of the day, evaluate how hard this exercise was for you. If it was tough, perhaps you should try again tomorrow and the day after that and the day after that until a new habit is formed. I guarantee your children will notice and will reflect a more peaceable spirit as well.

The good news is that on days when you do find yourself struggling to be cheerful, being around your cheerful children will perk you up! Cheerfulness is contagious.

Whoever said that parenting isn't easy was right on! We have to control ourselves as well as our children. Realization of the need for change in our own lives is the first step on the journey of our own transformation.

Step 2: Set Consequences

I must admit that the topic of obedience is a hard one for me to break down, as we just have always had obedient children because I would simply not have it any other way. Remember the story about how I was introduced to home education via a friend who had two respectful and well-behaved boys? Upon meeting this family, my attitude towards child rearing changed. I was so happy to see that yes, it *was* possible to raise children who love and respect their parents!

From the birth of our first sweet baby, we have trained our children to obey. Has it been easy? Not always. It takes an awful lot of follow-through and energy on the parents' part to extinguish bad behavior at any age. (Incidentally, bad behavior refers to any unwanted behavior in your household.)

Again, it is much easier to get rid of unwanted behavior when children are young. How does one do that? First of all, as we saw in step one, you and your spouse must have standards and expectations for good behavior. In step two, we focus on the consequences for misbehavior. It is imperative that you recognize the behavior you wish to eradicate, and that you address it every time it appears. Children *want* to know their boundaries, and it is our job as parents to set those boundaries and enforce them. You and your spouse need to get together and decide how to enforce the boundaries.

When my children were younger, our ground rules included being kind and loving to each other, no ugly talk, obeying the first time the child was asked to do something, and obeying cheerfully. Remember, reluctant obedience is not complete obedience. If I ask my daughter to please bring me a book from upstairs, she should not put on a pouty face and go stomping up the stairs. This type of behavior screams of disrespect!

Peace reigns in a home where love and respect for each other is the norm. Young children can be taught correct behavior, but it is up to the parents to make plain what the desired behavior is and have consequences for the unwanted behavior, while remembering to praise proper behavior.

The Power of a Praising Parent

Let's say you've gotten with your spouse, and you've discussed the things in your home that need to change concerning behaviors and attitudes. Hopefully, you've made a list of those behaviors and attitudes that you'd like to see in your children. Let's call it your Wish List. The only time you really need to make a Wish List is when you are in the beginning phase of learning how to train your children's hearts, and when you have a *bunch* of things to address at once.

If you had a handle on your children's behavior before reading this chapter, then you won't need a Wish List because you don't have major problems to correct. Congratulations! As any issue crops up, you simply deal with it directly, the way you have been doing all along. You, my friend, are in the minority. Many people probably wonder how your children got to be so well behaved, right? As if you are just lucky or something!

But now it's time to start a different kind of list. On this list, write down the good stuff your children do for which you can praise them. Perhaps your children are lax about cleaning up their own messes, but when you point it out to them, they cheerfully clean things up. The problem is that you have to point it out, and you'd like them to initiate the clean-up immediately following the mess-up. Remember, *it is always good to balance out a negative with a positive.* You may want to pop that statement on an index card and tape it to your bedroom mirror if you need reminding of the power of your positive words.

As you are preparing your list of things that need changing in your children, make sure you make a list of things that your children already do well. Shall we call this list your Happy List? Well, that is kind of cheesy, so feel free to call it whatever you want to call it. In step three, we'll utilize both lists and work some magic with them.

There is so much that our children do well in the course of a day that is worthy of note. A kind word such as, "Lilie, I really like the way you organize your things. You are such a good example to me," will uplift a child's heart.

"Adrienne, you probably don't know how much I love seeing you smile. Thank you for being your sunny self."

"Lydia, you always do your chores with excellence, and that makes me happy!"

Sincere praise and appreciation is even better than chocolate. Apply praise liberally, but sincerely, and your child will feel as loved and appreciated as he truly is. While you're at it, aim some praise arrows at your spouse's heart. We all deserve to be acknowledged and appreciated for the awesomeness we bring to our family's environment. Before long, your children will be following suit and letting you know what they appreciate about you. What goes around, comes around. It really does. Just watch and see!

A Thankful Heart is a Happy Heart

Along with praise comes thankfulness. One of the most important things to me as a parent is that my children develop thankful hearts. They won't develop thankful hearts if they don't have parents who have thankful hearts.

When I sit and think about all the blessings in my life, my heart is full. I can hardly stand it! What joy to count one's blessings! I love to thank my kids for blessing me, so I tell them frequently and sincerely—without being weird about it—that I appreciate the way that they (fill in the blank).

Sometimes I tell my girls, as a group, at breakfast time: "I really love the way you girls do your chores and then get busy on your school work every day without needing reminders—thank you!" They know I am sincere.

In return, almost every one of them—whenever I take them somewhere or even just cook a meal, will thank me for it. I love that! It blesses me to smithereens when they pepper me with thank-yous for everything from stopping for ice cream after piano lessons to going to the library. I don't fish for thank-yous. Ever. They just come at me. There is something about saying thank you that does the heart good, knowing you are doing someone else good by thanking them. Talk about a win-win!

Discipline

We've talked about the need for expectations and consequences, but how does a parent administer discipline? Obviously, the consequences for misbehavior have to be more unpleasant than the pleasure the child gets from the misbehavior, or else the bad behavior will not cease. There needs to be a consequence for *deliberately* doing the wrong thing. If I didn't gain weight from eating chocolate, for example, guess what I would feast upon daily! Some children only need a disapproving glance from a parent to correct them, while others need something more memorable.

It is not my intent in this book to advise parents on what type of discipline is best for their children. You know your children better than anyone else does. You know what makes them tick. You know what types of rewards and punishments will be most effective. Parents who love their children discipline their children.

Diligent discipline coupled with rewards for good behavior are necessary for the shaping of our children's hearts. Truly, I could write a book on discipline, but for the sake of our topic, I will simply say that you and your spouse need to have an effective system of consequences and rewards set up for your children, and the younger the children are when you begin correcting their behaviors, the better. Children are much smarter at a younger age than we give them credit for being. (You may want to highlight that sentence for future reference.)

Once you and your spouse have discussed the issues you have to work on within your household, the next step is to consider what consequences to offer if the rules of the house are not kept by the children who reside therein. In other words, formulate if-then statements. "If you do not do your chores with excellence, then you will receive another chore to do after you've gone back and redone the first one with excellence."

Be ready with consequences for the major issues. For example, honesty is such an important character trait to my husband and me that we reserve the most serious consequences if lying happens. My kids all know that they will fare much better by telling the truth because the consequences for lying are always the same and are not pleasant. In our home, there is nothing they can do to avert serious consequences if they lie to Mom and Dad. Save the most severe penalty for the most severe breach of conduct.

Conversely, most issues do not require severe penalty. One of my favorite—and probably most effective—consequences was devised back when our first five kids were little. I made up an annoying little song that the kids had to sing when they were not being kind to each other. While I wish I could sing it for you right here, right now, be very glad this is not an audio book.

The words to my annoying, yet satisfyingly-effective song are: "Be kind and loving to each other, be kind and loving to each other, be kind and loving to each other. Ephesians four, thirty-two." Nowadays, I jokingly threaten them with singing that song to each other—and at times I may still insist upon hearing it, so they don't know if I'm kidding or not—and that usually clears up any issues right then and there.

It is important to be creative in your discipline tactics. You know your children, and you know what works and what does not work as far as incentives go. Discipline is not a bad word. In our society today, discipline has a negative connotation; however, it is the wise and loving parents who keep a close eye on their children's behavior and discipline them when it is out of hand.

If you feel as though the discipline you are using is not working with your child or children, seek the counsel of a family who does have well-behaved children, and ask them what they do in their family to raise obedient, well-mannered children. We all need mentors, and in the discipline department, often parents just need confidence to know that they are not harming their children by disciplining them.

It is disastrous to the parent-child relationship if parents do not take authority in the home. If our children run our homes, it is because we gave them the authority to do so. Correct this as fast as you can. Loving discipline coupled with rewards for good behavior are major factors in exercising healthy parenting skills.

Other Discipline Issues

By the age of four, children should have grasped the expectations within the household; they know what is allowed and what isn't. There should not be a need for daily discipline on the parents' part. Yes, I'm serious. A four year old should be able to go through the day in a happy, obedient fashion without temper tantrums or fighting with siblings. The same should be true of the high school student. Sometimes stuff will happen in the course of the day where Mom needs to issue a warning, but then children should take that hint and straighten up.

This is a good time to inject that a warning should not be issued more than once. Why not? What is wrong with warning two or three times? If I repeatedly warn my child to stop a certain behavior several times before taking action, he will learn that he doesn't have to obey the first time he is warned. The more warnings I give before taking action, the lazier the kids become. Moreover, I am also being lazy by issuing more than one warning. Secretly, I'm hoping the child will just go ahead and obey so that I won't have to stop what I'm doing and follow through with consequences. Do what you say you will do.

Here is a scenario that may or may not sound familiar: the counting-to-ten-before-taking-action scenario. It goes something like this:

"Johnny, pick up your toys please."

"But I'm not done."

"One…."

"I don't want to."

"Two…."

"Why do I have to?"

"Three…."

Ugh! We only delay the inevitable by counting to ten. A child who obeys only when Mom gets to the count of three (or ten) has delayed far too long. Instead of allowing the child to argue, just apply discipline if he doesn't obey immediately. By doing so, you are saving yourself a lot of heartache and eliminating the opportunity for your young child to argue with you.

There are definite steps that must be taken to correct misbehavior. Each husband and wife must agree together on the standards and the consequences for behavior, and they must be willing to follow though together. There is no room for sloppy parenting in the early years because as we've seen, we reap what we sow. If we sow tolerance for whining, we will reap whining. If we sow the seeds of excuses for misbehavior, we will reap more and more misbehavior.

I strongly encourage anyone who is dealing with bad attitudes and general refusal of a child to cooperate, either in school work or otherwise, to get with your spouse immediately and devise a plan for dealing with the behavior. Children must know that they are not the ones in control, and their crummy behavior will not be tolerated.

Teaching and training our children's hearts requires discipline. It yields the peaceful fruit of harmony in the home. If you are faithful in loving your children, in letting them know that you love them enough to want to teach them right from wrong, then they will come to understand and see your heart in relation to the application of consequences. They will see that it is because you care about them that you take the time to pull the weeds in their lives before those weeds grow into oak trees and become much harder to remove. Do it while they are young.

Discipline and Guilt

I hear from moms who tell me that they do not like disciplining their children, or they do not like when their husbands discipline their children. This is a perfectly normal response. Parents should not enjoy having to discipline their children! Moms tend to be softies when it comes to discipline and prefer to give a child "just one more chance" as opposed to subjecting the child to discipline. In some instances, it is Dad who is the softie.

Sometimes wives think their husbands are too harsh with the children; that is normal. I believe one of the gifts Dads possess is the ability to be fair and balanced in the discipline department. I know my children much prefer to be disciplined by Mom than Dad. That tells a story, doesn't it? There are times when Mom needs to entrust discipline to Dad and allow him to deal firmly with misbehavior in the ranks, understanding that Dad loves the children just as much as Mom does. (Disclaimer: I am talking about consequences that are given in love, not anger. I do not condone child abuse.)

This may be a good time to mention that parents should share the responsibility for handing out consequences. Parents must back each other up. When Mom is on duty, she handles discipline; the same is true for Dad. However, at times Dad may need to step in—as Tim has done for me on several occasions—and reestablish the house rules when children appear to have forgotten them.

Sometimes, parents who don't spend all day with their children for whatever reason are reluctant to apply discipline out of guilt. They feel badly if the time they do get to spend with their children is centered around confrontation and discipline. Enter a bunch of trouble. What can parents do to lessen the feelings of guilt that may come from disciplining children instead of spending happy time with them?

1. Realize that you are the primary influence on your children, and if you don't discipline them, who will? Loving discipline is the right thing to do. Just do it, without guilt, knowing that your children have an advantage over those children who are seldom disciplined.
2. You reap what you sow. If you are faithful in setting consequences and enforcing them, your children will respect you all the more. If you do not discipline them, they will lack that respect, and they will, in turn, run the home by default.
3. A loving parent is a disciplining parent. Boundaries are healthy, and children need to know where those boundaries are.
4. A loving parent is a praising and thanks-giving parent. Balance discipline and praise.
5. Finally, as they say, catch your child doing something right. Don't overdo, but definitely do.

Self-Mastery and the Advantage

To extend children the freedom of self-learning, you must be able to trust your child. Period. Self-teaching allows room for the student to operate on his own, but obedience and trust go hand in hand when it comes to putting the burden of learning on the shoulders of the student. If you have been diligently instilling in your child immediate obedience without any questioning, whining, negotiating, or manipulating, then self-teaching will be a breeze! However, if you daily struggle with your children in the immediate obedience department, you may have some work ahead of you, but it is doable.

Do you find yourself giving in to your child's requests because you know he will not be happy if you do not give in? Do you repeat yourself several times before your children do what you have asked them to do? Are chores carried out well and done cheerfully? In other words, once again, who runs your home?

As parents, we are the ones who are to be in control; giving in to placate a whiny child means that child has just won, doesn't it? It is not a good thing to get anything less than happy obedience from your child the very first time you ask something of him. Delayed obedience is no obedience.

As you probably know by now, whining is not allowed in our home. It is a pet peeve of mine, actually. Because we made the effort to raise our first four children to respect Mom's and Dad's authority without question, our younger four naturally follow suit. Our younger children model the behavior of the older children, which is not always a good thing because we certainly do have our problem areas.

Tim and I are now reaping the benefits of having disciplined the older children in a timely manner when they were young and when *we* were young.

I remember spending countless days pregnant, exhausted, and crashed in a heap on the couch. As I would be about to drop off for a nap, one of my children inevitably would do something requiring swift and appropriate consequences. I would maybe hear unkind words being exchanged in the next room, or arguing over whose turn it was to clean up the toys.

How much easier it would have been to ignore the unkind behavior than to drag myself off the couch and deal with the situation, but I made a habit of addressing problems as they arose. Consequently, the children learned that just because I was lying on the couch, whether sick or resting peacefully, they still had to behave. That's not to say I didn't ever say, "Hmmmm…oh well," and go right back to sleep. There were some lazy moments, but they weren't the norm.

It is true that we reap what we sow. If we sow seeds of consequences for misbehavior, we will reap happy, obedient children as well as enjoy peace in the home. And eventually one can take a nap without a war breaking out in the family room.

The Behavior Barometer

If you have difficulty getting your children to obey you the first time you ask them to do something, you are not alone. Many parents allow this to go on in their homes on a regular basis, and I do not know why parents tolerate such behavior. Perhaps because it is easier to tolerate it than to discipline it? A bit of correction applied as needed can and will create a peaceful home environment.

Remember, it takes both parents coming together and setting expectations for the children, making sure the expectations, as well as the rewards and consequences, are laid out to the offspring. It is vitally important for Mom and Dad to be in agreement on a plan of action to change undesired behavior in the hearts of their children.

Actions come from the heart, so if we truly know the hearts of our children, we know if we have work to do in the area of discipline or if we are doing pretty well. The proof is in the actions and words we observe from our children daily.

One thing I make myself do from time to time is to closely observe the way my children are speaking to each other. I listen in when they do not suspect that I am paying any more attention than I normally do. Do I like what I hear? Do I like the tone of voice they are using with one another? Is there snippiness or impatience in the air in their interactions? Selfishness? This little exercise is kind of like a barometer in your home. If the results are good, the weather is fair. If the result of listening to their conversations with each other makes you want to scream, prepare for a storm.

I challenge you to listen well to your children's hearts as they reveal them to you via their conversations with their siblings or with their friends. If you don't like what you hear, you may want to choose a particular behavior to work on modifying.

The Fruit of Effective Parenting

Disciplining your child requires discipline on your part. This is a bit difficult to put into practice day after day, but consistency is the key to a child's behavior change. You must have more discipline than your child. This is hard work and progress is often slow, but progress can be made. There are often times when it would be so easy to give instructions a second time, count to ten, or be lenient just this once. However, requiring immediate obedience will save time, energy, and most of all, your sanity!

Children cry out for instruction whether they know it or not. We, as parents, daily choose whether to follow through in the consequences department or drop the ball. Each day is a fresh opportunity to turn our children's hearts toward self-mastery. The other option is to raise kids who drive you and everyone around you crazy! Who wants that? In the long run, it is very important to pay attention today to what is going on in your household. A peaceful home will be the result.

Does a teen just wake up one day and decide to be rebellious? No, rebellion in a young adult springs from a heart that has not been trained well in the early years. Rebellion in a four-year-old child is not cute or funny. If not dealt with, it will turn into rebellion in a first grader, then rebellion in a middle schooler, and then rebellion in a teenager. We cannot expect to break the cycle if we are not respectful towards our children and if we opt not to discipline them when they are young because "it's hard." Yes, it's hard. Expect it to be hard at first, but it definitely gets easier the more you invest yourself in the lives of your children.

At the top of this chapter, I mentioned that the day your child is born, you become a teacher (whether or not you were one before). Parents are qualified teachers simply by virtue of their love and allegiance to their children. The process of educating a child is not that difficult! Raising children to have the right attitudes and actions is by far the more difficult task.

Recently, a home-educating mom e-mailed me and remarked, "Teaching is easy compared to the child-training part of my job!" How true that is! School teachers do not possess some mystic knowledge bequeathed to them in the hallowed halls of a university. If so, I missed out on that part of my college education. A classroom teacher *can* teach a child's mind; the heart, not so much. A parent can teach a child's heart, mind, *and* spirit. We have that ability by virtue of being a parent. We have a love for our children that no one else has, and it is that love that will drive us to teach our children well in all three areas.

I remember being told by a woman in the grocery store, when she learned that I home educate, "I really admire you for doing that. It would never work with me and my child. We just don't get along that well. He would hate it." Those are some of the saddest words a parent could utter. Why? Because that parent is missing out on one of the biggest joys of life: a close relationship with her child. Home education could possibly be the best thing to recapture that relationship before it is too late.

Sure, it is possible to have a close relationship with your child if you do not home educate; however, it is much easier to maintain that relationship when outside influences are not present to interfere. I know my relationships with my children and young adults would be totally different—and not for the better—if I had spent 40 percent less time with them when they were growing up. To be home alone from 7:30 a.m. until 4:00 p.m. five days a week sounds totally depressing to me.

When someone says to me, "I don't know how you do it," in my mind I'm thinking, "No, I don't know how *you* do it being separated from your children all day." I would miss my children terribly!

Some parents lack the confidence to home educate, thinking their children would never *let* them. They hate having to fight with their kids and will give in to keep the peace. Others just have so many issues of their own that they don't have the focus and drive to educate their children at home. Until a parent has the unique vision and calling to do so, it is probably better for their children to stay right in the school environment where they are currently located.

Being around your children 24/7 is never an easy thing, especially when they are little and there are several of them. It's a sacrifice of sanity some days. Seeing the big picture—children who possess self-control, cheerful hearts, and are self-motivated—helps immensely. If you are in the season of life where you are training young hearts on a daily basis, remind yourself that you *will* reap a bountiful harvest for your faithful pruning. The more you fertilize and weed, the stronger the roots of your young plants become.

I want to encourage you that you are equipped to teach your children by virtue of the fact that you are the parent. You don't need a college degree to teach your child to read. You just need the desire to find out how to teach your child to read if you don't already know. Since we live in the Information Age, finding out what we don't know is a pretty easy thing to do. And by finding out what you don't know, you demonstrate self-teaching to your children. How about that!

Home Education Is No Silver Bullet, But…

I've met home educators who do *not* have their children's hearts. I've met home-educated children who are as discourteous as they come. Home education doesn't ensure that children will turn out any particular way. Show me parents who are concerned about their children learning proper behavior, morals, and ethics, and I'll show you parents who are raising their children to have self-mastery. These parents may educate their children in various ways, but their primary goal is that their children don't simply go through the motions of education for thirteen years and come out the other side looking and sounding just like everybody else.

Home education, by virtue of the fact that it is carried out in the home by the parents, is the best way to ensure that you are the primary influence in your child's life. If my kids go away from home to school, I am competing for their time and attention. I am located somewhere on the continuum of authority in their lives, but where? I can never be sure. And each of my children has a different source of authority—each has a different teacher—so we are not even all on the same page.

Furthermore, I don't even know what they are learning. I have no control over whether or not a teacher is going to decide to unveil issues that I, as the parent, am the one to unveil when I feel my child is ready. In our society today, bad is presented as good and good is presented as bad, morally speaking. Political correctness is rampant in schools. Did you ever dream there would come at time when recitation of the Pledge of Allegiance would come under attack? It's a different world than the one you and I grew up in.

Let me just say that it is a very cool thing to know exactly what your children know. Now, I'm not talking all the way through high school. My kids have experiences outside of us, their parents, but not until they are beyond the very young years. Call me overprotective. I've been called worse. I've had friends and relatives who years ago were very, very concerned to learn that Tim and I were going to home educate our kids.

Fast forward to today. Tim and I have been vindicated because our kids didn't turn out to be social misfits who can't get into college or find jobs in the real world. The opposite is true. Employers jump at the chance to hire home-educated kids, and colleges avidly recruit and pay them lots of money to attend their institutions.

If I want my children to turn out differently than the status quo, I had better do things differently than the parental status quo. Yes, I see it as my job to guard my children's hearts. I accept the responsibility for their hearts, and I make it my business to know what goes on in there.

I once heard a teen yell at her parents, "I hate you!" and then go stomping up the stairs, slamming the door to her room. From her room, I heard more muffled I-hate-yous and other assorted slurs aimed at her parents. What did her parents, who were sitting right next to me there in the family room, do? Not a thing. Seriously, not a thing. Why not? Because this was normal teen behavior to them.

It was appalling teen behavior! I wouldn't allow this from a two year old, let alone a young adult. Yet this scene is played out daily in many homes across America, and it is time for kids to stop abusing their parents. Oh, wait. Don't the parents have the power to break the cycle? Of course they do! Parents allow their kids to abuse them when they have the power to break the cycle. The norm in your home is what you allow it to be. Take action, and take back your home if necessary.

Let's look at *how* to take action in step three of the five steps to self-mastery.

Step 3: Family Meeting

Welcome to the easy step! I say it's the easy step because I like communicating with my family, and step three is all about communication. I love getting together, talking, laughing, asking advice on things, getting opinions on project ideas, and leisurely sitting around the family room with my kids. Family time is precious, especially when half of your children are grown and out on their own. Then the time you do spend together becomes priceless.

Group Discussions

Family meeting times at our house sprang out of Tim's and my desire to keep the lines of communication open with our children. We call a family meeting for many reasons, but most often it is done to discuss something important that is going on. Sometimes it is to hand out chores and make requests. These meetings may be called to discuss a problem that we are having that affects everyone, one that needs to be brought to the children's attention so the solving can begin.

A good family meeting is as positive as one can possibly make it. To give you an example of how we might proceed in our household, let's say that I am not happy because the kids are not doing their chores well. They've gotten sloppy. They are doing them, but not doing them completely and are leaving out several parts of the job. My husband and I would first talk together about the problem, just the two of us. In reality, I would most likely complain about how the kids are doing—or not doing—their work. He would listen, and together we would discuss how to solve the problem.

So in our discussion about sloppy-chore-doing, we would toss around a couple of if-then scenarios together. Should we give the kids a couple of options about how they will be punished for not doing their chores properly, or should we just give them one consequence to gnaw on the next time they are thinking they don't feel like doing their work?

What Tim and I usually do in our family meetings is present the problem and ask the kids to help us formulate a solution. Sometimes we offer consequences á la carte and have them choose the one they like best (or hate the least). Other times we let the offenders come up with their own ideas for consequences. Or perhaps we'll just let them know what-up and tell them what we've decided on their behalf. Offering choices is often the most beneficial solution because it gives kids a sense of control over their destiny and allows for more of a buy-in on their part.

Let's say before the family meeting, Tim and I decide to give the kids a choice of consequences with regard to the chores problem. We call everyone together, sit everyone down, and present the problem. We want to present the issue positively. How do you present an issue positively? First of all, start out with a positive statement.

Tim might say, "Your mom and I really appreciate your help with chores around the house. Generally you guys do a very good job."

Now it's time to state the problem. Your children are undoubtedly waiting for the proverbial *but.*

"But we have a problem. We're here to talk about it, and we want your help in finding a solution."

Now, after we present the problem, we want to give them time to discuss anything about the problem they would like to discuss. Perhaps the expectations for chore completion weren't clear when we first outlined what's involved. It's unlikely, but it is possible. Give an opportunity for them to talk about the issue—no finger-pointing, but a discussion of the issue. Sometimes they need some clarification of what it is that is not happening that should happen, or the other way around. Other times, they will know exactly what you are talking about. Be certain that everyone understands what the problem is.

Another point of a family meeting is to give opportunity for the children to realize what has been going on, and to apologize for it. Taking responsibility for one's actions isn't complete without an apology, even in a group setting. Usually one child will speak up pretty quickly after the problem is identified and apologize immediately (especially if Mom and Dad are pretty hot about the issue). The other kids will then apologize with rapid-fire succession. At that point, Dad will say something like, "Thank you. We forgive you." And I'll chime in as well.

If no one steps up to the plate to apologize, Tim or I might say, "Does anyone have anything they'd like to say?" It is not fun to have to drag out an apology. But we will, if necessary, because the apology stage is important for learning to take responsibility for one's actions. It can be a quick apology as long as it is heartfelt.

Once the apologies have been offered, and we have given the children our forgiveness, then we'll discuss how to fix the problem. In this case, we are going to give them two options if the same thing happens again. They can choose between losing their allowance for the week and going back and redoing the work, or receiving a whopper of a chore to do in addition to going back and redoing the work.

Because this meeting was meant to call a problem to their attention—more than one child was being sloppy with their work—*there is not going to be a punishment issued right now*. This session was designed to inform and to reset expectations, as well as to hammer out the consequences for all if they fail, individually, to do their chores with excellence. We don't punish the group for the failures of a few, but we do educate everyone all at once, get them on the same page, and then we walk on together. End of meeting.

Just to review, here are five steps to a positive family meeting to discuss a problem and find or present a solution:

1. positive statement
2. problem definition
3. apologies given
4. apologies accepted/forgiven
5. consequences determined

Everyone is now dismissed, or the topic is moved to something much more amenable.

The Parent-Child Meeting

What happens if next week one of the children does not do his or her chores correctly again? I'm glad you asked because it's such a good question. If I'm home and my husband is not, I ask the child to go hang out in my bedroom and wait for me. This is tantamount to asking him to chill while in the dentist's chair. I may even take my time going in to talk to him just to let him stew a bit. (Yes, I would do that.)

When I head into my room to talk with the child, I pretty much follow the five steps to a positive family meeting. I will make some sort of positive statement to start things off. "Nicholas, thank you for waiting quietly for me to come in." Then I will ask the child to tell me why he was sent to my room, which is the problem definition. I want to ensure that he understands what is going on. Always check for understanding, and have the child tell you why he has been called out.

Next, I am observing the child to see if he appears sorry for what happened. He should have an attitude of repentance; the child should not have any attitude other than being sorry for disobeying. He should not be cocky or defensive or sport an attitude of any sort. If so, you have a bigger problem on your hands, a respect problem. We'll get to that in a few minutes.

Expect a heartfelt apology from the offender. After hearing, "I'm sorry," I hug the child and say, "I forgive you." The offense is truly forgiven. In our home, we will pray together as well. My goal is for my child to leave the room feeling cherished, not punished. The air is totally cleared, and the child is ready to take his consequences.

What about consequences? The consequences already have been determined, remember? The child gets to choose between the lesser of two evils, as per our initial family meeting, but at least it is a choice. I am not telling him what he has to do. When he goes off to redo his chore that didn't get done properly, he needs to have a good attitude about it. No sulking, slamming things around, talking under his breath, or looking miserable. That is not repentance. Attitudes need consequences every bit as much as behaviors do. Don't be afraid to discuss attitude issues with your children and get those ironed out as well.

When you and your child are finished talking together, all should be well; you've forgiven him, and now you are ready to walk on peacefully together. If all is not well, don't leave the room until things are talked out. Trust your instincts on this one.

I didn't specifically say this earlier, but it bears saying clearly: be sure to take your child aside and speak with him or her in private. By so doing, you are showing respect for the child. I would never discipline one of my children in front of others, not even other siblings. My purpose should never be to publicly shame my child. Shame and humiliation have no place within the family. Children who have been shamed, humiliated, or ridiculed bear the bitter fruit of anger and resentment. A parent should never seek to shame, humiliate, or ridicule a child or teen. Discipline a child privately, meaning that just you—or you and your spouse—are present with the child.

Do your other children need to know what measures were taken with the offending child? Believe me, they will find out. Let the child be the one to give that information in his own way and in his own time if he wants to. The others already know what the penalty is for deliberately disobeying, so they won't be surprised. Moreover, they will see with their own eyes what punishment has been handed down if you issued a punishment that was a little out of the ordinary.

If there is a need for your other children to know what has transpired behind closed doors, saying to them, "Just a reminder that if you do _____, this will happen: _____," will suffice. Trust your instincts.

Natural Consequences

Sometimes, natural consequences will provide a level of embarrassment to a child, and that level of embarrassment will hopefully serve as a deterrent in the future. For example, if a child gets detention at school, he may be embarrassed about it. Embarrassing natural consequences brought on by a child's own doing are one thing, but parents should never deliberately embarrass or humiliate a child.

While natural consequences are not bad things, they are negative things that occur as a result of something else. If I poke my finger into an electrical outlet, I'll get shocked. The getting-shocked part is hopefully enough to keep me from doing it again. Of course, we don't want our children to get shocked, but let's be honest. Some children will not believe it until they actually do the thing and get shocked for themselves. Some children are just like that.

One of the most effective kinds of disciplinary action in the parent's arsenal is that of natural consequences. When my boys were in middle school, if they did not finish their school work before soccer practice, the natural consequence was that they would miss soccer practice. I bet you use this method of discipline as well. It works (unless the child doesn't like soccer practice). Natural consequences are effective for adults as well. If one doesn't go to work, one doesn't receive a paycheck, for example. We never outgrow natural consequences; they are inherent in the real world.

Of course, natural consequences should not endanger or harm a child. We wouldn't allow a child to learn, through natural consequences, that it is not a good idea to run out into the street after a ball. I just felt the need to clarify there.

Deferring Discipline to Dad

Earlier, I told you what I would do if my husband is not home and there is some correction that needs to be done. I want to point out that correction is best handled as quickly after an offense as possible. Saying, "Wait until your father gets home," is not always the best thing to do. As Mom, I should deal with things that happen on my watch, not pass them off to Dad when he gets home. If my husband and I have already decided on the consequences for misbehavior, and the children are aware of those consequences, I'm good to go. There will be exceptions, of course, where I feel an issue absolutely needs to be dealt with by Dad.

In the event that my husband and I are both home when an infraction occurs, I will happily defer to The Dad and allow him to handle step three. Seriously though, Dad should be involved in the heart-training process as much as possible. Dad should be the heavy, with Mom taking over when he is not present. His involvement truly sets the tone for the family. Unfortunately, a lack of involvement also sets the tone for his family.

Combining Steps

When engaging in steps two and three, you may find that there are times when you combine the two. For example, you call one of your children aside for something that has just happened that is outside the realm of acceptable behavior, and you have a meeting with him. In that meeting, you come up with the consequence on the spot. That is just fine. You won't always have the luxury of forethought.

It is possible there may come a time when you discuss a problem with a child or young adult, but at that moment you are not sure what corrective measures will be required. Sometimes you need a bit of time to think about a consequence or talk to your spouse about the situation once you get an opportunity to do so. Don't feel like the consequence will always be issued during the meeting because there are times when it won't work that way. Sometimes it takes time to figure out the best approach to take where consequences are concerned, and the child will need to wait a little bit until those can be determined. Expect the same attitude of repentance during this meeting, however. Offer forgiveness, but then the child will need to wait for closure.

Once the consequences have been determined, just meet up with the child privately once again and finish the conversation, expecting all the while to see the appropriate attitude from him or her. Then walk on together.

Discipline and the Single Parent

If you are a single parent, you have sole responsibility for the effective discipline of your children, and your job is a bit more difficult than mine. When both parents address a child and present a united front, the child is outnumbered. However, you do still have a set of effective tools to use. It's just that there is only one of you using the tools instead of two.

Remember that you are the parent; it is your responsibility to mold and shape the hearts of your children. Follow the five steps to self-mastery without fear. Don't be afraid to tackle the issues you see in your young children or in your older children. Be confident that you are doing the right thing by training your children's hearts.

In the event of a divorce, it is common for children to have two sets of house rules to abide by: one when they are visiting Mom, and one when they are visiting Dad. The best-case scenario is for both parents to agree to a standard set of house rules, but gee, I wonder how often that happens. I do not pretend to be an expert in this area. I also cannot imagine the energy necessary to be both Mom and Dad. (My best recommendation is for vitamins and plenty of rest. What do I know?) Don't be afraid to seek the counsel of those who have walked, or who are walking, in your shoes.

Remember my friend, Mary Jo Tate, and her blog for single parents? If you need the Web address again, it's http://singleparentsathome.com/blog/2009/06/10/ homeschooling-as-a-single-parent-how-you-can-make-it-work/. Mary Jo is a blessing to many.

The Past

You may be thinking, "I've made a lot of mistakes in my life. I'm not proud of some of the things I've done. How can I preach at my kids standards that I didn't live by in my past?" May I just say that I've done a lot of growing up since I became a parent? Almost all of us have learned things the hard way, but that doesn't mean our children must learn in that fashion. Our children do not need to know what has transpired in our past. Many things are best left in the past, and we walk on.

Perhaps an example here would be helpful. A mother who may have had her first child out of wedlock should not feel badly about teaching her children to abstain from premarital sex. The past is past. But what was learned from the past? The lesson is what's most important, not how the lesson was learned.

Pass on the lessons you've learned. You are not being hypocritical by doing so! It is natural to feel insincere when training our children in areas of our own personal weaknesses that stem back to our own high school or college years. Don't let the past be a reason to not train your children well today.

Step 4: Observe and Respond

Once the air has been cleared after a family meeting or an individual meeting, the next step is to observe behavior and see that changes are made in the upcoming hours, days, and weeks following your session. Praise your kids for the changes that your observe. Let them know you are—and will continue to be—watching and observing them. Thank them for earnestly making an effort to do better when you do see improvement.

If there is still sloppiness in the way a particular child is doing his chores, I will talk with my husband and see what he thinks we should do now. We'll discuss it, come up with a solution—perhaps giving the child a whole week of performing that particular chore to give him extra practice, plus extra chores—and let the consequences take their course. Eventually, the child will realize that it is a wise idea to do a great job the first time around.

Get creative if you have to, but always make the punishment fit the crime, so to speak. We don't want to be harsh with our children, but we do want to be firm. There is a definite difference between the two. Don't ease up on your standards; hold your ground.

Step 5: Repeat as Needed

The last of our five steps to self-mastery is simply to observe behaviors, and when you notice an off behavior or attitude, plug in to the appropriate step to address the issue. Talk to your child about the problem, set an expectation for change, and then watch for change. If, after setting the expectation for behavior, the child deliberately repeats the same offense, he's had his warning. Now it is time for a consequence.

Above all, maintain open communication with your children. We, as parents, are not dictators. We sometimes have to be firm, and other times we can be more flexible. Use the first four steps we've discussed to guide you and give you confidence that yes, you can control the behavior of your children. Yes, you can train their hearts now so that they have an inner moral compass to guide them as they enter the world beyond your front door.

Showing Respect

Not long ago, I was asked how parents *can show respect to* their children, so I decided to make a list for my own purposes and see how many ways I could come up with. Here is my list, although be assured, it is not exhaustive. Respect definitely is a two-way street. Showing respect to our children daily is vital to keeping relationships healthy and vibrant.

1. Listen well.
2. Give your children your full attention when they are talking to you. Make eye contact.
3. Don't interrupt.
4. Speak to your child like you would to a young adult—without a sing-songy little voice.
5. Speak kindly. Say please and thank you.
6. Don't deliberately embarrass your kids in front of people, including siblings.

7. Model the expectations you set for your children.

8. Apologize when you need to. Ask forgiveness.

9. Don't use "because I said so" with kids older than three. Take time to explain.

10. Spend time fully engaged with your kids, meaning put away electronic devices at times.

11. Knock before entering your child's room.

12. Don't air your children's shortcomings with your friends or relatives.

13. Ask before using something that belongs to your child. Don't give siblings permission to use an item that belongs to another child without that child's permission.

14. Allow children to do things differently than you would unless there is a good reason they should not.

15. Allow children to have their own opinions. Again, listen well.

16. Communicate, don't command.

Teen Issues

So what do you do if you have *not* been disciplining your children all along, and they are now teens with disrespectful attitudes? Effecting a heart change now is going to be like uprooting an oak tree, just to be honest with you, but it can be done. Both parents need to carefully consider together how to proceed.

Older children should understand if you say, "I am sorry that I have allowed this behavior to go on up to this point, but we are not going to tolerate your tendency to try to get out of your work, or your disrespectful attitude when I tell you to do something, or your whining and complaining," or fill in the blank. "We are not going to tolerate it," gets the message across in no uncertain terms. Remember, this is not a power struggle. You already have the power. You will need to be firm in setting new expectations for your teens.

Fine, but just telling the teenager this is not going to change the behavior, is it? Maybe, or maybe not.

Here is where you and your spouse are in touch with each other, and you go through steps one, two, and three. Determine the behaviors that your teen needs to focus on first. Pick no more than two at one time. Then determine the consequences for every time the behavior or attitude shows up. Both Mom and Dad need to stand together and have a meeting with the young adult at a time when everyone involved is calm and rational. (Bonus tip: if possible, don't make decisions when you are tired and worn out.)

Begin with a positive statement as discussed in step one. Follow that up by asking the teen if he realizes that when he does _____, it makes you feel _____. For example, "Jack, I don't know if you realize it or not, but when you roll your eyes when we ask you to do something, it makes us feel disrespected."

Give Jack time to respond to that statement. He is likely to be defensive and come back with something like, "But you ask me to do things that I shouldn't have to do!"

At this point, my husband might discuss what it means to be part of a team, a team that has respect for each of its members. We'd let Jack know that the expectation is for him to do what he is asked to do respectfully—without complaining, eye rolling, or anything else.

We would also let him know that when he is asked to do something, his response needs to include, "Yes, Ma'am," or "Yes, Sir." (We live in the South, and this is commonly how one responds to an older person.) Tim would probably then throw in something to the effect that if Jack can't show respect on his own, we will have to assist him by giving some consequences if he chooses not to change his responses.

Obedience is a choice. Make sure your teen understands that he has the power to control his own destiny in this situation. Avoid sarcasm. Your tone of voice should be firm and calm. Your eyes should reflect your loving, concerned heart.

"Jack, It is unacceptable for you to complain (or sigh, or roll your eyes) when we ask you to do something. You need to work on breaking this habit, and your mother and I will help you to do so. Every time you fuss or complain at your mom or me, you will (insert consequence here)."

Perhaps the teen loses a privilege. Perhaps he spends time in his room without screen time or whatever he usually does in his room. Don't be afraid of your teen. I know, that is a weird statement, but some parents—moms especially—are afraid of the confrontation that arises when they talk to their teens about their behavior. That is why it is important to get with your spouse first, devise an approach to the problem, and then both talk with your teen.

The flip side to negative consequences is to reward the desired behavior when it shows up. This is much more effective for most young people. "Jack, I like the way you just took out the trash for me this afternoon. It meant a lot to me that you are trying to do better in this area." Don't be creepy or cheesy about it, just be sincere.

You know your child and what makes him tick. Do not make excuses for his misbehavior, but covenant together with your spouse to find the right pressure to apply to effect change. You have to apply pressure if you want to see a change.

If you are currently experiencing issues with your teenager, all is not lost! But you have some serious work to do. Don't despair about where you are, but try to see how you got there, and work with your spouse to turn the ship around immediately.

I want to encourage you that having joyful teenagers is a possibility! It is not the norm with children whose primary influence has been those outside of the family core. Peer influence is a destructive force if children spend large amounts of time around others who do not hold the same values you do. It takes strong family ties to withstand the onslaught of influences that go against the values that you and your family hold dear.

While Tim and I have had to discipline a teen upon occasion, we have not had a young adult rebel against our authority to this point. And all of them are bigger than we are. No, I don't believe we are just lucky. I know in my heart it is because we deeply respect our children, and they respect us back. There is a hierarchy of authority in the home, but love is at the center of everything we do. Our young adults know that when we make a decision and they don't agree, we will listen to them heartily and then make the best decision for all. There is a trust that is based on the knowledge of being loved and respected, and happily, it goes both ways.

The Link

Is it just by chance that the kids in my laboratory (house) not only exhibit self-control resulting in good behavior, but they also excel academically? No, I don't believe it is by chance. Please know that I don't say that proudly. There is a link between self-mastery and high academic achievement, and it has taken me years to draw this conclusion. My students have good study habits and a good work ethic; they also carry high GPAs. *There is definitely a link between self-mastery and the ability to work independently and with excellence.*

Trustworthy kids can easily become self-teaching kids. The converse is also likely to be true. Children who cannot be trusted to be honest and work independently will not be able to work without micromanagement. Remember, if your children's hearts have not been well trained, you will not be able to trust them to work without your constant monitoring. Children who are lazy and unmotivated will require lots of prodding. Can you see how a student's behavior most definitely has an effect on his education?

Our children are our life's work; they are our *magnum opus*. It takes time and attention to detail in parenting children, but good things will come as a result of our efforts. The biggest thing to remember is that while we are not perfect, we are the parents. Have fun with your children, love on them, and make sure they know how proud you are of them, but continue to work on their areas of weakness with them. You will be rewarded with a peaceful, loving home and with children who will grow up and thank you for your investment in their lives.

Self-mastery is the most important element of the self-propelled advantage. If you can only plug in one of the three elements into your child's world, make it the process of self-mastery. Constant self-improvement is an art, and we are all works in progress. While self-mastery is elusive and can never be completely achieved, we should always be moving forward on the path towards greater and greater self-mastery.

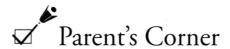

Parent's Corner

1. Do you and your spouse share similar expectations for your children's behavior?

2. How did your upbringing contribute to your views on discipline?

3. On a piece of paper, write the name of your oldest child. Make a list of all the things you like about him. Repeat this exercise with each child's name. Heck, go ahead and make a list of what you like about your spouse, too. Put this paper in a safe place. Retrieve it during times of frustration so you can remember the good stuff along with the momentary not-so-good.

4. How do you demonstrate respect towards your children?

5. Are your children respectful towards you? Do they need to improve in this area?

6. Are there currently any negative influences in your child's life? If so, what steps can you take to minimize those particular influences?

7. Take a few moments to listen to the way your children interact with each other when they don't know you are listening. Do you like what you hear? If not, are you willing to put in the time and effort to effect change?

8. If you haven't already, meet with your spouse to discuss steps one, two, and three. Make lists of expectations and consequences. Have a family meeting. Start today to experience more peace in your home!

CHAPTER 5

ELEMENT 2: MASTERY MINDSET

Only one who devotes himself to a cause with his whole strength and soul
can be a true master. For this reason, mastery demands all of a person.
—Albert Einstein

The second element of the self-propelled advantage is mastery learning. Mastery is indeed a mindset. In the realm of home education, it is a secret weapon in terms of giving children an educational edge unlike any other. How is mastery defined? Mastery learning simply is the process of learning any given material to an A level. A student does not move on to subsequent lessons until he has fully grasped the current one. It's such a simple concept!

Mastery learning just makes sense unless one is in a classroom setting where the teacher does not have the time and the resources to ensure that each child understands a lesson totally and completely before moving on to the next lesson. It does not take an advanced learning theorist to see that if a child moves on in, say, subtraction before he totally understands how to borrow, he is going to have a rough time of it. In fact, chances are good that if he does not completely understand the borrowing concept, he is likely to do poorly on the next concept that is introduced because each concept builds upon the previous one. Before long, an I-can't-do-math attitude develops which can shadow a child throughout life.

Mastery ensures that children build success upon success. Mastery, however, is totally dependent upon readiness, especially in a child's early years. Just because a first grader's math book says it is time to learn how to tell time doesn't mean that the child will have the ability at that exact moment to learn such an abstract concept. In a classroom, the teacher teaches time when the curriculum dictates, not when she determines the students are ready to tackle time.

What happens if a student in the class doesn't have the ability to grasp the concept of telling time yet? He fails. The teacher moves on. The student carries that sense of failure with him as the class approaches the next element in the math curriculum.

In my home, I had children who were not ready to study time when our math curriculum said it was time for time. Instead of wearing myself and my student out by going over lessons on time day after day, trying to think of new ways to approach the concept (which my student simply was not mentally ready to dissect), I merely skipped the unit on time and went on to the next thing in the book. After a couple months, I came back to the time unit and checked for readiness. Eventually, the child was ready and easily grasped the material. All my kids can now tell time, in case anyone is concerned.

We do our young children a disservice when we plow through the curriculum and allow the curriculum to tell us what the child should be ready for and when. It is so important not to let the material dictate readiness. A child is ready when he is ready and not a day before. With young children, mastery of a concept may not be possible at this very moment. Giving children the gift of time to mentally grow and mature is one of the major advantages of home education.

Is Teaching to Mastery Cheating?

If a student misses more than 5 percent of a lesson, he or she needs to go back and study what was missed and recheck for mastery at that point. This means that at times a student is given more than one chance to take a test. Is that fair? In public school, students generally only get one chance at a score, so why are home-educated students given credit for relearning? Isn't that cheating?

Uh, no. It is not our fault that the public schools do what they do. They actually allow students to miss 30-, 40-, and 50 percent or more of the material and then just roll on to the next level. "You didn't understand it? So sorry, so sad, but we have to move on." The teacher lacks the time to help the individual student reach a complete level of understanding before advancing. Just because it is done this way in a public school doesn't mean we have to do this in home education.

It makes absolutely no educational sense to say, "Well, Joey, I see that you missed eight questions in your chemistry lesson today. That is a C (which supposedly means average), so as long as you are not getting a failing grade, let's move on."

What a crazy thing to do! Move on when the student obviously is missing a good portion of the lesson? The home-educated student doesn't have to be satisfied with only understanding 70- or 80 percent of the lesson! He can take the time to back up and reexamine what wasn't understood the first time through, doing more study until he *does* understand it all.

Should he still be given a grade that reflects his knowledge the first time through, or should he be given a grade which is a true reflection of his knowledge *now*? I say that a child has to earn the grade, but if it takes a couple times through the material to master it, so be it. Does he totally and completely know the material right now? If so, then I am going to reward that knowledge. I don't care how the student acquires the knowledge; I want him to know it completely! What is the purpose of education? Thorough understanding of each lesson should be the outcome of education.

You know your child. If in first grade he is presented with something brand new in a math unit, and he doesn't understand the lesson, and he misses everything on the page, you will probably both be 100 percent frustrated. If you work and work and work, trying to help him get it, but he still doesn't, guess what! He is simply not ready yet to learn those concepts. Skip that unit and catch up on it in a few weeks. Don't force the child to fail. There should be no such thing as failure! Switch things up a little. If you can't progress in the math book without the child understanding this particular concept, then take a little break from math for a while.

Don't allow your curriculum to be your master. It is only a tool, after all. Reteach the concepts in a different way and see if that helps your child. If it does not, it is definitely a readiness issue. I am assuming that the child is not trying to play games with you here. All children are different and may require more time to master any given concept, so if the readiness to learn isn't there, put the work aside for a while and come back to it.

What Is the Goal of Education?

Grades are not the ultimate goal in learning, although they usually are a reflection of effort. Certainly we want our children to understand what they are doing, whether it is a lesson in math, reading, science, or anything else. The goal is not an A. However, an A should be the *outcome* of mastery learning every single time.

When my student reworks the math problems he missed on his test, I make sure that he knows *why* the problems were missed. Once the problems are corrected, I either retest, or I give him at least partial credit for the corrected work. (The amount of credit given depends on the reason the problems were missed in the first place.) I am rewarding the student for the knowledge he now has; for the effort he has shown.

If he misses more than 10 percent of his work the next day, then there is a problem that needs to be addressed. If the issue is sloppiness, then the child does not get the chance to increase his score. He takes a hit in his grade *and* the work is redone. But if the issue is lack of understanding, then once the student goes back to relearn the material and shows that now the understanding is there, the grade reflects that outcome.

Accepting less than A-level work from our children sends them the message that either the material isn't important enough to be learned, that it isn't important to do your best, or that excellence isn't worth the trouble.

If something is worth doing, it is worth doing well. By setting a standard of mastery in home education, we are teaching our children to learn thoroughly for the sake of learning, not for the sake of a grade. It should bother them to *not* understand something. They should not shrug their shoulders and just move on. We have to fight against "a B or C is okay" mentality. The only way to do that is to insist that everything done in the student's school work be done to a high standard of actual understanding. Encourage relearning, and reward work well done.

Michelangelo said, "If people knew how hard I had to work to gain my mastery, it wouldn't seem so wonderful at all." Michelangelo, one of the greatest artists in history, had to work at his craft. It took intensity to create his masterpieces, even though art was his passion. When we are passionate about something, it still takes hard work to live out those passions. The end result of mastery learning is an adult who searches for understanding and wisdom and does not give up easily. A yes-I-can attitude shadows him throughout life.

That is precisely what I want for my children.

Why Don't Schools Teach to Mastery?

The entire point of mastery learning is to make failure obsolete and to prevent cracks in a student's educational foundation. Why, oh why, would schools—both public and private—not want to ensure that each child learns to a mastery level? The answer? *Teachers don't have time* to ensure that every child learns the material before the class moves on. It is as simple as that. It is as sad as that. However, home-educating parents certainly should have time to see that their children learn to mastery every single day. Advantage: home education.

Not to be repetitive, but mastery learning entails learning everything in today's material to an A level. All self-propelled students should be learning every single subject, every single day, to an A level. If there is a problem, the student just gets extra practice until he comprehends the lesson in its entirety, and then he moves on.

If a public school student in a tenth grade chemistry class fails a quiz on balancing equations, what is the chance that this student will fail a test based on the same subject matter later? The chance is close to 100 percent that the student will fail unless there is intervention on the part of the teacher, the part of the parent, or some other influence in the student's life.

I'm sure you remember my chemistry rant from earlier, so I will not spend a lot of time re-ranting. Because my chemistry teacher accepted the fact that the best I could do in chemistry was D-level work, I also came to the conclusion that the best I could do was D-level work.

The reason I love home education and mastery learning so much is because students do not need to be embarrassed or ashamed if they do not get a topic the first time it is presented. It's okay! Isn't that exciting? Students are not set up for failure! If one of my kids does not understand a math concept or a language concept, I am going to know right away by the grade he or she gets on the day's work. A red flag is raised, and it is my job at that point to find a way to help the child understand the material that was just presented. Older students generally do not need help. They just go back to the content that was just covered, and review it to glean what they did not catch the first time around.

Success Motivates!

Here is another thought on mastery learning, and it is a very important thought: success motivates! By not allowing your student to move on to the next lesson until he has mastered today's stuff, you are ensuring that your child builds success upon success. And remember, success motivates like nothing else.

Perhaps this would be a good time to share some information on how to instill the love of learning. Keep in mind that school work is still just that—*work*. Children do not genuinely love work, do they? Come to think of it, I don't genuinely enjoy some types of work, but other types I do enjoy. We all have those gray areas where work doesn't seem like work. With that said, and with the understanding that there is no magic formula which causes children to enjoy every subject you set before them, let's get to the good stuff: the love of learning.

How to Instill the Love of Learning

Let's take a look at an old approach to education in hopes of illustrating a more effective way to foster learning. That approach is the teach-and-test mentality, the old-school rule that children must be tested after something is taught to them in order to ensure that learning indeed took place.

Think for a moment about one of your passions. Perhaps it is a hobby, such as scrapbooking or knitting or gardening. Maybe you spend your spare time woodworking or painting or organizing. I am passionate about gardening. I love growing and nurturing flowers. Not vegetables, but flowers. I have a love-hate relationship with vegetables and prefer to ignore most of them. But flowers soothe the soul.

Let's say I order a new book on gardening from Amazon, and of course I am terribly excited to dive into it when it arrives in my mailbox. However, before I can crack open the book, my husband takes it and decides that he will create a syllabus to go along with the book for me, just to make sure I cover all of the bases. He also devises a chapter test to follow each chapter, and he provides me with a notebook in which to write out the answers to his questions. And when I finish the book, he wants me to write a ten-page paper on the history of gardening.

Do you think I am excited to read the book now?

Absolutely not! Inwardly, I am a bit resentful that he thinks I need to do all of that stuff in order to learn. All I want to do is read the book on my own and absorb it for myself without jumping through any hoops to prove to him that indeed, I have gotten my money's worth. Why can't he just trust me to study the book on my own? If I am honest, I am frustrated before I even crack open the book. I set it aside, and the dust immediately begins gathering on the cover.

Of course, my husband would never do this, but I have done it in the past to my children. For years I have done this to my children! I've given them a shiny new book full of interesting information, and then required that they show me proof—every three pages or so—that they are indeed learning. Why not just give my students the books? Why not let them read them as I would read anything set before me as an adult? Why chop a book up into twelve segments with quizzes and tests and papers to write?

The answer to these questions lies in our fundamental perspective on how children learn. We have been programmed to expect that children will chafe at the opportunity to learn, that their default setting is "I don't want to learn," so we have to regulate their every lesson with testing of some sort. When we take this approach, we steal the love and joy of learning from our students! We weigh them down in order to enforce learning.

A Mindset of Trust

It is time for a new mindset—a mindset of trust. If we trust our children to learn what we set before them, we do not have to legislate learning. Children must be trustworthy, of course, but when they are given the freedom to learn without restrictions, children become motivated and interested in what we set before them. Doesn't that just make sense?

Aren't you more inclined to work or to pursue an interest if you are allowed to attack it without restrictions on how it must be done? Perhaps you need instruction along the way, but you are apt to try to figure things out on your own first, which is exactly what I want my children to do—attack a problem or question, look at it from various angles, and try to solve it on their own. They will take responsibility for learning if I don't demand that they do things from an old-school mentality.

So why do we chop up subjects into little bite-sized pieces for our children, and then require that they regurgitate their learning in the form of a test or quiz? It is because we don't believe there is a better way. All we've known from our own experience is the teach-and-test mentality. We think we have to bring the classroom model into our home and act as a teacher to our students.

When you think about a classroom teacher, she has a classroom full of students whom she truly doesn't know, doesn't have any real authority over, and doesn't have time to teach to mastery. I used to be that classroom teacher, and my M.O. was teach, test, and move on. Sure, there were gaps for some students who had difficulty with a subject area, but I couldn't *require* that the students learned, which was frustrating. Some wanted to learn, and some didn't. Some struggled, some didn't. I didn't have the authority to change the poor attitudes that many students possessed. My job was to present the material and try my best to get students to cooperate and learn.

Self-propelled students deserve a totally different set up. As parents, we have the authority to insist that learning occurs. I set the expectations for my children, and I have authority to give consequences if mastery learning does not take place. There is no way around it for my children: they have the opportunity to learn material presented to them to an A level each day. That is the expectation, and it is a realistic one. They meet these expectations naturally and cheerfully.

Sometimes parents are happy if their children achieve a B or a C in a subject, and that just does not make sense. If a child has to learn something, why not require that they learn *all* of it? Students will rise to our expectation levels. Sure, we all have bad days, and sometimes readiness is an issue for a child. We know our children intimately, and we know when they are being lazy and when they are just struggling and need additional time to work before moving on to the next lesson. We can make the necessary adjustments and give additional help when necessary. Just as important as giving help is setting high standards. Those high standards are the framework within which students should work and work well.

Am I against testing? Not at all. Testing is a tool that measures learning, but it should not be the only tool. Too often we rely only on testing to measure learning. With younger children, it is necessary to ensure that they are truly learning the material. With math, we can easily tell if they are learning a concept just by looking at their daily work. Reading is easy to assess as well. Phonics and language skills are built upon day after day. The more reading-intensive subjects such as history and science are where we tend to require written quizzes and tests after every two or three pages in the book. This writing often weighs children down and interrupts the flow of what we want them to be learning!

I suggest allowing children to do quizzes in their heads and look back in the lesson text if they are not sure they remember the answers. Then they fluidly move on to the next thing. I trust my children to make sure they know the answers before they move on, and when they have earned this trust, they are not likely to abuse it. I also allow them to mentally take tests in history and science at this level. Sometimes they *want* to write the answers down as they go along. Sometimes I ask my students to see me when they get to a test, and I give it to them orally. Once again, I have seen that if a lot of writing is required, children get bogged down, they lose interest, and they do not remember what they have read. By setting them free from all of the written work, they enjoy the material and retain it better.

This type of freedom to learn doesn't make sense from a classroom teacher's standpoint, and never once in my classroom teaching days did I give students the freedom from writing everything out, but that is because I *had* to require all that writing in order to measure learning. I didn't have time to spend individually with the children, discussing what they had read, nor did I trust that they would just naturally want to learn.

As a home-educating mom, I *do* trust that my children will learn without having to stop every couple of pages and write out answers to questions that they already know the answers to because they just took the time to learn it! Why weigh them down and hold them back by requiring so much writing? Accountability is necessary, but writing is not the only way to measure mastery. I firmly believe that not trusting and not allowing our children to learn independently steals the love of learning right out from under them.

To my high schoolers I grant even more freedom. There are some subjects that are required, obviously, and then there are some that they may choose. We sit down every nine weeks to set goals for the upcoming quarter, but then I give them freedom to decide how much they need to do each day in their subjects. They know the expectations for the quarter, and they are trusted to meet those expectations.

I check in on my high school students regularly to ask a few questions about what they are doing in this or that subject, and I ask for a math grade every day. I trust that if they do not understand something, they will ask for help. My high schoolers have always preferred to work things out on their own first, and I see that as a beautiful side effect of self-learning. Do I ever have them write things out? Not as proof of learning.

I do require the writing of short essays twice a week using vocab words, but I don't grade the work. I read their work and enjoy reading it, and I will let them know if they need to work on a particular area, or if they have misspelled a word. I enjoy reading their thoughts, and I want them to enjoy writing. Again, I set the expectation that writing takes place, and then I allow them to meet that expectation responsibly. If they do not, then I will be much more invasive in their school work.

My children appreciate this freedom, and seldom have I had to rescind that freedom. Why? Because at the high school level, they have spent years earning my trust. I still hold them accountable, but because they have proven to be trustworthy, my job is extremely easy. My role is that of coach, not teacher. School days are enjoyable and unstressed for my kids and for me.

Charlotte Mason (1842-1923) said, "Let them get at the books themselves, and do not let them be flooded with diluted talk from the lips of their teacher. The less the parents 'talk in' and expound their rations of knowledge and thought to the children they are educating, the better for the children. Children must be allowed to ruminate, must be left alone with their own thoughts."

I simply love this quote! It supports my view of education as being a responsibility on the part of the child rather than the responsibility of the parent or teacher to teach the child. However, because Charlotte was never a parent, she did not possess the confidence that her children were reading and absorbing information on their own, so one of the methodologies she required was narration, the oral summary of a passage that was read.

On occasion I have my students provide me with a loose summary of what they are doing in their work; however, I do not require a narration following every single reading assignment. That is terribly burdensome to both parent and child. I strongly hold that narration as a testing method falls into the category of being an unnecessary burden on our children, weighing them down and sapping their motivation. In a natural learning environment, the child will spontaneously share his excitement without the sharing being mandated by the parent. Required narration is the counterfeit to happy discussion.

Recently I spoke at a home school convention, and I talked about the joys of self-learning for both parents and students. Afterward, a woman told me about her sixth grade daughter who reads over her science book, writes out the questions at the end of the chapters, but takes an enormous amount of time to finish the work daily. The mom told me she spends a lot of her morning cajoling and nagging her daughter to get her work done. Mom suspected that she was just moving her eyes over the words, not really learning anything. Her question to me was, "How do I get her to learn this without me having to holler at her every day? She is just not interested in science, or so she says."

To me, it was obvious that by switching up the approach to learning, the student would be able to shift into true learning mode. I suggested that she make a deal with her daughter. She does not have to write out all of the answers to the questions at the end of each little section if she can mentally answer them; she should look back at the lesson to find out anything she didn't know the first time through the reading. Mom would ask her questions about her work initially, and if she didn't know the answers, she would need to go back and write them down.

A week later, I heard back from the mom, and she was amazed at the change in her daughter! Not only did the student know the answers to the oral questions her mom asked her, but also she was *taking her own notes* on the material along the way, writing down what she wanted to remember versus what she felt the book was dictating that she remember.

Do you see how Mom was giving the student freedom and trust? She began allowing her daughter the freedom to learn without written interruptions, and in response, her daughter actually started writing things down of her own volition. By putting the onus on her daughter to learn in exchange for being set free from the burden of writing out everything, a fire was kindled in the child's heart for learning science. The child rose to the occasion and showed herself to be faithful in learning independently.

If a child is given freedom to learn on his own, but the parent learns that the child is not doing the work and is not able to tell the parent what he has been learning that week, then the child simply loses the freedom to work independently and has to go back to writing everything out. Before long, the child realizes how much better it is to work independently and will meet expectations the next time he is given that freedom.

Independent learning is a privilege to be earned, and it can easily be taken away. The fact that Mom can take it away and send the student back to the miserable realm of having to write out everything is what motivates my students to be responsible students.

The Gift

Trusting my children to do their work and do it to an A level is my secret to being an underwhelmed home-educating parent. I have confidence that the kids will speak up if they need my assistance. By setting high expectations and enforcing those expectations at a young age, a parent teaches a healthy respect for learning that carries over into every area of life. By not permitting a job to be done to anything but an A level, chores included, you teach your student that quality is extremely important, as is the resolve to do one's best.

Why not give the gift of trust to your children? Why not give them freedom from the shackles of the teach-and-test mentality? Trust them to soak up a book without endless interruptions to test their learning, and see if they do not become more motivated and interested in what you set before them.

Mastery is all-important in the early, foundational years of a child's education. *Not* understanding a concept may spell disaster for a young child because he will be building upon that concept in the future. If the foundation is not stable, the whole building is at risk.

I hope you can see how naturally mastery can occur once a parent and student possess the mastery mindset.

Mandated Mediocrity Versus Mastery

I recently finished an excellent biography of Harriet Beecher Stowe entitled *Harriet Beecher Stowe: A Life*. Harriet was the author of *Uncle Tom's Cabin*, and she lived in the early-to-late 1800s, during our young country's turbulent years encompassing Pre-Civil War, Civil War, Reconstruction, Prohibition, Women's Suffrage, and the emerging educational system.

I shot off an e-mail to the author of the book, Dr. Joan Hedrick, who won a Pulitzer Prize for *A Life,* expressing how moved I was by her depiction of the life and times of women in the nineteenth century. I must have mentioned home education somewhere in my note, for Dr. Hedrick acknowledged my note with a thank you, explaining that truly, "Education has come full circle." Alas, Harriet Beecher Stowe had home-educated her children in the 1830s and 1840s.

Full circle. Interesting choice of words, I thought. In Harriet's day, children were educated by Mom around the hearth and in the parlor. Basic education was provided for at home by the settlers of this country. Granted, education was more rudimentary at the time, but the home-education opportunity existed. People taught their children things they wanted them to know, things they would *need* to know to get along well in life.

Today we have resources galore from which to choose in the education of our children. We have many and varied types of schools and institutions available, yet today, many parents are bringing their children back home—into the parlor and around the hearth—in order to give their children an excellent education. Full circle, indeed.

Government Regulations

Here in Tennessee, we currently enjoy great liberty in the realm of home education. There are, however, some things the government feels the need to mandate, and one of those areas is the need for high school students to spend a total of one hundred fifty hours on each subject in order to receive one credit for having completed a course.

Counting hours of work is one of the stupidest state requirements I have ever heard, and I am a former classroom teacher and have heard a lot of stupid requirements. Just because required hours are put in by a student in a classroom, be it public or private school, doesn't mean that mastery has ever occurred. And if a student masters his course material in ninety-nine hours, why should the student be denied credit because it didn't take him one hundred fifty hours to get through it? Mastery isn't the goal; credit hours are the goal.

I expect and trust my kids to master their material regardless of the time it took them to do so. True education means the students *master* the material and then move on at their own speed and not at the speed of a government-imposed regulation. Hours have absolutely nothing to do with mastery. Finishing books *does* have a whole lot to do with mastery, however. Funny, but in public school, we never once finished a textbook. Ironic, isn't it?

Public schools are not concerned about mastery; they are concerned about test scores. Don't settle for anything less than mastery in your world. Mastery means thoroughly digesting the presented material and demonstrating that understanding according to set standards—and not necessarily just tests, either. Mastery is attained when a student reaches the goals set by the curriculum, or the goals set by you, or the goals set by the student himself as he uses the curriculum.

Tips for Students in a Classroom

If your children are educated in a public or private school, mastery is most likely the *ideal*. The reality is that when a student gets a B or a C, the teacher is not likely to raise an eyebrow.

You can instill the standard of mastery by asking your young children to bring home their tests and quizzes for you to look over. Have them go over the correct answers with you, as much as you possibly can without having the teacher's manual right beside you. Encourage them to find out the right answers in class by asking the teacher or looking up the answers themselves. Help them develop a thirst for knowing the correct answers, as well as seeing where and why they made their mistakes.

Older children can get on the mastery train by redoing anything they miss on a quiz or test; looking up the answers, and doing their own research to find out what they did not know the first time around. Encourage the mastery mindset in your children. Help them see a reason to go back and find out what they didn't know the first time around the block. By relearning material, they are plugging potential holes in their foundation.

In Conclusion

Mastery makes a difference in our children's lives. Children who work to an A level are confident, high achievers because they know it is okay to not get everything right the first time through. They have the luxury of going back and relearning, although it certainly requires commitment to do so. They still aim to hit the target the first time around, but if for some reason they do not, they are not satisfied until they have been able to go back and finish strong.

Mastery causes students to stand out in the crowded landscape of college candidates. Coach your children to run the race, to finish the course by overcoming all the hurdles. The way is over, not around. Teach them to run the course with excellence. Your expectations of your children today will shape the final outcome of their education. Expect mastery, and live it yourself with passion!

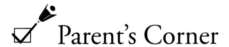

☑ Parent's Corner

1. How can *you* demonstrate mastery to your children in your daily routine?
2. If you home educate, how do you check for mastery in your children?
3. What are some ways to see how much your child has learned aside from testing?
4. Do you think it is an advantage for your child to learn his lessons to an A level? If so, are you willing to put in the work necessary to instill the mastery mindset in your home?

CHAPTER 6

ELEMENT 3: SELF-TEACHING

Learning how to learn by learning how to think makes a well-educated person.
Learning how to learn not only expands the mind. It also gives you a lifelong
asset. Once you have it, it stays with you for the rest of your life.
—T. Kaori Kitao

The third element of the self-propelled advantage is self-teaching. Why is self-teaching the third element and not the first or second? Parents first begin teaching self-mastery to their child at a very young age, long before the child is ready for kindergarten. As the child becomes kindergarten age, he is ready to venture into the land of mastery learning. He should begin learning his lessons, each and every one, to the best of his ability before moving to the next lesson. Once the child begins to develop standards of excellence through mastery learning, he is ready to begin working independently. Self-mastery and mastery are prerequisites to self-teaching.

What Is Self-Teaching?

Let's take a moment to define our terms before we get too far into this chapter. First of all, the terms *self-teaching* and *self-learning* are interchangeable. But what do they mean by way of definition?

A student is a self-learner or a self-teacher when he learns any new concept, idea, or skill independently—without acquiring the information from a classroom teacher's mouth. An independent learner can learn a concept, idea, or skill from a book or from the Internet or from an interview. How else do self-learners learn? Let's look at an example. If I'm studying horticulture, and I need help, some things I might do as a self-learner are:

- scour the Internet for answers
- look up material at the library
- talk to an experienced gardener
- download a relevant MP3 file (audio) from iTunes
- join an online forum for gardeners

A self-learner employs the tools at his disposal. He has options! He does not *require* a teacher to stand in front of him, tell him what he needs to know, and then test him on the knowledge acquired via lecture mode. Furthermore, a student can retain much more material if he plays an active role in delivering that information to his own brain. That's just common sense. Or is it? It doesn't seem to be common in the realm of modern-day schools.

Self-learning is not the only way to learn, but those who can work and learn independently possess an enviable skill that will cause them to stand out in a crowd. Being skilled in teaching oneself is often paramount to success. Why? Successful people know where to go to find out what they don't know. Unsuccessful people are likely to hit a wall and quit.

Self-teaching requires a student to have the ability to work independently, and self-taught students are motivated by the sense of a job well done. They are self-motivated because they have the confidence that if they don't know an answer to a question, they know how to use available resources to find out the answer. Self-teaching students can often finish their courses in a fraction of the time it would take to study the same material in a traditional classroom setting.

The opposite of self-teaching is teacher-teaching, which sounds kind of silly, but that's exactly what it is. Back when I taught school, I was responsible for many things in my classroom, but one thing for which I was *not* responsible was choosing curriculum. I was given the books from which I would teach. In the home-educating environment, the parents (or the parents and student) choose the materials.

My job as a classroom teacher was also to teach material to my students within a certain time frame. Teachers usually follow the directions in their teacher's manuals, which explain how to present individual lessons to all students in the classroom at the same time. I love how teacher's manuals assume that all children are on the same page as one another.

As a classroom teacher, it was my job to assign homework and then to give quizzes and tests to make sure that learning occurred. I would never have handed the teacher's manual for mathematics to the students in the classroom environment so they could check their own work, yet I do it all the time with my own children at home. Why is this? How do I know my children aren't giving in to temptation and cheating?

The difference is that unlike the classroom teacher, I know my children intimately, and I know when they are truly doing their work and when they are not. There is a relationship of trust balanced with accountability. Such relationships do not exist between a classroom teacher and all of her students, and she generally uses a test format to check for learning.

Self-Teaching and the Classroom Environment

How much self-teaching did you do in high school? How about middle school, or elementary school? If you are like most people, self-teaching was not a part of your educational upbringing. Teachers get paid to teach, not to teach kids to teach themselves. In most classrooms today, teachers set the pace for learning. It's their job. They get paid to run the classroom. Gifted children may have opportunities to pursue the occasional self-led lesson, and a few teachers here and there will sometimes offer a student-led classroom environment. By and large, however, self-teaching and self-paced learning are the exceptions in a public or private school classroom.

Because it is so rare to find a school that supports a student-led initiative, self-teaching is not an option for children who are students in a classroom environment. I can just see the look on a teacher's face if a parent were to march into a classroom one morning and announce, "My son prefers to learn independently. Can you please just give him his work each day and let him do it on his own?" That's simply not how things are done in institutions. If your student is currently in a public or private school, you likely don't have the luxury of structuring your child's learning environment to foster self-teaching.

If self-teaching is such an integral part of the self-propelled advantage—which it absolutely is—and your child is unable to develop a self-teaching and self-paced approach to his education in a classroom setting, it is apparent that something has to give. Either you have to settle for utilizing the first two elements only, self-mastery and mastery learning, or there needs to be a change in the way your child's learning environment is structured. As you'll see as we go along, the student-directed model yields incredibly good fruit. The teacher-directed model may as well, but I believe the side effects of being told what to do and how to do it subdue the student at best, and prevent him from learning with excellence at worst.

An Overview of Self-Teaching

Self-teaching is ingraining in the student a concept of continual success; the gradual and steady success that results from diligence and the pursuit of excellence. Students who are allowed to work independently are motivated by the freedoms they possess as self-learners. They are trusted to meet expectations without daily parental intervention.

One motivational aspect of self-teaching is goal setting. Short-term goals can be set just four times a year, and goal setting is never tedious within the self-teaching process that I will outline for you. When your student is predominantly self-teaching, you should be able to quickly pull out a few short-term goals for the upcoming nine-week quarter (or whatever length of time you choose), or better yet, have your student set short-term goals himself once he is acclimated to your expectations.

Once the nine-week quarter is over, his work is evaluated. At this point, the student should see how far he has come and also be rewarded for his progress. This is hopefully a happy moment!

Planning equals motivation. The more control a student has over planning and goal setting, the more motivated he will be to meet those goals because they are *his* goals, not Mom's or Dad's. Make sense? Ownership is priceless! We'll talk a lot about planning over the course of the next two chapters, but it is important to understand that an ownership mindset is the key to your student's self-teaching success.

Who?

Who can be a self-learner? Anyone with a good grasp of reading can be self-taught. Self-teaching is a gradual process that begins around age eight and continues for life. Some curriculum lends itself better to self-teaching than others. Generally, unit studies are not a self-teaching curriculum model, but perhaps a creative individual could adapt unit studies to the self-learner. I've found that most curricula can be used in the self-learning home environment.

Just a brief notation: it can be difficult to encourage a student who has recently been pulled out of a school system to become self-teaching. The more years spent in the system, the more difficult the reversal can be. It may be more difficult, but it is certainly not impossible! Being given control of one's education after being in the public school system could be like a breath of fresh air to some kids. Just be aware that the fact that a student has been *taught at* for years could mean that he takes more time to adjust to working independently.

Where?

Self-teaching can be done anywhere at any time. It is unlimited learning, but it is not unstructured learning. A good record-keeping system is required so that the student can look back and glimpse the steady progress he is making, which is definitely motivational. This planning system can be as loose or as structured as you and your student desire.

Why?

We've already discussed several benefits of self-teaching from the student's point of view, but what about from the parent's point of view? What's in it for you? Perhaps the biggest benefit to the parent is the fact that self-teaching can drastically reduce—or even eliminate—a phenomenon known as *burnout*. Have you ever experienced burnout? I see you nodding your head, especially those who have been home educating for a year or longer. If you have been doing all of the teaching to this point, I know you are tired. The good news is that you are about to learn how to take the burden of education and put it squarely on the shoulders of your student, where it belongs. That means no more weekly (or daily) lesson planning for you. Sound too good to be true? I assure you, it isn't!

Avoiding burnout is a major advantage to raising self-learners. There definitely are more advantages of having a self-teaching student. Keep in mind as you read the list below that some of these advantages are immediate while others will develop over time—once your child is walking with steady footsteps along the self-teaching pathway.

Here are more advantages to you:

1. Your student becomes an independent thinker.
2. Your student learns to accept responsibility.

3. Your student gains the freedom to learn without boundaries. (He doesn't have to stop and switch subjects after forty-five minutes.)

4. Your student becomes trustworthy and accountable.

5. Intrinsic rewards become the focus—that good feeling inside that comes from a job well done.

6. Your student tests well because he is used to tackling problems on his own, which builds his confidence level. Testing becomes much less intimidating.

7. Your student retains material more naturally when he does the work himself versus parents or teachers spoon-feeding him.

8. Your student learns what to do and where to go when help is needed. There is no need to worry about gaps in his education because if he needs to know something down the road, he'll research it on his own. He doesn't panic if he doesn't understand a lesson on the first read-through. This builds confidence and a yes-I-can attitude, which is crucial to becoming a lifelong learner.

9. Your student has the courage to delve into an area of interest to study it without waiting for a teacher to teach it.

10. Your student becomes more than prepared for college.

11. Self-learning gives the opportunity to develop a good work ethic.

12. Self-learning allows the student to go as deeply into a subject as he would like to.

13. Self-learning enables the student to limit the number of interests undertaken so as not to be spread too thinly.

14. Self-learning allows the family to function as a family without trying to reproduce an institution in the home.

15. Your self-learner is accountable to the goals he has set for himself; Mom is not a slave driver. A student really does become motivated by the freedom granted to him!

16. Self-learning means that Mom can read great books rather than teacher's manuals and text books.

17. Self-learning means that babies and toddlers get more attention from Mom because she is not busy playing teacher.

18. Your student actually cares about the quality of what he produces. He owns his education right now and for the rest of his life. Once he has a taste of educational freedom, he will not want to go back to playing school.

19. Your student can enjoy challenging himself. A challenged student is a happy student.

How?

Believe it or not, the answer to "How does a student become self-teaching?" is simple. Set some short-term goals with your older student, give him the materials, including the answer keys, and then step back and watch the transformation. You will be amazed at the simplicity of this process! Students who are not yet reading independently will need more guidance, but the process is still simple, as you will see in chapter 7.

Of course, you need to check your student's work periodically; how frequently will depend on the individual. Make sure goals are being met. Otherwise, stay out of the way.

When?

Today! Or whenever you are comfortable with the concepts. Start slowly and allow your child to gain your trust and respect. Give more and more freedom until you reach the point where your child rarely needs you in order to complete his assignments. Don't worry, he still needs you, just not in the same way that he did before.

Negatives?

The only negative to the self-teaching method of education is that your children may become smarter than you are. That is pretty much true here in my household— where most things mathematical are concerned. No students over the age of ten waste time asking me a math question. If they can't figure it out on their own, they ask an older sibling for help, or they will seek out their dad.

In my defense, I wasn't taught to enjoy math. I didn't know that I could do math! I was one of those late bloomers where logic is concerned. I never was enabled to practice mastery learning, the building upon a solid foundation of one learned concept after another. Thank heavens there is a better way to learn. Now, if I wanted to, I could go back and learn math to my heart's content. Unfortunately, that desire is long gone; it was snuffed out years ago by my sense of failure.

Leonardo da Vinci stated, "Poor is the pupil who does not surpass his master." My children *should* be surpassing me. Okay, I feel much better now.

Remember, a benefit of having self-teaching students is that you are not doing lesson plans day after day and teaching every subject, day in and day out. Moreover, you are now free to walk about the house. You can be attentive to your toddler or baby or both. You can run a business from your home. You can do whatever needs doing without worrying about whom is doing what in your absence, or if your *whoms* are even working. You know they are learning. That is educational freedom for everyone.

This is a good time to let you know what I consider to be the cornerstones of a self-teaching home. These are the basic building blocks of education with which a strong foundation is built.

Cornerstones of a Self-Teaching Home

1. Proficiency in Reading—The better the reader, the more likely he or she is to seek out information and internalize it.
2. Proficiency in Mathematics—Math is the language of the sciences.
3. Proficiency in Writing—The better a student is at expressing himself, the more respect he will gain from anyone he meets, especially future employers.

I see these three areas—reading, math, and writing—as the foundation of an excellent education. Keep in mind that children will grow and flourish in these areas when they are naturally ready. I have had three-year-olds who could read, and I have had a child who was seven years old before she really showed a delight in reading on her own. Mathematics, like reading, is one of those areas where, with a young child, you cannot push it.

I don't subscribe to the better-late-than-early theory where children are not introduced to formal learning until ages eight to ten. I don't think late is better, by any means. I believe that learning should happen when a child shows readiness. If that happens later, then so be it. Out of eight children, I haven't had a child who has not been ready to read by age seven, and then that particular child caught up quickly. My daughter was so used to being read to that she was reluctant to do the work necessary to read independently. One day, she found a series of puppy books in the local library. A burning desire to read suddenly came upon her! It happened just that quickly.

Sometimes we do need to help our children find something that lights their little fires, so to speak. When the time is right, the fire takes off and burns brilliantly.

A child will read when he is ready. At what age will he read? All children are different, so as parents, we just need to relax and trust our instincts.

What are you passionate about? I bet you taught yourself most of what you know about it. Or perhaps you sought out people on your own who could teach you what you wished to pursue. How many of us wish now we could go back and study different things in high school than we actually studied? I wish now I had taken horticulture, studied computers, or learned typing. Instead, I was put on the fast track to college. When I graduated from college, I thought I was finally through with learning. Seriously! I thought I was done learning. What I didn't realize was that it was just my years of mandated learning that were over.

Thirty years later, I value every spare minute I have to read a book on something that interests me. I love learning about various things that I never dreamed I would be interested in back when I was in high school. I never enjoyed studying history, but as an adult, I have discovered a real interest in reading biographies of early Americans, especially U.S. Presidents and their wives. My love of biographies has turned into a learning experience for my kids, whether they like it or not, because I order DVDs from Netflix on all sorts of presentations by the History Channel and other such companies. Yep, I mandate that they watch some of them with me every now and then. Hopefully my passion for history, which has lain dormant for forty years, will perhaps spark an interest in them. If not, that is fine; their passions may lie elsewhere. But I am exposing them to my passions anyway, and they will be exposing me to theirs as time goes on.

Allow your children to be a part of your passions, and show an interest in theirs. Enjoy the journey as you travel down the path of learning together. Your children will be inspired by your determination to learn and grow.

Record Keeping as Motivation

Record keeping is an important part of self-teaching or any type of home education, for that matter. You want to know what your child is learning. You want to know at the end of the year what has been accomplished. The older the child, the more important it is to have a thorough system of recording subjects and grades. It is important in the high school years to maintain careful course records for college prep purposes. I recommend *The Home School Student Planner* and *The Essential High School Planner* because they are expressly designed for the student to keep track of his work. These planners are the perfect tool for use by the self-propelled student (or any student, for that matter).

Give your younger child a planner with a list of daily requirements for the week, and watch him take great pleasure in completing and crossing off the assignments. It is such a good feeling to cross something off your to-do list, isn't it? Same thing holds true for students. Sometimes one of my children will ask if he can do his Friday's work on Thursday (after completing Thursday's work), so he can have a long weekend, and I highly encourage that. That's motivation! Make sure the work is done well, however, and not slopped through.

Give your older student a planner, and let him be in charge of writing his own goals and daily assignments on a quarterly basis. You'll need to give a bit of guidance by helping him set appropriate goals for the quarter, but then let him work out how he is going to accomplish these goals. Your students will be much more motivated because they set their own goals. The planner is a record of where they have been, and it's a map for where they are headed next.

Before long, you'll see an unbelievable change in the way your child approaches his assignments. There will be no more, "Mom, what should I do next?" because each activity is right there on the planner pages.

A Sometimes-Overlooked Benefit of Self-Teaching

As I mentioned earlier, I spent four years working full-time outside my home at a time when I had eight children at home. I also had a home business to run, I might add. I can honestly say that I was only able to work outside of the home due to the self-teaching method of education, and the assistance of all of my children. The older ones took care of the younger ones, cooked meals, did laundry, and many of the other assorted tasks that were placed on their chores list.

Things ran pretty smoothly without either Mom or Dad at home. My co-workers just could not believe that I was actively home educating my children while working forty hours a week. My self-teaching children definitely kept me from drowning during that particular season of life.

As I do more and more traveling and speaking in the current season of life, my children are once again entrusted to attend to their chores, as well as to their scholastic endeavors, with excellence. They don't require my presence (or nagging via cell phone) to carry on. I love being home, and it is always a sacrifice to be away from my family for days at a time, but thankfully, I can have peace of mind during those periods of time.

If you are a stay-at-home mom, you are wonderfully blessed! Many moms would love to be in your shoes. However, I would never judge women who are out in the work force helping to pay the bills while home educating their children; I understand that sometimes it is necessary. Self-teaching children—if they are old enough to be home unsupervised, *and* you have raised them to be trustworthy and competent in your absence—can achieve educational excellence even if Mom and Dad are not home all the time.

Conclusion

Self-learning students develop a sense of personal responsibility toward their school work as well as toward their very lives. They also become competent at tasks at a young age; consequently, they are apt to develop a strong work ethic that yields dividends both now and in the future.

In short, self-learning is for those families who want to give their students an educational edge in today's society, as well as in life itself. Raise a child to be self-teaching, and not only will you have a young adult who possesses the tools to succeed in whatever he sets his mind to, but also you will have cultivated a passionate individual who will pursue his purpose with exceptional ability.

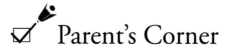

Parent's Corner

1. What is self-teaching, and why is it the third element of the self-propelled advantage?
2. If your children currently are in a teacher-directed setting such as a school classroom, do you think that self-learning is enough of an advantage to warrant a change is their learning environment? Why or why not?
3. If you work outside the home but are interested in home education for your children, do you see how self-teaching can not only enable your child to learn independently, but also how he can go further, faster as a self-learner?
4. Could your children learn to work independently?
5. What are some of the advantages of raising self-learners, both to you and your student? How would the student-directed approach make your life easier?

CHAPTER 7

SELF-TEACHING
AND YOUNG CHILDREN

The object of teaching a child is to enable him to get along without a teacher.
—**Elbert Hubbard** (1856-1915) American author, editor, and printer

As any parent knows, a toddler loves to do things independently. If you have older children, I bet somewhere in the recesses of your mind you can still hear the echoes of "I can do it by myself!" And as children grow and become school-aged, they still like to do things on their timetable and in their own way. Children can be pretty insistent about their abilities. Give a youngster a bicycle with training wheels, and there is no stopping him! He will ride for hours upon hours by himself, confident that he needs no help to enjoy the ride.

Where my kindergartener's education is concerned, my function is similar to that of the training wheels on a bike. I am there to support my child, to go places with him each day (figuratively and literally), and to give him confidence in his rapidly-developing skill levels. I'm there to assist him in learning how to stand on his own two wheels. I provide the hardware—the learning materials—and he provides the locomotion. Wherever he goes, I go with him, but this is only for a season. Before long, he is ready to move on without leaning entirely on me.

In the educational realm, once a child learns to read, he can really dive in and enjoy a whole new world—a world of being able to read signs, books, cereal box panels, as well as other things; but most importantly—the ability to "read" the words that mom and dad spell out loud because they think he won't understand them. (Ha! Reading certainly opens doors!) Reading well should signal the beginning of educational independence for the child.

Self-teaching is a privilege children earn as they develop reading skills *and* prove themselves to be honest and hard-working. Self-learning and self-mastery are closely intertwined. But shouldn't we be reading to our children, helping them with their math lessons, going over the parts of speech in their grammar lessons, and then making sure that they have done a thorough job each day? The answer is yes! Self-teaching does not mean we abandon our children to sink or swim on their own. Rather, self-teaching is the end result of a trusting and nurturing relationship with a child. Step by step, the child begins to see that he or she *can* learn things independently. It is precisely that feeling of independence that motivates the child to want to attempt more and more work on his own. Before long, the student is only coming to the parent to ask minor questions on an intermittent basis.

Young children are not expected to be self-teaching. However, we *can* start them on the pathway by giving them responsibilities in very small increments. Young children naturally have a desire to please their parents. They are motivated by praise for a job well done. If you have a young child, age two to five, try giving him a small task to accomplish, and watch your child beam with pride as you give praise when the job is completed.

As parents, we are always available as resources for our children, but we want to eventually become their last resort, so to speak. The older student should be choosing other sources for information before asking for parental help, either searching more diligently in the text for the answer or looking back a few pages in the math book to remember how to work a certain type of problem, or reading the directions a second or third time until comprehension is achieved.

The I-can-do-it-by-myself attitude that toddlers exhibit when they are ready to attempt new tasks on their own should never disappear. Rather, it should blossom and grow. We should be getting out of the way and allowing our children to become independent learners at an early age instead of relegating curious young learners to desks and chairs in a classroom setting to be taught at.

The Five Steps to Self-Teaching Success

Teaching young children to teach themselves is a simple five-step process. I'll list the steps for you first, and then we'll discuss how to plug them in.

1. *Provide* each student with his own planner or whatever record-keeping sheets you find work well for your family.
2. *Gather* the curriculum you will use for each student.
3. *Set* short-term goals with your student in each subject, being sure to notate the goals for future reference. Show the student how far he will get to go in the upcoming quarter (or whatever length of time you choose). This should be a positive statement!
4. *Monitor* the student's progress by checking up on him at whatever interval you deem necessary. This will vary according to the student's age.
5. *Let go* of the bicycle seat, and watch your student ride like the wind!

That sounds easy enough, right? I assure you that if you have a firm hold on your child's heart, as discussed in chapter 4, self-teaching will be a breath of fresh air for you and for your student. I cannot emphasize that fact enough. If your young child does not obey you in everyday matters, you can expect to have difficulty with regards to schooling as well. With a grip on your child's heart, education is easy.

A Parent-Directed Approach

A parent-directed approach is what I refer to as the approach you will take when working with the young child who is not yet reading. It will be hands-on for you at the beginning, but you will see, somewhere around second grade or even earlier, that the transition from parent-directed to student-directed begins to magically occur with your child.

I remember when my last child, Lilie, began to make the transition from working with me to wanting to work more on her own. When she was in second grade, every morning after breakfast I would wait for her to finish her chores, and then she would bring her planner and tub of books into my office or into the family room or wherever I happened to be when she was finished. Together we would look at what she would be doing that particular day.

One morning she brought me her materials, and she had a silly grin on her cute little face. She announced that she had already done her math upstairs at her desk. I gave her a huge hug and kiss, and my heart literally was flooded with joy.

She had caught the bug! She was learning intrinsic motivation—working on her own with excellence for the sake of enjoying the feeling of not only surprising her mom, but also realizing that yes, indeed, she could do her work by herself! It was a charming moment that I am not likely to forget.

I don't remember that same moment with my other seven children, but I will with Lilie probably because I was beginning to think she would never want to work on her own. As the baby of the family, she still enjoys being the youngest, and she takes her time with things that the others just rip-roared through. She is every bit the little math whiz that my other children were, but it just took her a little longer to get to the same point. That is truly 100 percent fine!

The light bulb will go off with children eventually. Stick to the parent-led approach and allow your child to blossom into the student-led model on his own timetable. He will.

Step 1: Provide a Planner

Step 1 is to get your child some sort of planner that is *his own*. This is vitally important for the child to feel as though he owns his schooling. While you will be the one to write in it at first, do all that you can to make him understand that this book is a collection of everything he accomplishes in his schooling this year. Give ownership as much as possible to your little student.

Step 2: Gather Curriculum

At the very beginning of the year, you literally sit down with your student's textbooks, workbooks, or whatever curriculum you will be using. Step 1: grab the planner. Step 2: grab your stack of curriculum and sit down on the floor with your child. How easy is that? Okay, well choosing curriculum can be a challenge by virtue of the fact that there is so much available on the market today. (Curriculum help can be found in chapter 9.)

Step 3: Set Short-Term Goals

A little planning is a good thing. You will want to see where your younger students are headed. Each home-educating family has its own method of schooling. What does your school calendar look like?

In order to work through step 3, you need to know how you are going to break up your school year, how you are going to segment your time. For example, I like to divide our school year into four quarters, each containing nine weeks. A typical school year consists of thirty-six weeks, so if you do the division, thirty-six weeks divided by four quarters equals nine weeks per quarter.

Now, we don't usually go nine straight weeks without a break. In fact, right now, as I am writing this, we are on a two-week fall break. It is wonderful to take breaks whenever you feel it is necessary. When we start back to school next week, we will be on week number seven of our first quarter. Three more weeks and we are done with the quarter entirely! I probably shouldn't sound so excited.

It is important to remember that the process you are about to go through in step 3 will be a longer process at the beginning of the year because you are getting an overview of where your student is headed for the entire year. You are not going to set anything in stone. You are just going to guestimate for right now.

For simplicity's sake, let's assume you are going to use a quarterly system of record keeping. Grab your child's math book, and look at how many lessons there are in the book. Take that number of lessons and divide by four. This is the number of lessons that need to be tackled *each quarter*. We'll say there are 160 lessons in the math book. 160 ÷ 4 = 40. Now I know that my child should complete forty lessons in the first nine weeks of the year.

A quarter contains forty-five days if you are doing five school days a week, so I will make a note under the First Quarter Goals section in my young student's planner that our target goal is to complete forty lessons that quarter. Obviously, that is less than five lessons per week, so he may finish early. Or perhaps a lesson may take more than one day to complete. There is some flexibility built in there.

You're done with the math book, so you move on to the next subject—phonics—and perform the same mathematical operations. Look at how many lessons are in the entire phonics book. There are 120. Divide by four, and you know how much must be accomplished in nine weeks' time or in one quarter: thirty lessons. Then take that quarterly portion, and divide by nine weeks. There you have the amount of work that must be accomplished per week, which in our fictional phonics book comes out to about three and a half lessons per week. Write this on the Short-Term Goals section of the planner or notebook you are using.

Feel free to do this for your kindergartener before you sit down with him on the first day of school. But I would go through the process with your first or second grader so he can see your thought process. He may not totally understand it, which is fine. You just want to be acquainting him with the process.

What Does the First Day of School Look Like?

On the first day of school—which is a very exciting day, by the way—sit down with your student, lay out the planner, and go over with him what he is going to *get to do* in the upcoming nine weeks. (Remember to use the words *you get to* instead of *you need to*.) Don't overwhelm him with information, but share enough so that he is excited because he can see where he is headed.

The quarterly goals are merely a road map. Be sure not to let your curriculum be your taskmaster. Remember that you are master over it, and that mastery is always the goal. If a student takes more than one day on a lesson or concept, go with that. Don't worry about it! There is no such thing as being behind in home education unless you spend your days perched on the couch in your PJs, watching TV, and eating bon bons. If you are on the couch because you are sick, that doesn't count against you, okay? It is okay, especially if you have a chronic illness or are pregnant or need to take it easy for a legitimate reason. But if a parent is just lazy and unmotivated, the student *will* soon be behind as a result.

Back to sitting on the floor with your student on the first day of school. Write out a week's worth of work in each subject, one day's lesson per square, per subject, and then as you go through the day, allow your student to cross off what he has done. He may not be able to read, but if you point to the square under the math column where you've written, "Do pages 1-2," allow your child to cross it off on the schedule. This is the most exciting part of the day—crossing off or checking off work that he has done!

Think about you and your to-do lists if you make them. Isn't it a wonderful feeling to cross an item off the list when you complete it? I get excited just thinking about crossing things off my lists. In fact, sometimes my sole motivation to actually complete a task is to cross it off the list! Know what I mean? The same is true for students of all ages.

As far as deciding whether to write out lessons for a day at a time or for an entire week at a time, the choice is really yours. I prefer to write them out for a week with my younger children, especially the kindergarten-through-first-grade crowd. If you prefer to do daily lessons, go right ahead. There really is no right or wrong way. I am sharing what we do in our home. Your needs may be different.

Work through the subjects for the day with your student, allow him to cross off completed items as they are finished, and then celebrate finishing the day with a dish of ice cream. That is how I celebrate all things great and small—with ice cream!

A Note About Lesson Times

With children in grades kindergarten through first grade, be careful not to overload the student with table work such as math, phonics, and handwriting. The early years are perfect for doing short bursts of work. A kindergartener can do all his subjects in about forty-five minutes. Just as you don't want to be ruled by your curriculum, you don't want to be ruled by the clock either. It really doesn't take very long to go through phonics, handwriting, math, social studies, and science for a young child. Time does not matter. The shorter your lessons the better at this age.

I was once asked for advice by a mom who was upset that her five-year-old little girl would not sit still long enough to complete anything. I asked her how long each lesson was, and she said that often a math lesson was a half-hour long, and a phonics lesson took forty-five minutes. Wow. That is way too long. Of course a lot of that time was spent fussing with her little one, and I am guessing that only a fraction of that time was spent actually teaching.

If you have a wiggler, you have a normal child. Young children are built to move, to explore, to play, to laugh and giggle. Work your educational program around that knowledge. Do half a lesson of math in one sitting if your child needs a break. This goes for older kids as well. Break up the work into tiny pieces at first if necessary. As the child matures, he will be able to do more at one time before needing a break.

Even though you are the teacher in the parent-directed setting, remember that you do not need to play teacher or bring the classroom into your home. Where your children do their work is up to you. It can be done on a trampoline, in a fort, in a bedroom, in a family room, or at the kitchen table. Location depends, of course, on the age and maturity level of your child. A kindergartener may work better at a table than he would if he is sitting on the trampoline in the backyard. I'm sure there are kindergarteners who can sit on the trampoline to do math. Trust your instincts, and find what works for your children.

It is true that variety is the spice of life, so don't be afraid to allow your children to work in different locations from time to time.

Working Ahead

Here is a cool thing that happens with the parent-directed model. Let's say you go ahead on Monday and write out what you would like your young child to complete this week. What if he finishes his math early today and wants to work ahead on tomorrow's math? Should you allow this? Certainly! Go over it with him first to make sure he understands what to do, and then let him go!

Now that he has finished Tuesday's work on Monday, he would like to do Wednesday's, Thursday's, and Friday's so that he is done with math for the week. Is that a good thing? By all means! This is self-motivation at its finest! As long as you go over the instructions with him and he is doing well on the work, let him go ahead and do his entire math for the week. High-five time!

Suppose on Thursday your student would like to work ahead for Friday so he doesn't have to do anything on Friday. I bet you know what I am going to say. High-five time again! Of course you will need to sit down with him, look at his planner with him, and help him get through the next day's work as well. He will get a taste of the intrinsic motivation we've been talking about. He will most certainly have a great feeling inside from doing his work and doing it well.

Readiness

In the elementary years, you probably will find that your curriculum presents your child with something at some point that he is not developmentally ready to tackle. Perhaps it is a phonics concept. Perhaps it is double-digit addition. You will know your child has hit a wall when you try and try to explain the concept a hundred different ways, and he still doesn't get it, resulting in frustration both for you and for him.

When this happens, take a deep breath, step away, and trust your instincts. You may have to leave math for a little while. I remember that Lilie really struggled with double-digit addition. She could add anything together unless the sum was great than thirteen. I tried using coins to demonstrate the concept, I tried using beans and other manipulatives, but we got nowhere. You'd think that with my eighth child I would have known what was going on right away, but I had to get to the frustration point, unfortunately, before I realized that she wasn't going to grasp that particular concept right now. So I apologized to her for being frustrated, and told her that she was doing a wonderful job in math. In fact, she was doing such a wonderful job that we were going to take a math break for a while. That was it; I put math away for a while. It was probably for an entire month—I don't remember exactly. From time to time I would nonchalantly quiz her while we were shopping or doing something mundane during the day. I gradually noticed that she was beginning to get it, so I got the math book back out.

We could have gone on to another section in the math workbook, but there really wasn't much we could have done until she was able to master her addition facts above ten. Once I realized what was going on, I was cool with it. I was able to create a different plan, which in this case mandated setting the subject completely aside for a time, and when the readiness was there, we went back to math. She was then able to master the facts, and there was no sense of failure.

Again, if she had been in a public school setting and wasn't able to master the double-digit addition facts, she would have experienced failure. It's not that I don't want my kids to fail; I don't want them to fail for reasons that are completely out of their control. Home education definitely allows us to work with the individual readiness factors that are inherent in each child.

Step 4: Monitor

Step 4 involves monitoring your student's progress. With the parent-directed method of presenting lessons, the parent will obviously know how the student is progressing each day because Mom or Dad is looking over the child's work daily in order to check it and/or grade it. You do not have to grade everything. I only grade spelling, phonics, math, and language in the early years. Science and social studies do not require formal testing before grade three. You can simply question the student from time to time to get a feel for his retention level.

However, as a student matures and begins to move into the realm of self-learning, you will still want to look over his work to make sure everything was learned to an A level. My second grader may do her math lesson independently if the lesson isn't something brand new. She will run off and do her work, but then I would like her to bring her math workbook page to me so I can look over it to ensure that she has mastered the lesson. Then we'll go over anything she may need to revisit.

After Each Quarter

Once you complete the first quarter, look over the goals you set together with your student or perhaps that you just wrote out for your kindergartener, and see how far you've come. Celebrate with your student! Woo-hoo! Progress has certainly been made. If you didn't quite get as far as you'd hoped, no problem. When you sit down to do the next quarter's goals either with or for your student, take that into consideration. Do not stress over it. Simply readjust your goals as necessary.

Chances are good that your student exceeded his goals. When this happens, make sure you praise the child extravagantly. Well, not too much, but you know what I am saying. Praise sincerely when you do give praise. It may be time for more ice cream.

Parent-Directed Learning with a Reading Child

Here is a snapshot of what Lilie and I did when she was beginning to read in second grade. I would write out what she was to do each day a week in advance. I was careful to go over each subject with her during the day to make sure she understood what to do. Real parental teaching goes on at this level. However, since she was able to read, she crossed off her assignments when she had completed each subject for the day.

I would say, "Lilie, once your math is finished, drop it off at my desk, and then you can take a break and go play outside." I'd then look over her work and go over it with her if there were errors. If it is 100 percent correct, then she gets something out of the candy jar. Then Lilie is off to do the next subject, which may be reading. If so, I would have her read to someone: to a sibling, to Daddy if he was home, or to me. I stress oral reading up to about third grade for my children.

When Lilie was at the in-between stage between needing me and not needing me, I would look over her work with her before she did it to make sure she understood what she needed to do. Sometimes she would flag me away, insisting she knew what to do. And she usually did. I was, at this point, beginning to allow her the opportunity to read directions and try the lesson on her own. Then she would write down what she had done.

Often she would ask if she could work ahead in a subject, and how I love to be asked this question! She was completely self-teaching by third grade, meaning she and I could sit down once a quarter and develop attainable goals together, and then she and I would together plan out a whole week at once instead of a day at a time as we had done when she was younger. Again, you can plan one day at a time or a whole week at a time. Do what works best for you and your child.

Don't expect too much of younger ones. I still needed to check Lilie's work daily when she was in third grade to ensure that she was learning her new concepts well. I checked over everything every day. She took an oral spelling test once a week. Lilie was now able to move through her list of weekly work which we planned out together on Monday mornings, and little help was needed from me except to check over her work daily to reinforce concepts as well as to check for mastery.

When I was working full-time outside my home, my eldest daughter, Lauren, was the one who oversaw my two younger girls' work. The girls knew they could seek help from their older siblings if help was necessary, especially if Tim and I were not at home. The older kids were happy to assist. This increased the pleasant ties between brothers and sisters, a nice side effect.

Once Lilie got to the fourth grade level, I began expecting her to be able to plan out quarterly goals with me. At this point, she had access to the answer keys to check her own math, language, and so forth. Now I am just looking over her shoulder on a semi-daily basis, allowing more and more independence as I feel she can manage it.

Step 4 is a constantly evolving process. Her planner is her lifeline and mine too. Especially when I was a working-outside-the-home mom, I relied on the recording of work done in planners in order to check the progress of my crew. The planner is still the center of our self-teaching home.

Transition Time

When my students show a readiness and have a clear understanding of my daily expectations for them in each subject, then they are ready for the student-directed process which allows *students* to write down what needs to be accomplished each day. Now it is getting exciting! Not only am I going to be freed up to spend more time with other children or with other things that I have on my plate, but the students are ready to experience more fully the joy and privilege of working much more independently.

Step 5: Letting Go

With students up to grade three and perhaps beginning grade four, we are not completely letting go of their bicycles yet. Why not? We are not completely letting go because fourth graders are still learning foundational concepts in their lessons; they still are learning the rules of the road. But as their ability to read and comprehend develops, we are finally able to take off the training wheels. In chapter 8 we will completely let go of the bicycle. For now we are running alongside, keeping an eye out for potential problems.

Are you seeing that there is a great deal of hands-on with younger children? A child certainly needs direction when learning to read. I still experience the wonder and joy when a little one starts to read because I am right there helping the child along. Of course self-teaching does not mean that we are abandoning our role as teacher with our little ones. Rather, we slowly begin allowing them to do on their own those activities that they would have previously asked for help with before tackling. Then we praise them for a job well done!

You can expect a third grader who is reading well to work more independently. The child now is beginning to understand your expectations from the short-term goals that you've set together. Sometimes a child is ready to transition to self-directed learning earlier than third grade, but third grade is the target age for a child to truly begin entering the realm of independence.

In the kindergarten through second grade years, we are actively teaching our children about the world of learning, observing the glorious moment when our young ones realize they can do things by themselves! But we don't neglect the cuddle-up story times with this precious age group. There is a natural balance between your child's need for you and his need for independence. Finding that balance is what schooling this age group is all about. Trust your instincts above all. Oh, and enjoy your little ones like there's no tomorrow.

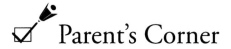

Parent's Corner

1. How do you like to break up your school year?
2. What kind of planning pages work best for you?
3. How much of your child's school work has to be done with you? Is there anything he can start doing on his own today?

CHAPTER 8

SELF-TEACHING AND OLDER CHILDREN

I am beginning to suspect all elaborate and special systems of education. They seem to me to be built up on the supposition that every child is a kind of idiot who must be taught to think.
—Anne Sullivan

At what age can children be given the freedom to self-teach? That is a question I hear frequently, and as you may have guessed, the answer will be based on a student's individual circumstances. Usually a child who is about the age of eight can begin to work on some subjects independently, still with supervision, however. After this age and provided the student is trustworthy, you can begin to really let a student go to begin working independently.

In our last chapter, we took a look at the *parent-directed* approach of self-teaching where the parent is the one who sets up the schedule, and the young children cross off their work as they complete it. With the *student-directed* model of self-teaching, the student is already acquainted with the self-teaching approach; he is mature enough to handle being given more and more freedom, and he's allowed to work on his own with much less parental intervention as a result.

Student-Directed Learning for Middle School Students

Students from fourth grade and up should be able to plug right into self-learning and run with it. Remember though, it is a process, and if you are just starting out with the self-teaching method with your family, you will probably not want your students to jump right in to working independently in every subject.

Begin to incorporate the five steps to self-teaching success (which we'll review and discuss in this chapter), but just give your student maybe one or two subjects to work on independently when starting out. Choose a subject that you know he is interested in and will easily be able to pick up and go with. Add more subjects as you feel he is ready. On the other hand, once you go through the first four steps, your student may be ready to just dive in and work independently. All kids are different. Trust your instincts.

Student-Directed Learning for High School Students

Ninth through twelfth graders should be able to focus in and work on their own for the most part. Again, if your older student is just now being exposed to self-teaching, start slowly and monitor his progress. If your student has been working independently through the middle school years and now is ready for high-school-level work, you are not really going to see a change in activity. The subjects will be different, of course, but students should be able to read the directions and get to work.

There are certain subjects that you may opt to do with your high schoolers that will involve you. Perhaps you would like to teach a literature course to them which would require your hands-on assistance. If that is what you would like to do, by all means, feel free to do that. Everything in a student's day does not have to be self-learning. Just make sure that you are not holding your students back with your desire to work with them. My students would much prefer I give them their materials and leave them alone to work at their own speed. They will let me know if they need me.

There will be times when your student is working on a subject that is challenging for him, and he needs your help. That is fine if he has already exhausted the resources for help that are available to him. His first reaction if he doesn't understand something should not be, "Moooooooooom!" If bellowing for you is his knee-jerk reaction to a problem, gently inquire what steps he has taken to resolve his problem on his own. Remember, we want to be working ourselves out of a job. By reinforcing your belief that the student is totally capable of digging deeply and finding out the answers on his own, you promote confidence in his ability, thus making him more likely to do something else first—such as re-reading the introduction to the chapter or looking back over the materials—instead of immediately asking you for help all the time.

Certainly, we must be available to help when our students have exhausted all of their other resources and truly need our help to dissect a problem. I don't turn my kids away when they ask for help. I will ask them what steps they have taken to figure out what they don't know. When one of my kids hits a wall, I know that he probably does need my help, and I am happy to give it at that point. However, my ability to help my high schoolers may be limited. If there is a mathematics issue at the high school level, for example, I will direct the student to my husband. Same thing with chemistry and higher-level sciences. I'm the mom; I don't have to know calculus! This is not about me and what I know. It is about my high schooler and what he needs to know. I've already earned my diplomas.

If neither you nor your spouse feels equipped to handle a certain subject area, there is probably some sort of video tutorial available from a curriculum publisher to help you and your student through the rough spots. Another resource is the library. I've found that the Internet can be a home-educating parent's best friend. You can also find someone who can help through an online home school message board group like a Yahoo Group. It really isn't hard to find an online home education forum that has a qualified person willing to give some advice.

Another option to find someone who can help your student through any rough spots is to check within your network of friends and see who is gifted in your weaker areas. I am blessed to know several local moms who have engineering degrees, so I would not hesitate to go to one of them (or ask my student to politely inquire with one of them) to see if someone would have a minute to take a look at something he has a question on. Knowing where to go to find out what you don't know is an important skill to have. This skill will serve our students well in college and in life beyond college.

Courage to Face High School

Sometimes parents think that they could never home educate their kids through high school for one reason: they have little knowledge in certain areas such as literature or writing or higher math. As a result, they think they can't possibly teach such subjects to their kids. Lack of parental knowledge should never be a concern because with self-teaching, the student is going to be working independently.

Nine times out of ten, he will find the answers to his questions in the textbook he is using. If he can't find the answers and you don't know the answers, then together you can look for a resource person locally, or perhaps borrow or purchase educational videos on the topic in question. Where there is a will, there is a way. *High school kids can easily be home educated.*

Earlier this month I was speaking at a conference in Ohio, and two of my girls accompanied me on the trip. At the conference, I was talking with a home-educating mom who was feeling a lot of stress over her eighth-grade daughter entering high school in the fall. I asked Olivia, my daughter who had just completed ninth grade, how she thought the transition to high school had been for her. Olivia simply said, "High school really is not any different. I use different books, but what I do during the day is the same as what I did in middle school. Nothing really changed." It's so true!

Home education in the high school years is not a big deal. The big deal is the record keeping if students are college bound. But even record keeping is not extremely difficult once you understand your state's requirements. *The Essential High School Planners* solve that problem for you, and self-teaching allows your students to work independently. My high school kids are basically invisible during the day while they are working on their daily lessons.

C.S. Lewis once said, "Anything I've ever done that ultimately was worthwhile initially scared me to death." If you find yourself overwhelmed and stressed about the prospect of home educating your high school student, write this quote down and refer to it often. And then remember my daughter's comment about high school being the same as eighth grade to her, just with different books. I want to encourage you to relax and be confident that the high school years *are* the best years yet. You don't want to miss them!

Focus on Strengths

One year I had a daughter who simply hit a wall in advanced math about halfway through her senior year. She never had issues with math prior to this, but now she was doing just half a lesson a day, and it was still taking her upwards of two hours to work through half of it. She was mastering the material; however, it was taking her so much time to do half a lesson that I began to question the value of having her finish the book. I stepped back and took a look at the situation. Here is what I concluded: this student was already accepted to college and her intended major was English. She had done extremely well on the math portions of the SAT and ACT, so I knew she had very good math skills. Was there a good reason why she needed to complete this level of math? Would she really need to know calculus down the road? I had to admit that the answer was no.

I know this will most likely knock you off your chair, but I allowed her to retire her advanced math book. I think my daughter was as surprised as I was at the suggestion. I had done some deep thinking; I did some soul searching to determine if I should find her a tutor or just let it go at this point in her high school career. She was already well prepared for college with the math she had behind her. I consulted with my husband, he agreed with my conclusion to call it quits on math, and the rest is history.

When this same daughter went to college, she had to take a math class of some variety her freshman year, so she signed up for college algebra. She was a little nervous going into it, but early in the semester she was already tutoring other students in her class on a regular basis. She knew much more advanced math than was taught in the class, and she was very successful in meeting her college qualifications in mathematics. I feel that we made the right decision to let her stop with math in high school so she could focus on other areas that were of greater interest to her—and which would be more helpful in the course of her future studies.

I am not saying that one should let a child off the hook if he or she complains that a subject is too hard. That is not what happened in this case. There was honest effort on my student's part, and we were faced with a decision to make as far as what was the best road to take *with her*. I have a son in college right now as a pre-med major. Did I allow him to stop with advanced math in high school? No, he went on to study calculus. First of all, he loves math, so that wasn't an issue. Because of his giftings and abilities, doing higher math was extremely important to him. On the other hand, I didn't have him do more than two years of Spanish because there just was no point to it. Each student is an individual, and his or her academic needs will be unique.

How Does This Mesh with Mastery?

It's possible you may be thinking, "So, Joanne, if your high schooler struggles in something, you just toss it out the window?" No, that is not what I am saying. My daughter was taking two hours to get an A on half a lesson of advanced math. She was mastering the material, but it was such a difficult thing for her to do day in and day out that she was worn down and frustrated beyond belief.

Like I said, she had easily mastered her math work up until her senior year. I decided that it was not worth her time to focus so hard on something that obviously was so difficult for her. If she was thinking about being a pre-dental major in college, then obviously the math would have been vital. She did not have the desire to engage in a career that involved high-level math. Some subjects are necessary for high school graduation, and even though they may be difficult and challenging to a student, I still will have the student go through the course. No breaks are given there. But she had already had plenty of math and had met her graduation requirements, so dismissing the math book was not going to hurt her in any way. I want to be perfectly clear on that point.

Know you children; know their hearts, know their abilities, and encourage them. But when something happens and you know your high school senior isn't cut out for a subject above and beyond what is required for graduation, you may want to look at your reason for having the student proceed. Trust your instincts.

One of our most important roles as parents is that of coach. Coaches look at a player's strengths and weaknesses and place players at the position for which they are best suited. One wouldn't choose the shortest guy on the basketball team to play center. A lot of times, players are chosen for their suitability at one position, not at a multitude of positions. A pitcher on a baseball team is not likely to be an outstanding batter, and a hockey goalie is not going to be scoring goals for his team. Athletes generally have an area of expertise. As a coach, you look at each of your students and help them discern their gifts and abilities. Focus more on those in the latter high school years, especially the senior year. What position will he or she be playing in life?

The senior year is a good time for your student to be shadowing a local adult professional in the student's prospective field of interest. When Taylor was a senior, he was trying to decide between engineering, dentistry, and medicine. He shadowed a local dentist for two days and had the opportunity to see a root canal procedure, a bridge procedure, and some other rather icky stuff, in my opinion. Taylor was very happy to get to see behind the scenes in a dental office. He realized that he really was interested in not only dentistry, but also in medicine in general.

It would have been laughable (and a waste of time) to arrange for Taylor to shadow a professional harpist since he has no desire or expertise in that area. Why make him study a year of music history in high school if he is not interested in music? Sometimes we think our children must be well-rounded, when in reality we are doing them a disservice by throwing way too much information at them in the high school years. Having one particular passion is a good thing.

A high school student is not lacking if he doesn't excel in everything. He needs to master his work, but he doesn't have to go deep in every single subject. Here is perhaps my favorite C.S. Lewis quote: "I think this wise; the greatest service we can do to education is to teach fewer subjects. No one has time to do more than a very few things well before he is twenty, and when we force a boy to be a mediocrity in a dozen subjects we destroy his standards, perhaps for life."

I am constantly looking for ways to encourage my high schoolers and seeing how I can help them to realize their potential. Our kids need us to say, "You seem to enjoy debate and researching for debates. What kind of jobs would include this type of thing?" Help your young adults discover their strengths and focus on those versus stressing about perfection in a totally unrelated area that's not critical for their potential career choices.

Oftentimes a high school senior doesn't know what course of study or what direction he would like to take after graduation. That is totally fine and normal. Just continue to encourage the student in the areas of strengths that you find apparent. The rest will unfold in time. The purpose of the high school years is to continue building success upon success, mastering skills and gaining knowledge in key areas. We should be enabling our young adults to become an independent thinkers who are self-motivated and steeped in excellence.

The Five Steps to Self-Teaching Success

Let's now go through the five-step process of self-teaching for middle and high schoolers. Before going over these steps, I am going to assume that your student has the maturity level to carry out tasks on his own. Here we go.

1. *Provide* each student with his own planner or whatever record-keeping sheets you find work well for your family.
2. *Gather* the curriculum you use for each student.
3. *Set* short-term goals with your student in each subject being sure to notate the goals for future reference. Show the student how far he will get to go in the upcoming quarter or whatever length of time you choose.
4. *Monitor* the student's progress by checking up on him at whatever interval you deem necessary. This will vary according to student's age.
5. *Let go* of the bicycle seat, and watch your student ride like the wind!

Recognize these steps? I hope so. They are the same ones we used to introduce self-teaching to young children. Let's look at each of these steps individually and in more detail to see how they relate to the older crowd.

Step 1: Provide a Planner

Step 1 requires some sort of planning system. Once again, I highly recommend *The Home School Student Planners* and *The Essential High School Planners* simply because they are designed specifically for self-propelled students. They are essential to providing the student with a feeling of ownership of his education, and as tools, planners are extremely important.

Feel free to use what works for you. If you have a different record-keeping system that works well for your high school students, by all means, stick with it. You will see as you go along that the planner system, whether it is one of the ones mentioned above or whether it is simply a big notebook, will be a key factor in motivating your students. Think of it as providing each student with a place to record his to-do list as well as his done list. Don't forget the planner or notebook or whatever your student uses! *It truly is the most essential piece of equipment for self-teaching purposes.*

A little planning is a very good thing. A planner equals organization and yields a sense of ownership. But use whatever you choose to use. Just be sure it belongs to your student and has a place for keeping short-term goals several times a year and has a space for recording work done each day.

Step 2: Gather Curriculum

In Step 2 you will gather the materials your student is going to be using this year, and I recommend that you sit down together with a stack of books as well as the student's planner. Both my middle school students and high school students will literally begin their new year with a stack of books. What do my kids need to do this year? Well, see that stack of books there? The goal for this year is to get through those books. I don't care how they do it. I don't care if they read everything out loud to themselves, if they have music playing while they are working, if they work outside in the van where it's quiet, or if they stand on their heads to master the material that is stacked in front of them. They understand that the expectation is that they will plow through this stack of books I've given them. When they are done with the last book, they are done for the year.

I will, however, sit down with them and help them devise a plan for working through those books so that they can see how they are going to get through all of them in thirty-six weeks' time. Once they have their curriculum, they know where they are headed. In the next step we'll help them get there, step by step.

With just a little help at the beginning of the year, your student can grab the baton and run the course independently throughout the rest of the year. Before long your student will not need you to break all the work down for him. That is when self-teaching really begins to pay off. A self-motivated student is going to want to jump in headfirst and do the work laid out in Step 3 by himself. Why not let him?

Step 3: Set Short-Term Goals

In a student-directed environment—which is what we are talking about with middle and high schoolers—I recommend that at the beginning of the year you take a look at the materials and help your student set his short-term goals for the quarter (or for whatever length of time you are using).

At this point, you need to know how your school year is going to be broken up time-wise. Are you going to do a quarterly schedule of four nine-week segments, or perhaps three semesters containing twelve weeks each? It is totally up to you. We like to use a quarterly grading system, so for clarity's sake, I will share how we schedule our school year from the very beginning of the year.

Our year is divided into four quarters with each quarter containing nine weeks of schooling. We take days off in the middle of the week out of necessity sometimes, and I will have my students fill in the make-up days utilizing the Saturday and Sunday spaces that are included for each week in their planners. We always take a break after week number four or five of each quarter, depending on what else is going on in our household. Then we take two weeks off at the end of the quarter. I love this schedule! It gives us a lot of flexibility, and the time off between quarters is so refreshing.

Middle school and high school students can easily become self-teaching once they understand your expectations. Sit down with the students individually at the beginning of the quarter, and initially you will need to go over with them how much can feasibly be accomplished per subject within the nine-week time frame. Allow for interruptions in the school week. It is best to set goals that leave room for a day or two of inactivity within the nine weeks. Life happens, and interruptions will come along.

In this planning phase of the quarter, it is better to set goals that you are sure will be attainable for your student at first, and once they have met the goals you have helped them to set, allow the student more freedom in setting the next round of goals when the next quarter rolls around. This provides the student with a feeling of being in the driver's seat which equals motivation. You should witness gradual and steady success on the part of your self-teaching student. It is exciting to watch!

Fleshing It Out

I allow and actually desire for my fourth graders through high schoolers to write down in their planners what they have accomplished in each subject every day as they finish it. I am no longer writing out what needs to be done for an entire week at once and then allowing the student to cross off the spaces once the work has been completed.

Why should we begin to modify the record-keeping process in the first place? What happens if we keep going with the weekly to-do list format? Let's say a high schooler sees that he has three chapters to read in American history this week. On Monday, he speed reads through it in order to be done with that subject for the week. Mastery is not usually attained by moving one's eyes over the words as quickly as possible, if you know what I'm saying. Also, there is no additional learning taking place in history for another whole week.

We want the student to be immersed each day in the subjects at hand. If Monday's a rainy day, and the student is curled up with her American history book and just keeps reading out of interest and ends up doing three chapters in one day because she was caught up in the excitement of the material, then she would write down in her planner that three chapters were read on Monday. She knows she is not off the hook for tomorrow. She will most likely realize she is ahead of her projections for her nine-week goals, and that is a good thing! Being ahead is a very motivating factor for a student.

This same student who has done more than usual in one day in history may do just the bare minimum in this subject for the remainder of the grading period Yes, this could happen. But when I am reviewing with that student after the quarter is over, and we are looking at what goals were attained, I look for spurts of energy in a subject and gently point out and praise that student for accomplishing so much in one day. When the student sees that I notice such things and verbally reward her for it, she is likely to repeat this behavior.

While I prefer to have my middle and high schoolers write down in their planners what they do in each subject as they do it, you can have your students record their stuff any way you choose. The important thing is that they are doing the work, seeing their progress, and writing down what they've accomplished, so you can see what they have accomplished as well.

A perfect place to keep a student planner is to keep it open on the sliding keyboard tray of a computer desk. My kids all have computer desks, and I always know where to look in their rooms for their planners when I go in to check their work. That makes my life that much easier. And my kids don't misplace their planners, which makes their lives easier as well.

Breaking It Down

Let's go into detail about how to figure out the amount of material a student must complete each day in order to finish a textbook by the end of the school year. You want to work backwards by choosing one text book—let's say biology—and peek at the table of contents to see how many lessons there are in the entire book. Science and history can be a little tricky to figure because the material is generally presented in units, each consisting of a varying number of chapters. Generally, look at the number of pages in the book and divide that number by thirty-six weeks in order to get a rough idea of how much material will need to be covered each week.

Let's say the biology book has 375 pages. If we divide that by thirty-six weeks, we get roughly twelve pages per week. There are five days in a week, so that is roughly two to three pages of biology per day. Wasn't that easy? Often goals just look like this: "Plow through the first six chapters of history." It is assumed that the student will be working to a mastery level. You will want to incorporate time for quizzes or tests if you use them; just something to keep in mind as you plan out the quarter.

With a subject such as math, which is usually divided up into individual lessons, the process may be just a bit different. I don't want to know how many pages are in the book; I want to know how many *lessons* are in the book. Let's say the math book has 140 lessons. If you are doing a quarterly schedule, for example, you would divide that number by four quarters, and you get thirty-five. That tells you that thirty-five lessons must be done each quarter. (If you are doing a twelve-week semester schedule, you would divide by three, and you end up with just under forty-seven lessons that must be completed in each twelve-week segment.)

Now you know how many lessons must be accomplished in one segment of your thirty-six-week year.

From there I just divide by the number of actual school days in one unit or one quarter, and that would be forty-five days. (That's nine weeks times five days per week.) I take the number of lessons I found that we had to cover within each quarter (35), and divide that by the number of days in the quarter (45), and now I have the number of lessons that need to be done each day (three-fourths of a lesson). Instead of having my student doing less than one lesson of math each day for five days a week, I would rather he does one full lesson a day, four days a week. This builds in some flexibility. If the student prefers to do a lesson of math per day all week long, that just means he will finish his book before the end of the year and be done with math early!

Goal setting is just that easy.

Hopefully your student has been watching you do this process of figuring out how much work should be done per day. Allow him to help with the next subject and so on until you have a short-term goal set for each subject. This shouldn't take more than twenty or thirty minutes. Bam! That is your planning for the next nine weeks! It is done! There is no need to spend hours on lesson plans. Say good-bye to Sunday night panic. My kids set their short-term goals once every nine weeks, and that is that.

At the End of a Quarter

Once you reach the end of your grading period, get with your students individually and look over their progress for the quarter. Praise them for a job well done. Of course you will be keeping tabs on them throughout the quarter, but use this time to really focus on your students' accomplishments. It is also a good time to go ahead and have your students set the next quarter's goals. It is your job to look over the goals and ensure that they are attainable; not too stringent nor too easy. Then take a well-deserved break from school work for a little while, if desired. As I said, I love taking time off between our quarters, but do what works for you.

Step 4: Monitor

This next step is on your shoulders completely, and I have found out the hard way just how important it is to check up on your self-propelled students regularly. Kids are human, and even the students who demonstrate the most self-mastery may give in to the temptation to take advantage of the system. I have had that happen only on a few occasions, but it can happen.

What Is Accountability?

Accountability is *not* being a helicopter parent, hovering over the student's shoulders, checking up on everything, every minute that he is working; making suggestions, rearranging the pencils in his pencil cup, and doing other over-motherly things. We want to allow the student the freedom to work independently, after all. We are giving our students the gift of our trust, but we still must do periodic inspections.

Accountability is inspecting what we expect, I like to say. If your fifth grader is to be reading her science book independently, stop into her room every couple of days at first and ask her some questions from the chapter she is on. Better yet, ask her some questions from a chapter she did a month ago to test for retention.

I have found that when I do not require that students write down the answers to every single quiz section in the more reading-intensive books such as science and history and just allow them to enjoy the material, they retain much more than if they are reading just to satisfy a bunch of questions. I allow my kids to read freely, but when they come to questions at the end of a chapter or section in history, science, health, etc., I want them to quickly answer the questions in their heads. If they can't remember an answer, then they need to look back and find the answer. That way they are mastering the material every day.

When I sit in with them and look at their planners, they know I am going to be orally quizzing them on the material they say they have completed to a mastery level. If they do not know the answers to my questions, they are penalized by now having to write in a notebook the answers to every test and quiz until I feel they are ready for another chance. You know your kids, and you know if they really read the material or not by how they answer your questions.

I had to discipline one of my girls once when she was just doing the move-the-eyes-over-the-page thing and was not really concentrating. This apparently had been going on for a couple of days because when I quizzed her on the chapter she claimed she had just completed, she didn't know many of the answers. In my book, that is the same as lying. If you tell me you read something thoroughly, and you truly did not, you just lied to me, and lying is a serious offense in our home. There is a punishment that automatically accompanies lying. In addition to that particular punishment, this student lost her freedom to self-teach in that subject. For the next month, I had her write out the answers to the tests and quizzes, and

I looked over her shoulder every single day of that month. That, I think, was the worst part of it for her.

But after the month of time had been fulfilled, I gave her back the freedom to self-teach in the subject with which she had been having difficulty. You have to use your best judgment here as there is no magic formula to use as punishment. Set up your boundaries beforehand so that the students know what to expect if they are not faithful in holding up their end of the self-teaching bargain. Children have to understand that they must earn the freedom to self-teach, and it is a privilege. It is a privilege that will be taken away if they don't keep up their end of the bargain.

We know if they are keeping up with their end of the bargain by looking in on them, comparing what is in their planners to what we find is in their heads when we quiz them. Because my children so enjoy working on their own, I very seldom run into situations where they have not been working to a mastery level when I checked them.

There was one time when one of my seniors claimed to be much further ahead in his math than it turned out he was. When I realized the truth of what was going on—that this student had not been doing a subject at all for a very long time—I felt almost ill. First of all, I had slacked up on checking his work because he had always been so gosh-darn responsible! I mean, I never would have expected this student to do what he had done. But he had, he felt terrible, he apologized, and we had quite the parent-student conference.

On the other hand, I hadn't been checking in on him. I was just assuming that he was doing his work completely and with excellence. Don't do that, I learned! Don't assume anything ever. I learned my lesson, and believe me, he learned his. For the next month, he went nowhere until he was completely caught up in the subject. Thankfully, this student was absolutely repentant and actually felt much better once his secret was out. He had been walking around with a burden on his shoulders because he truly was not the deceitful type. He got behind in the subject, and after a while, he couldn't catch back up so he didn't even try. It was a life lesson for him, and it was quite a lesson in the importance of accountability for me.

See, my kids certainly aren't perfect. We deal with heart issues as well. How thankful I am that because we have our children's hearts, when something like this happens, it does not separate us or come between us. Forgiveness is easily given when a child repents and asks for forgiveness. The incident is forgotten (until Mom goes to write her book), and life goes on. However, the consequences still have to be paid at the time.

So be sure to inspect what you expect from all of your kids, no matter how much you trust them. We all are human, after all.

To Test or Not to Test

I'd like to talk a little about the concept of quizzing and testing. If you remember, in chapter 5—the mastery chapter—I give the example of purchasing a book from Amazon.com on gardening, my particular passion. Then the book comes in the mail, and I am excited to plow into it! But my husband takes it from me and devises some quizzes and tests he thinks I should take along the way to make sure I am truly learning the material. Remember that? Once I realize that I have to take quizzes and tests on this book (which I was initially so excited to receive) as I'm reading it, all I want to do is pitch the book across the room! Why can't I just read it for my own enjoyment instead of having to prove to my husband that I got my money's worth out of the book? Why, indeed!

Don't we do the same thing to our kids when we test and quiz them to death on every single thing they do every day? The same thing happens with our students in a very real way. Give your student the American history text you would like her to read. Then let her read it without obstruction. Pop into her room from time to time and ask her what she is reading about. Maybe ask a few questions, but give her your trust and the freedom to enjoy the book. See if she doesn't enjoy *and* retain the information! I do have my children mentally go through the chapter quizzes that follow the reading sections, but they do not need to write the answers out for me.

I do think that tests and quizzes can be valuable tools for measurement of learning, but they certainly are overused, in my opinion, which detracts from a child's learning experience. As a teacher in a classroom setting, I had to use tests and quizzes because I didn't know what was in every student's head. I knew there were some kids who wouldn't do the assigned homework no matter what, and there were other kids who might do the work, but I cannot know if they learned anything or not until I test them. Somehow, scoring well on tests has become the sole motivation for learning.

I desire that my children learn to be knowledgeable, not to score well on a test. "Teach to the test" is exactly what I was trained to do in the classroom realm because it meant the kids could memorize only what they *needed* to know; no more, no less. I remember as a student asking my teachers, "Do we need to know this for the test?" Did you ever ask that? By asking that question, I was really saying, "What am I forced to know if I want an A?" And teachers were happy to tell us the answer because that would make them look better if students' test scores were higher. It is a vicious circle of fake learning. Ugh.

Yes, sometimes I use tests such as spelling tests. I take grades every day in math. In fact, when we are sitting around the supper table, I will ask the kids to tell me how their math went. Yep, we even have honest-to-goodness peer pressure in home education!

When it comes to deciding whether or not to test a student on his daily work, consider my example of the gardening book. If you do quiz and test, have a good reason for doing so. "Because this is how they do it in schools," is not a good enough reason for me, and I hope it is not for you either. Trust your instincts.

At the End of the Year

When you are ready to pack it in and call it a year, you will probably want to complete a simple assessment of the school year. How does one analyze a whole year of home education? Is the best way to look at the goals we may have set before the year began? Sometimes we must adjust our goals as we go throughout the year. What I thought would happen at the beginning of the year may not have happened at all because the goals changed mid-way, or maybe we accomplished more than I thought we might. Either way is absolutely fine. Home education needs to be fluid and flexible as the day's challenges and opportunities dictate. Goals are great to have and reaching them is wonderful, but they are not the only standard by which we should assess.

Should you assess the year by the number of books that were finished? Did your students finish all of their books from the stack at the beginning of the year? If not, know that this isn't unusual, as we don't need to measure out education in terms of time. High schoolers face more pressure in this area, as the educational system in America tells us that subjects must be finished up within a 180-day time frame. Real life often doesn't work that way, however, so if your students did not finish every textbook by the time the clock runs out, just start up where they left off when you begin anew. Or high school students can work on a particular subject during your break if there is a need to press on within a given time frame.

I don't know about you, but I don't recall ever finishing a book during my school days—not one! The difference is that as home educators, we do have the luxury of finishing our materials because we can start up wherever we left off. As I say repeatedly, there is no such thing as being "behind" in home education. You are where you are, unless you've been negligent in your duties and allowed your children to do anything but school work for half the year. Then there is an issue to be addressed.

I would like to repeat that statement for emphasis: there is no such thing as a child being behind in his work. He is where he is. We as moms tend to think that we must mimic the very system from which we have removed our children. Textbooks are designed to fit the traditional school setting, and classroom teachers feel a lot of pressure to get through as much material as possible with the large number of children in their classes.

I know that when I was a classroom teacher, mastery never was my goal. It was a dream. There just wasn't time to hang around on one subject until all the kids learned to an A-level before moving onto the next thing! Consequently, some children fell between the cracks. Fortunately, the reverse is true in home education. We can take all the time our students need to digest and truly learn their lessons before moving on, or the students can progress more rapidly if they are able.

Sometimes we fall behind our schedule. Recently, I listened as a four-star mom lamented that her child is behind where he should be in two subjects. Mom is now feeling guilty and losing hope that she can ever teach her children well at home. She would undoubtedly feel a load lifted off her shoulders if she could see that her child is right where he *should* be.

Sometimes things happen in our lives that sideline schooling for a day, a few days, or even a few months. Nothing has been lost except that our plans may have been thwarted, but that is when you just jump back in without guilt and keep right on going. It is so important to not have the *behind* mentality, as that is a negative mindset. You have not failed in any way by adjusting home education to meet the real-life needs of your family. Wherever you are, this is where you should be. If adjustments need to be made, make them without guilt. Life happens, and we certainly are not perfect. Don't expect yourself to be.

Now, there *is* such a thing as a student (or, in some cases, even a mom) simply not applying themselves diligently to the task at hand, and thus not being where they otherwise could have been; in that case, the heart attitudes need to be dealt with. However, that's not primarily what I'm talking about here. I'm simply talking about the different rates at which students learn material and the various life circumstances that can impact our schedule. We don't need to feel guilty when our student honestly has a hard time grasping a certain topic, or when an illness or family emergency puts studies on hold for a while. These types of things don't cause us to be behind; they simply require adjustments to our plans and expectations. Life happens, and none of us is perfect.

Grades

One of the most common ways of assessing the school year is to look at the grades that children have achieved. Is this a good yardstick to use? I would say that absolutely, grades are an important factor as they show *demonstrated competency*. However, I do not grade every little thing my children do. Let me stress that I am looking at work and mentally grading *all the time*. Mastery of the material is of the utmost importance, and I know whether a student has mastered the concepts or not simply by looking over his work as often as I deem necessary. How often I look over a student's work will depend upon his age and his level of self-mastery.

With the mastery method of learning, the student does not move on to the next activity unless he completely understands what has been presented today. If he did not do well on today's work, this indicates a problem that needs to be addressed. That problem could be a readiness issue; the child is not developmentally ready for the task. This happens much less frequently than the other causes of problems, which include laziness, lack of concentration, or the child simply requiring more information or more practice to understand the material. The necessary time needs to be taken to attain mastery.

Children will rise to meet our expectations, and we need to expect them to learn their daily material diligently. With this said, it would follow that children who have the benefit of mastery learning will achieve high grades in every area that is measured simply because they do not move on until the comprehension is demonstrated. We need to be careful not to train our children to work for a grade like a puppy obeys to receive a treat. A self-propelled student works in order to learn, and yes, in some cases, works to just get through the work and come out the other side. A student is exposed to so much in twelve years that it would be silly to expect him to love learning everything he is handed. It just won't happen. The goal is for the student to learn and to be self-disciplined enough to learn despite the fact that the material may not thrill him. It still must be done and be done well.

If you have been disappointed with your student's performance in one or more subjects this year, I urge you not to move on and just think that things will be better next year. Unless something changes, the results will most likely be the same. I also urge you not to feel guilty, but rather, look at the situation objectively.

I firmly believe that grades are a reflection of a child's attitude about learning and are often a reflection of the heart as well. I hesitate to make such a sweeping generality, but I have seen time and time again where a stubborn or strong-willed child who does not want to work will not do the work completely, will not do it properly, or will not care how he does it at all. This is not a reflection of ability; rather, it is a reflection of a heart problem that needs to be addressed by the parents. If poor grades are an issue in the home-educating environment, and there is no physical problem causing them, there is most likely a lack of peace in the house as well because the child has behavior issues that are not being addressed. There is most likely a self-mastery issue or two to examine and remedy.

If we assess our school year according to actual grades and look at how well children have learned the material we presented to them, we will have a more accurate picture of achievement than if we concentrate solely on how much material was covered. It is the old quality over quantity thing.

Step 5: Let Go of the Bicycle

For some parents, this is the most difficult step of all—letting go and trusting their students. Some parents just find it hard to believe that there is a better way than teaching *at* their kids for all thirteen years of the home-education experience! If self-mastery/heart training is developing from an early age, letting go of the bicycle can be done by parents with confidence.

By the middle school years, a student should possess a high level of self-control which wins him the freedom to work independently. The self-propelled high schooler is going to ride to places perhaps his parents have never been, figuratively speaking. How does he get to those places? He uses self-learning and mastery learning as tools, and because he has self-confidence and is conscientious, he can find his own way, asking for directions if needed.

If a parent has a student who has a tendency to be sneaky, who can't be trusted to do anything without supervision, and who lacks motivation, the self-teaching method of education is not going to work. In fact, this parent has a much bigger issue to look into: the heart issue. Much work still needs to be done in disciplining and training this child. Kids do not just grow out of these kinds of stages. In fact, I don't believe in stages. Children will rise to your expectations, but if a parent doesn't set expectations of quality work and diligence, the child is not going to just magically inherit those characteristics. Self-mastery is much more important than any school work anywhere.

Ultimate Goals

My ultimate goal for my students each new school year is that they know what material needs to be covered, they set attainable goals for themselves, they work with excellence to master the material, and they enjoy their accomplishments. Because they are self-propelled, they tend to finish their work in optimal time and have free time to spend pursuing their interests on a deeper level. They also have time to help around the house and time to spend with their parents and siblings. They also have time for socialization.

 Parent's Corner

1. Are there any subjects your student has this year that should remain parent-directed?
2. Decide how often you want to check in on your students to see if they are learning what they say they are learning. Mark it on your calendar.
3. How does the five-step self-teaching system compare to what you are doing now with your students?
4. If your children currently are in a teacher-directed setting such as a classroom, do you think that self-learning is enough of an advantage to warrant a change in their learning environment? Why or why not?

CHAPTER 9

WHAT ABOUT CURRICULUM?

The philosophy of the school room in one generation
will be the philosophy of government in the next.
—Abraham Lincoln

When I was a school-aged youngster, my parents would never have questioned the curriculum that was used in my public school classroom. It just wasn't done. Of course that was three decades ago. My classmates and I used whatever books were chosen according to the school board's standards. Times change, however, and today there is a lot of hollering and fussing and fighting that goes on over public school curriculum choice. I am just glad I don't have to be involved in determining what to use for hundreds—perhaps thousands—of children in a public school system today. One size can't possibly fit all. What a job!

I understand why there is so much fuss over what curriculum is used in the classroom today; I definitely want to have control over what my children learn and how material is presented. That is why I've chosen home education. I use certain curriculum because it is challenging for my students, among other reasons. I've seen some public school curriculum that is not even remotely challenging, and I wonder how students can get an edge in today's world. Curriculum can certainly dictate the quality of learning, and not just any old books should do. Curriculum is the starting point of an excellent education.

Many parents do not consider well what types of materials are being used to instruct their children. Truly, there are only so many ways you can present mathematics. However, children can be challenged or not challenged, depending on when concepts are presented in a textbook. I want my kids to use challenging math materials that present logic and reading problems at a young age to develop their critical thinking skills, for example.

Those of you whose children are in a public school, take a look, if you haven't already, at what materials your student uses. Is it challenging for them? Are they bored in class because the material is simple? Are the materials interesting to look at and aesthetically pleasing? I don't know about you, but I like color in textbooks. Maybe I'm just funny that way, but if the text is pleasing to the eye, it interests me from the get-go. We do judge books by their covers, and children do too. On the other hand, I wouldn't sacrifice the challenging aspect for the eye-pleasing aspect. I look for both.

If you don't like the curriculum being used in your child's classroom, the bad news is that you have zero influence. Tough beans. Too bad. Since public schools are run by the government, the curriculum tends to be chosen in a rather political manner. Even teachers have little say over what materials they use to convey information to their students in their classrooms. That is just weird, isn't it? What's worse is that parents basically have *no* say.

In the private school realm, curriculum has a better chance of being challenging simply because the private school's board doesn't have as many hoops to jump through or as many people to please as the public school's board. Private school students' parents may have some input on curriculum decisions in some cases, but generally they do not. While curriculum in the private school is likely to be more challenging than that of the public school, parents still need to consider the curriculum's suitability before blindly sending their children away each day to be submerged in it.

If I am a parent with a child in a private school, and I am paying a lot of money for my child's education, I'm going to speak up if I have issues with the curriculum, but only if I have very good reasons for having issues, and only if I have a recommendation for replacement material. I encourage you to look at what your student is learning and how it is being presented. If the materials are too easy for your student, he is not being challenged. If he is not being challenged, time is being wasted. This is time that you and he cannot get back.

Public and private school parents should consider carefully whether or not their students' academic needs are being met, and see that they are being challenged and stretched through the materials being used in the classroom. There is a delicate balance here because too much stretching yields frustration while not enough challenge yields boredom.

Worldview

Every day we are presented with information from a variety of sources. One can hear the same event covered on *Fox News* and *CNN*, yet both news reports about the event may come from totally different vantage points. The vantage points will be reflective of the reporters' perspectives.

As parents we naturally want our children—especially when they are young—to see the world through the lens of the beliefs that we hold—our worldview. Many parents choose a private school for their children based on their worldview. For example, Catholic schools teach Catholic values. Parents who want their children to learn through the lens of a Catholic worldview are apt to send their children to a Catholic school. The curriculum there is going to reflect their values. Often the teachers will be nuns.

It goes without saying that children in the public school will be taught through the lens of political correctness via curriculum that reflects politically correct values. Government schools promote lifestyles and activities that many parents do not condone. A parent should choose wisely what worldview will be presented to the young child, remembering that worldview comes through a curriculum as well as through the teacher's own perspective.

One of the reasons my husband and I home educate our children is our dissatisfaction (and disgust) with the reigning politically-correct atmosphere in public schools today. However, we currently have a college student in a public university. We've raised our young children with a distinct worldview that will enable them as adults to hold to those values and thrive amidst a culture which tends to make destructive choices. In America, we have the right to choose the worldview from which to educate our children. It is every parent's right to do so.

Home Education and Curriculum

If you are a home educator, you have complete control over your student's worldview and his curriculum. However, this freedom can scare the life out of any self-respecting mom! How does a home-educating mom avoid becoming overwhelmed when it comes to deciding what curriculum materials to use with her children? If you are new to the wonderful world of home education, may I just offer a word of advice? Try to relax. I know there is a huge world of book publishers and a plethora of methodologies from which to choose when considering home education for the very first year. (And I want you to *relax?*)

Just how should you go about choosing curriculum anyway? If you are a first-time home educator, I recommend asking for suggestions from friends who have children who are excelling in home education. Take a look at what your friends are using, and see if you like what you see. Recommendations are extremely valuable, but keep in mind that what works well for one family may not for another, as we all have different likes and dislikes as well as different goals for our children.

It seems nowadays that there are massive curriculum fairs going on all year around. You may want to seek out a curriculum fair to visit. You can see different types and varieties of curriculum from secular and non-secular publishers. Visiting a curriculum fair may or may not be helpful because the curriculum choices out there are staggering, and at this point, you don't need added terror, especially if this will be your first time at the helm. Curriculum simply needs to be user-friendly, not too easy, and it must present information in a logical and memorable fashion.

I chose a lot of our curriculum sight unseen from a catalogue years and years ago, thinking I could return it if I did not like it. I kept it. Start somewhere without worrying about whether or not you have found the perfect thing for your children. The perfect curriculum does not exist on planet Earth. Every brand of math program or every brand of spelling or science or health or phonics has its limitations, and our children should learn to learn within those limitations. Choose a program that looks as though it will be interesting and will meet the needs of your students and run with it. Trust your instincts.

What's More Important Than Curriculum?

Curriculum, while important from a worldview perspective, is not the cornerstone of education. If a student possesses a good attitude and willingness to work hard, the particular brand of materials he uses will not make much difference.

However, if a student has the perfect curriculum, but he lacks the drive and determination to master this so-called perfect material, learning—especially self-learning—won't happen.

As a former elementary school teacher in a classroom environment, I learned that curriculum alone does not an educated child make. I never had the opportunity to choose the curriculum for my students when I taught in a private school; I used what was available to me to the best of my ability. The students who did well in my classes were the ones who came from homes with parents who were supportive of education, which led to good attitudes on the part of the students.

Home education is wonderful in that it provides parents with the marvelous opportunity to choose what type of worldview will be presented in the education of the children; this is extremely valuable. There can be no downplaying of the validity of using high-quality curriculum that we as parents hand-pick for our children. But this wonderful curriculum will be useless unless we train our children's hearts to best use these tools.

How to Use Curriculum

In the home-education realm, many well-meaning parents fuss and worry over whether or not their young child will *like* his spelling book, or his handwriting book, and they will go off looking for a different program if little Susie states a dislike, or worse yet, will not do the work. There are innumerable programs and systems out there, and most any one of them has validity. As a curriculum specialist, I can tell you that I have never met a curriculum that I thought would *not* work for my children. Sure, I have preferences, but if the student is cheerful, obedient, and trusts the parent's judgment, most any math or spelling or science program will be more than suitable. Learning can happen with just about any curriculum if one is determined and committed to making it work!

When my children were young, I used to wonder if the particular curriculum I had chosen was adequate. Were they actually learning? To find out, I had my oldest two tested, and they tested way above grade level, and both had areas where they tested off the scale. Whatever we were doing was working. When I saw how well they were doing, I relaxed. I needed that measurement to help me relax, for some reason. I just did not trust my instincts yet. Several years down the road and eighteen years of home education later, I still use the same curriculum for my elementary children that I used for my children who are now college students. Why? *Because I know it works.* I have found what works, and I have stuck with it, despite the almost-suffocating desire to look and see what the latest, greatest thing is that has come down the pike in Home Education Land. If you have curriculum that works, by all means, stick with it!

You now have freedom from the compulsion to attend every curriculum fair in your tri-state area. I advise parents not to attend curriculum fairs if they have systems that already are working for them. Going to a curriculum fair to browse is like peering into a candy store window. You know you are going to see something you have to have right here and now. But do you need it? Chances are, nope.

How many of us have shelves and shelves full of resource materials that we have picked up thinking, "Wow, this could help us in geography," or "I might be interested in more science experiments," and before you know it, you have a bazillion or more books that you forgot you have, let along use regularly? Don't feel like you have to be up on all of the latest trends in curriculum because I assure you, what you have been using successfully right now will not go out of style. Moms are especially susceptible to being curriculum shopaholics, and it causes confusion with your children and possibly causes wasteful spending when you are constantly changing programs.

Virtual Schools and Curriculum

I want to take a minute and discuss a very viable option available to many home-educating parents: virtual academies. (We talked a bit about virtual education back in chapter 3.) K^{12} curriculum is an interesting option that I've recently been exploring for my own research purposes. While K^{12} is a privately-owned company, K^{12} works in tandem with the public school systems in a number of states in the U.S. K^{12} is an online curriculum that is free to parents who choose to educate their children at home through their system which is, in essence, a public school program.

I think that K^{12}, and other companies such as this which are virtual, are very good options for parents who want to home educate their children, but they prefer to use programmed instruction. I'm not saying that it is for everybody. If you have been home educating for a while already, you may not like the more rigid K^{12} approach in your home education environment. But I would choose public school *at home* over public school in a classroom on the other side of town any day. Why? Obviously, if your child is learning at home, he can learn to a mastery level, he can build self-mastery skills, and he can utilize self-teaching with the K^{12}

approach. Win-win-win. You can also discuss any worldview issues that may arise, and discussion is oh-so-valuable.

You can check out K^{12} by googling them online. I encourage you, if you feel the tug to bring your children home to learn, to look into this virtual alternative. There are caveats as far as there being governmental input in the standards and the testing methods, so look into it from all the various aspects. There are definite pluses to using a virtual school.

When You May Need to Change Curriculum

If you have been home educating for a while, one reason for changing curriculum may be because you have chosen a different methodology, a different type of approach. For example, there are some materials which are not suitable for a self-learning approach. If I have been doing unit studies, for example, which is a very parent-intensive approach, and then I decide I want to train my children to become independent learners, I will need to change my curriculum. If you drastically change the method of instruction, you will need to change a brand of curriculum in some cases.

What I refer to as curriculum-hopping is entirely unrelated to this type of change in *approach*. Changing my science curriculum because my son whines and complains about not liking the current one would be an example of nefarious curriculum-hopping. And the whining and complaining is indicative of a totally different problem that has nothing at all to do with the materials I am using, which we have already talked about at length.

The underwhelmed mom finds what curriculum works for her children, and then she sticks with it, confident that her children can and will adapt themselves to it and work to the best of their ability. Notice I said that the children will adapt to the curriculum and not the other way around. I firmly believe that the learning styles concept is completely overrated. I believe that with all my heart. All eight of my children have, for the most part, used the same curriculum. Of course they have learning *preferences*, but I do not specifically cater to them. Why? Once our students reach college level, what kind of input do they have on the curriculum their professors choose? Exactly! None. They may choose their classes, but the professors will not care about individual learning styles in the college classroom. Employers don't care about learning styles either, do they?

Why do we spend so much time and energy trying to discern exactly how our (non-learning-challenged) students learn best? In the realm of adulthood, it is a moot point. Perhaps it is because I have to institute a certain measure of crowd control because I have a lot of children, but I do not look for learning styles. I look for my children's ability to adapt and work through their weaker areas. Results speak more loudly than anything, in my book, and we have had and continue to have excellent results by utilizing mastery learning, having expectations for each child, and my husband and I tailoring our time to coaching and helping each child reach his or her potential.

To restate, I feel that curriculum-hopping is nonessential. Find what works for you, and stick with it. There is no reason why all of your children cannot use the same materials! Going back to my days teaching in a school system, the curriculum was non-negotiable. I never had a fourth grade student complain to me about the social studies book or the math book we were using. It never happened. Why not? Because the students would never think to complain! It wouldn't change anything even if they did complain, which they wouldn't do because they understood that they had to push through what was put in front of them.

Why do we think differently in the home-education realm? I am the mom; I have chosen what I think is the best curriculum for my children via philosophy and presentation of the material, and I am going to *expect* my children to work with the tools I have provided. My children would not even think to complain.

I approach my high school students a little differently. For the most part, I choose what brand of materials I would like to use, but the students have a lot of say in what they study and when. Of course we have the standard courses that must be covered, but each child's abilities are taken into consideration. My oldest child studied calculus, but I did not require the next student to do so, as her post-high-school pathway would be different than the first child's. Yes, I have the final say in what brand of chemistry book is purchased, but I get input from my high schoolers and respect their viewpoints as I make the choice.

Contrast that to what I would do if my nine-year-old daughter came to me and said she didn't like her spelling book. I would certainly listen to her reasoning; however, her reasoning will most likely have nothing to do with the educational value of the book itself. Perhaps she doesn't enjoy handwriting, and she is complaining about the book in order to avoid having to actually do the work.

Again, it wouldn't cross my younger children's minds to complain randomly about the tools we have given them with which to work. If your children complain about curriculum, look at the root of the problem. Does what they are saying have validity? If so, then the problem may warrant a change. More often than not, the problem is not with the curriculum; the student needs to pour on the effort and work through the situation.

With younger children, there may be readiness issues. For example, just because Susie's first grade math book says it is time to study clocks and how to tell time doesn't mean Susie is mentally ready to tackle and understand time. Young children may not be prepared for what is being presented by the text at that moment in time. This is where you have the freedom to not be a slave to the curriculum. Skip past the unit on time or on calendars, and come back to it a couple of months down the road and try again. This is a whole different issue than what I mean by curriculum-hopping.

When I examine our home education process, I see that my husband and I have the same expectations for all of our children. We expect all of our children to be kind and loving, to respect each other, to do what is asked of them cheerfully, and to work to the best of their ability. We expect each student to maintain an A average in every subject. Each child's ability to do this is the same: *they possess the ability*. Some are more motivated at earlier stages than others, but they are all capable of mastery learning. It is my job as the coach to enable them to set goals and work towards them each day, not by standing over them and cajoling and begging them to do their work, but by challenging and rewarding their efforts.

One of my favorite quotes is by Albert Einstein: "I never teach my pupils; I only attempt to provide the conditions in which they can learn." You may want to post that prominently on your desk. Or write it in hot pink lipstick on your dining room wall. Truly, your job as a parent is not to teach your children for thirteen years. Your job is to provide the conditions in which your children can self-learn. Do I hear an amen?

Einstein also said, "It is a miracle that curiosity survives formal education." Why is this? I believe it is because formal education attempts to institutionalize learning. Education is not a one-size-fits-all endeavor. Our parental responsibility is to provide the tools for learning as well as an environment conducive to learning. The attitude training is often the biggest challenge. Once your children are cheerfully doing their work with the tools you have provided, the learning part is easy! They are ready to be set free to wholly absorb their lessons in an environment over which they have a measure of control.

An attitude that says, "I can do this, I will do this, and I will do it well," is invaluable to any human being, and a child who grows up with that kind of thinking will have an advantage that reaches into every corner of his life. Curriculum is a tool in the education process, but attitude is the heart of education. Curriculum plays but a small role in the overall education of students.

While choosing curriculum is an essential step in the home education process, it is not a do-or-die decision. Quality instructional materials are necessary, but often we waste so much time and effort worrying about and looking for the perfect thing in every subject to thoroughly delight our student when delighting the student is not the point. If delight is a side effect, great!

Pulling Back the Curriculum Curtain

If there is one thing I get asked repeatedly, it's "What curriculum do your children use?" I have never before pulled back this particular curtain because what works for one family may not work for another. But in order to give you a starting point, I will list the curriculum I have personally used with my children. I will also give you recommendations of materials that are self-teaching in nature that I have not personally used, but which I know have been used with excellent results in other self-teaching homes.

The asterisks (*) beside the materials listed below represent curriculum I have personally used with my students. Note that materials for children in grades kindergarten through third grade will not be self-teaching unless the children can read and follow directions on their own.

Math
Modern Curriculum Press (K-3)*
Saxon (4-12)*
Jacob's Geometry*
Math-U-See
Life of Fred
Saxon Dive CDs

Spelling
Christian Liberty Press (K-4)*
Spelling City (free Internet version)

Handwriting
Zaner-Bloser*
Italic Handwriting*

Phonics
A Beka (K-2)*

Language
A Beka (3-6)*

English
A Beka Literature (9-12)*
Lots of reading of student's choice plus my own book list for them.*
Language Alive (see description below)*

Reading
Pathway Readers (K-3)*
Scaredy Cat Reading System
   We encourage reading all the time from sources of the children's choosing for the most part. The more choice we give in reading material, the more children will enjoy reading. Of course I know what they are reading and must approve it.*

Grammar/Writing
Analytical Grammar
Writing Strands
Easy Grammar
   We've used a curriculum I designed for my own children called Language Alive that includes writing, grammar, and vocabulary for grades seven through twelve. (Available for purchase in late 2012. Check www.URtheMOM.com for updates.)*

Science
A Beka (K-8)*
A Beka Physical Science (9)*
Apologia Biology (10)*
Apologia Chemistry (11)*
Saxon Physics (12)*

History
A Beka (K-12)*

Foreign Language
Rosetta Stone*
Power Glide*

Miscellaneous
Switched on Schoolhouse
Mind-Benders
American Adventure History Series
Mavis Beacon Typing Program*

Student Planner
Equally as important as your curriculum is *The Home School Student Planner* or *The Essential High School Planner* (Available from www.URtheMOM.com)

Curriculum Conclusion

If your children are in a public or private school, take a hard look at the curriculum they are currently using in each and every subject. Check out the worldview presented, especially in history and science. If you have any discomfort at all with the worldview, talk with your children about it. Ask your children if they are bored with any particular subject. Find out if they feel challenged. If there are red flags in this area, get with your spouse and discuss any changes you feel may need to be made either now or down the road.

If you home educate, take whatever curriculum you have that has been working well, and be confident that you are working with the appropriate tools for learning. If you strongly feel that a curriculum change is warranted, make the change. Most importantly, make sure you are teaching, enforcing, and modeling the attitudes necessary for your student to be a motivated learner. Have great expectations for children, while keeping in mind that no curriculum can accomplish true learning without the user bringing it to life through a yes-I-can attitude, commitment, and determination.

☑ Parent's Corner

1. Are you happy with your child's curriculum? Why or why not?

2. What worldview does your child's curriculum present? Does it reflect your own worldview?

3. What is even more important than the curriculum you use?

4. Make a list of the curriculum you already have and use. Is there any reason to change? If there is not a pressing reason, I recommend sticking with what you already have.

5. If you are the parent of public or private school students, amaze your children by closely examining their textbooks. They'll be happy that you are interested in what they are learning.

CHAPTER 10

HIGH SCHOOL AND BEYOND

We are what we repeatedly do. Excellence, therefore, is not an act but a habit.
—Aristotle

I confess that I do not understand why some parents think that once their home-educated children get past eighth grade, the kids now must obviously go to a "real" school, "so they get everything they'll need for college." My family is an example of a family who has children who were educated at home from kindergarten through high school, and they lived to tell about it. There are many other families whose children are living proof that kids can be well educated at home all the way through high school with excellent results.

If that isn't enough to gird you with confidence, know that there are many teaching resources and options available to you aside from books and textbooks. In this day and age, there are resources which can be utilized in high school to continue to give your students a much better education via home education than a public or private school can give. Some of those options are video classes, satellite classes, accelerated classes at local community colleges, and accelerated distance learning.

Self-Teaching in High School

This particular section of the book is written specifically to parents of home-educated students who have been using the self-teaching method of education long enough for the student to be comfortable with it. If your student is just starting to self-teach in the high school years, that's great! Keep in mind that you may have to start them slowly and give more freedom to self-teach as the readiness presents itself.

Our experience in transitioning to high school has been most non-traumatic. Once I learn what course of study my kids want to pursue, my husband and I then begin to map out or shape the course we would like to see them take; we also give them the opportunity to choose courses that they would like to take. Let's face it: four years of English is a graduation requirement. Three sciences and four math courses are also expected. Factor in history and geography, plus economics, foreign language, physical education, and electives, and you are looking at a pretty full high school schedule.

Perhaps you are thinking, "I could never teach biology, let alone calculus!" If you have been with me up until this point, you will realize that it isn't about you teaching them. Your high schooler should be self-teaching by now. You are the mom; you don't have to know calculus, or biology, or fill in the blank. The self-learner can take a physics book, accelerated though it may be, and work through it if he has built a solid foundation of self-teaching. He won't suddenly need you to do the understanding of physics for him just because it is a high school class!

If your student has a question about a particular subject, remember, we have taught our kids where to go to find out anything they don't know. We have taught them how to use their resources to dig into a question that is plaguing them and find the answer for themselves. This yields a high level of confidence. High school is the time for your self-learner to soar! I want my kids to love their high school years, and so far, this is exactly what has happened as they've earned more and more freedom through the natural maturation process.

Speaking of maturity and freedom, once kids are old enough to drive, not only can they have a lot more interaction with their friends, but also they can follow their passions outside the home. As a high school senior, Franklin would drive two-and-a-half hours, twice a week, so he could play hockey with predominantly college-age players. He would have been unable to pursue this passion at all if he had attended the local high school his senior year. No schools in our area of

Tennessee have ice hockey teams. So you see, there are more than academic benefits to home educating through the high school years.

Our self-teaching teens can and should be able to work through their high school courses on their own. They will need our guidance in setting the course load and perhaps in record keeping, but aside from that, we should be inconsequential when it comes to doing their actual school work on a daily basis. Come the junior and senior years, you will need to be thinking about college if your student is college bound, and you will probably begin contacting various institutions of higher learning to do your own college research on behalf of your student. This is where the going gets fun! Helping your teen choose a college is a relationship-building experience.

The climate for home-educated graduates being accepted at universities across the country has never been better. Why? Because admissions counselors have had ample time to watch the successful performances enacted by home-educated graduates who have come to their particular schools and out-performed many other students from traditional high school backgrounds! Universities actively recruit home-educated students today.

More than anything, I want you to be confident that your student will not be penalized at all for being home educated through high school as far as eligibility for college entrance is concerned. Remember, many colleges embrace these students. What you *will* need to do as your student hits ninth grade is to take record keeping more seriously if you have been a little laid-back in that department to this point.

High School Record Keeping

Ninth grade is the time to start preparing for college via record keeping. Scary? It doesn't have to be, and here's why. *The Essential High School Planner* has all the record-keeping components your student needs for each year of his high school career. I have not seen any other planner that is tailored to meet this specific need. (I've had college students ask to use these for college as well.)

At the end of each year, your student will have a complete portfolio to set aside for future reference. Four of these planners are all you need to keep your sanity throughout the next four years. Enjoy having neat and organized portfolios for your student to take with him to college admissions interviews. This is an absolutely shameless plug for these products because we believe in them! Not sure? Check them out at <u>URtheMOM.com</u> and follow the link to the high school editions.

I have been talking about setting a course for your high school student. What do I mean by this? You will need to map out what courses you want your student to take, and what year you plan to plug each course into the scheme of things. If your student is not planning on going to college, there is a different course of study he may choose to follow. Both of these planning sheets are in the planner mentioned above, and they are truly essential for planning out the entire four years' worth of course work.

Advantages for the Self-Propelled High School Student

What are the advantages to having your student continue education at home for the high school years? The advantages vary somewhat according to what type of learner you have. For example, many students can pack enough credits into their first three years of high school (utilizing summer school time) to graduate a year early.

All of my students who have graduated from high school to this point could have graduated at least a year early. A lot of times parents will advise their high school student to dual-enroll at a local college or community college so the student can get both high school and college credits at the same time which may enable the student to graduate from high school early. If there is a specific reason for the student to graduate early, I think it's a viable option. If there's not a good reason for early graduation, what's the rush?

With each of our four high school graduates to date, we supported their decisions to enjoy their senior years. Why hurry off to college early? One of the advantages of doing high school at home is this: you have your son or daughter around you for four whole years! Sure, all four of our graduates were extremely motivated and could have missed out on their senior year in exchange for beginning college earlier, but they also enjoyed being a part of our local educational co-op, being on a debate team, designing the yearbook, and playing sports. Why miss out on what could be the best year of a high school career merely to run off to college? I'm sure in some cases there are perfectly good reasons to do so. I would just advise parents to weigh those reasons carefully.

I remember Nick getting an e-mail from Caltech during his junior year in high school that began, "You have captured the interest of Caltech." Yes, I was happy to hear that Caltech had heard of Nick's accomplishments on all the College Board exams he had taken. He also received unsolicited recruiting from Harvard, Princeton, Yale, Georgetown, and too many other schools to list. However, during his junior year, Nick decided that college would still be there after his senior year. He had aspirations to fulfill before he felt he was ready to go away to school. That's maturity. The realm of higher education was pretty much at his feet, but he was not even daunted.

Here is an important advantage of home-educating high school students: we, as a family, got to be together for the duration of all of my first four children's high school years. Of course time waits for no mom, and college has been stealing away my children, one by one, with no signs of letting up. Each has left home with loving relationships with their parents and siblings to support them even while away. Tim and I find it hard to release them, not unlike releasing doves into the wild, but the joy of the experiences awaiting them on the journey of life is in our hearts.

We're a close family because we have a strong foundation built upon both hard times and good times, and we have shared values and a shared faith. We would not have that strong foundation if our family was splintered by some of our kids heading off to an elementary school building, some to the local middle school, and the rest to a high school to be educated by people we don't even know, five days a week. It's safe to say that my kids would not have the self-motivation, self-discipline, and commitment to their education if they did not have as much control over their environments as they do when they are self-teaching at home. They are self-propelled as a result. Their own energy is what pedals the bike.

In the high school years, students are able to study more than just their required courses because they have the time and inclination to do so. They can concentrate on their interests once their regular work is done, as Franklin was able to do at the ice rink twice a week during school hours. Students can study in various ways, not just via lectures or textbooks.

The College Admissions Process

Let's change gears here for a little while, shall we? Let's take a look at what admissions counselors will be looking for when a student is in one of their offices, being examined under an electron microscope. The goal here is to win scholarships or entrance to special programs, and in some cases, simply admission to the university itself.

Many, many colleges and universities will just require a scholarship application to be filled out and sent to them for processing in order to apply for entrance to their schools, but some of the more elite schools will personally interview applicants who show particular promise. It is always necessary to keep accurate records for your high school students over the course of their four years. You will always be prepared if you have kept careful records.

Admissions reps will be looking for:

- high SAT/ACT scores
- high school transcript: how rigorous are the courses?
- excellent writing skills/communication skills
- heavy course load the senior year even if graduation requirements have been met
- academic and extracurricular pursuits outside of the box
- leadership skills
- demonstrated talent in a specific area, if vying for music, athletic scholarships, etc.
- volunteer work done
- a memorable and distinctive interview (if required)
- excellent letters of recommendation

Sounds scary, doesn't it? Again, it doesn't have to be scary. If your student is self-propelled and has been working to mastery and self-teaching for years, he is very likely to get above-average SAT/ACT scores. You will have used challenging curriculum for him, so that won't be an issue. (See chapter 9 on curriculum advice.) He'll have excellent communication and writing skills simply from his years of reading on his own. It is likely that he has pursued unusual interests and has some sort of demonstrated talent that he has been honing in his free time. The interview and letters of recommendation are all he needs to prepare. Please breathe.

Preparing Your High School Junior for College

I want to focus for a moment on an important segment of the high school population: the college-bound junior. There is a lot that can and should be accomplished in the junior year to prepare the student for college. If you have a junior in your household, what should you be doing now to make sure he will be ready for the college-application process? Here are my tried-and-true steps to whip your junior into shape for graduation next year and college next fall.

1. *Talk with your student about his areas of interest.* Share with him the strengths you and your spouse see in him, and brainstorm how these giftings may translate into a career. You can also have a family meeting and invite siblings to chime in. Positive input only! Perhaps he does not have a clue what he would like to study in college; that is normal, but your input as to his strengths will help him begin to formulate ideas. Surely he is interested in something. You may just have to dig to get at that something. This is an ongoing process. Lather, rinse, and repeat.

2. If he has not already done so, *have him take either the SAT or ACT,* ASAP. It is important to get a baseline score on these exams. I actually recommend taking either the SAT or the ACT earlier than in the junior year, but it is not a life-or-death thing if the student has not taken any yet. During the spring of the junior year, it is essential that the college-bound student takes one or both of these exams. The more tests, the better. A student simply cannot test too often.

   Quick tip: Ideally, it is great for the student to take his first SAT or ACT once he has completed Algebra 1. That may mean a student takes the exam after eighth or ninth grade, which is great! There is no pressure on a student at this age. Who expects an eighth or ninth grader to be competitive at this age? Ah, but they will most likely surprise themselves when they can relax and take an exam for fun as an eighth or ninth grader. It's a great way to get the student acclimated to these tests, and I bet the student will also be surprised and encouraged by the results, especially if he is self-propelled.

   Unless your family is independently wealthy, merit-based scholarships are a godsend, and these scholarships are most often awarded to those with excellent College Board exam scores. Additional things to keep in mind: technical colleges often prefer the ACT to the SAT. Check with individual schools to be sure, but other than the tech-y schools, either exam is usually acceptable. If your student has a particular school in mind already, check the school's website to see if it has an exam preference, or give a quick call to the admissions office to see if it prefers one test over another.

3. *Make a list with your student of potential college choices.* How do you come up with these choices? Start with location. Does your student want to attend a school in-state or out of state? A four-year school or a two-year school? Based on interests and location, do an Internet search to see what

is available and what tuition costs are. Gather as much information as possible about the schools that offer the areas of study in which your student is most interested.

Franklin, our fourth young adult, had a prerequisite for his future college of choice. If a college didn't have a hockey team or hockey club, he was not interested in looking at it. He also was looking for a college in Tennessee. Believe me; those two requirements narrowed the field immensely.

4. Once you have a list of schools in which you and your student are interested, *contact the admissions office* of each school to set up a time to visit the campus. This can easily be done via e-mail or online. There is nothing like a campus visit to give you a feel for the true spirit of the school. Brochures are nice to look at, but they don't tell the whole story. While on campus, talk to a professor or department chairman in your student's primary area(s) of interest.

When my son, Taylor, was looking at colleges his junior year, he was interested in engineering and medicine primarily. He also wanted to stay in Tennessee, and he was looking for a school that would reward his academic achievements with scholarship money. We visited a school that was known for its engineering department, and it offered substantial scholarships, but we weren't terribly impressed with the faculty member who represented the school's pre-med department.

Another school we looked at together was farther from home, but it offered a very rigorous pre-med program. We found this out through meeting with the chairperson of the pre-med department and doing some of our own research. The school had no engineering programs at all, so Taylor would need to be pretty sure he wanted to pursue medicine if he chose this school. Scholarships were also readily available as a result of his high SAT scores, and ultimately, Taylor chose the second school. I should add that we looked at a third school, but there were things about it Taylor didn't like, so we crossed that one off during his junior year.

Do you see the process there? By visiting campuses during the junior year, your student has a chance to think about the various aspects of each one without the pressure of having to make a decision within a few months' time. There are so many scholarship deadlines during the fall of the senior year that it is extremely helpful if the student already has an idea of where he would like to attend by the beginning of the senior year.

Take your time in the junior year to look around at potential schools. It's kind of fun, too. You may want to re-visit a campus or two during September of the senior year just to be sure. Choosing a college is a major decision, but you and your student will *just know* when you find the right one.

Remember, if you visit several schools in the spring of the junior year, you'll have time to go back and make another visit in the senior year if desired. If you have other high schoolers who are younger than your junior, be sure to drag them along for the campus visit as well. It is never too early for a high school freshman or sophomore to be reminded of why he is working so hard in high school.

Check out each college's scholarship information and deadlines for scholarship applications (which will arrive before you know it). I like to put these deadlines on my fall calendar while I am thinking of it. Have the student put any deadlines on his calendar as well.

5. The final thing I do with my high school junior is to *look over the high school transcript thus far and compare it against what needs to be accomplished before graduation.* We use an umbrella school which recently started sending a transcript to parents in the junior year and highlighting any courses that need to be taken before graduation. It is extremely helpful to have this kind of information before the senior year is upon you. You don't want to get into the senior year and find out the student is lacking some requirements that you didn't know were necessary. Thoroughly check your student's list of completed subjects against your state's graduation requirements to ensure that next year holds no surprises in the credits department.

6. *Tell your student how much you are going to miss him and beg him not to leave.* Just kidding. High school graduation is a wonderful beginning for your student, but it also means an ending to a chapter, which is bittersweet for those left behind at home.

Senior Year Sanity Tips

The senior year can be a little on the stressful side if your student is college bound. Here are two ways I have found to cut out much of the stress:

1. Do as much stuff in the junior year as possible. This includes going college shopping as mentioned in the section above, and have a good idea where the student would like to attend. Plan for your student to have taken the SAT or ACT more than once in the junior year, if not earlier.

2. The second stress-buster for the senior year is to use a calendar and write down all deadlines for tests, scholarship applications, and of course the college application itself. You will thank yourself over and over again if you do this step.

Because each state is different, make sure your senior is on track to meet all the necessary graduation requirements, and check out his transcript if you are with an umbrella school. If you prepare the transcript yourself, make sure it is ready to send off to universities during the application process. Admissions departments will happily take a look at the transcript through the first semester of the senior year. If your student is accepted to the college of his choice, they will request a final copy of the completed transcript once your student graduates.

Scholarships and Financial Aid

Usually colleges and universities have fall deadlines for scholarship applications which include applications to honors programs as well. Keep those deadlines on a piece of paper on the refrigerator if you must!

Not only are all states different in the types of scholarships they offer to students who earn a benchmark score on the SAT or ACT, but colleges and universities also have various types of scholarships that may be applied for. Don't forget to ask about these if you make another trip to visit a school of choice the senior year. Another option is to research scholarships online at the school's website. Athletic scholarships are a whole different ballgame, as the requirements vary from division to division. The school will most likely offer *merit-based scholarships* which are based on GPA and College Board test scores, for example, and *need-based scholarships* which are based on financial need. There are also private scholarships available, and I highly recommend searching the Internet for funding sources. Since this is not a book on college entrance information specifically, I will not go into detail because there is just so much out there via Google.

There is, however, one main government financial aid website to which almost all colleges desire that students apply, and that site is the FAFSA portal: Free Application for Federal Student Aid. Be sure that you use the official web address, as there are businesses out there who purportedly file the FAFSA for you. I do not recommend using these sites. Filling out the application is simple once you have your current tax information in front of you. Visit www.fafsa.ed.gov to apply for federal student aid.

When you file the FAFSA, you are applying for a wide variety of scholarships, grants, and state aid all in one fell swoop. Also available are low-interest student loans. I recommend visiting this site to familiarize yourself with this important option.

Here is an important tip for you: your high school senior can file his FAFSA as soon as January 1st of the year he will be going off to school. He will file using your tax return information from the previous year since obviously, you haven't filed your taxes for the current year yet since it is only January 1st. After your taxes are done for this year, then he can go back in and file a correction.

The earlier you file the FAFSA, the better, as some student aid programs are based on a first-come, first-served basis. In other words, file ASAP in order to ensure that the student is at the head of the line. If you wait until you have your taxes prepared for the current year, it may be too late to receive some federal grants, as the money may have run out.

Filling out the FAFSA online determines your student's eligibility for federal student aid. As I said, many state programs such as grants and scholarships are figured through your student's FAFSA application. The government will report your financial information directly to any school you list on the application. This is a kind of one-stop shopping, but there will be other aid sources. Check with your local home education support group or websites online to get advice on specific scholarship information that is pertinent to your state.

If what I just told you didn't make any sense, here is an illustration that may help. As of January 1st of this year, 2011, Franklin filed his FAFSA information online. He is going to be a freshman in college in the summer/fall of 2011, so this was the first day he could apply for scholarships via FAFSA online. Because my husband and I had not filed our taxes yet for the year 2011, Franklin used our tax information from last year. Then when we *did* fill out our tax return for 2011 (a month later), Franklin went back to the FAFSA site and filed a correction.

This is precisely how the government has set up the FAFSA system to work. There is nothing illegal about it. Few people are aware that one does not have to wait until the current year's return has been filed before their college-bound senior files his FAFSA information. This means your student is ahead of the game and in the front of the line for scholarships and other financial aid.

Once your high school senior has sent off the scholarship applications, the college applications, and he has filed the FAFSA information, you really can relax. The work is over! Of course there is graduation to plan for down the road, but I have found that the first semester of the senior year is the busiest with so many decisions to be made. Usually by December we have sent in all applications and the waiting begins. The second semester of the senior year is much calmer. But the fall is rough. Be prepared for things to be busy, but if you're prepared, everything should go smoothly.

Some colleges have a rolling admission process whereby they will accept applications up until the summer following a student's high school graduation or even later. However, the best scholarships usually are awarded by December of the senior year, so be prepared to apply early if you are looking for the maximum amount of cash for college.

If college is not in your high school senior's picture, then the senior year will be considerably more relaxing. Continue to support your student and enable him to get a good snapshot of his or her abilities. Help him find a way to get where he ultimately would like to go. If he is interested in a technical college, research this as well in the junior year. Visit the campus. Ask questions. Plan ahead.

What About CLEP Tests?

My experience with CLEP tests is very limited. We haven't used them at all, and for good reason; I'll explain that statement in just a minute. First, let's look at what these tests do and don't do for the college-bound student.

To start with, CLEP stands for College Level Examination Program, and it is a program run by the College Board folks. The idea is to study for any one of thirty-three exams in five subject areas, then take the CLEP tests to "CLEP out" of classes in college (if the student's score is high enough, that is).

CLEP exams are seventy-seven dollars each, but there is also a testing center fee to add in which is not standard. I've seen fees listed anywhere from fifteen to twenty-five dollars by testing centers, so there is a hefty monetary investment involved *per test*. Keep in mind that these fees do not count the cost of the prep material. Yes, I think it is an expensive process. However, if your student can get college-level course credits, you are saving him the cost of credit hours at the university level.

Another thing to keep in mind is that not all colleges grant credit for CLEP exams, so make sure you check with the colleges your student is interested in attending to find out if your student can indeed test out of lower-level courses in the freshman year.

Another thing to consider is that if your student enrolls in the honors program at his college, he most likely will not even need to take lower-level classes in the first place. He'll be taking the honors courses which generally he cannot test out of anyway. Many universities will not even require a freshman to take lower-level courses if his ACT/SAT test scores are high enough. For these reasons, my first three high school graduates did not even have to take a single lower-level course their freshman years in college, so CLEP tests would have been a waste of their time and my money.

In Franklin's case, he didn't score quite high enough on his ACT to test out of pre-calculus, but he wanted to take the lower-level pre-calculus class anyway as a refresher during his freshman year in college. Factor in that he has scholarships to cover his tuition, and taking lower-level classes costs him nothing out of pocket anyway. So for all of my first four kids, CLEP tests were not worth doing. But if your student does not think he will get high enough scores on the SAT/ACT, and if the schools he is interested in will accept CLEP scores, you may want to look into having him take a couple of them.

I recommend that if your student studies for the CLEP exams and takes one or more of them, have a very good reason to do so. He may not need them his freshman year, depending on his SAT/ACT scores, and especially if he will be enrolling in his university's honors college. Why waste time and money if you don't have to?

AP Exams

What is the difference between the AP and the CLEP? First of all, AP classes are offered at many public and private high schools. These classes are advanced in the sense that they are designed to simulate the difficulty level of the freshman college classroom. At the conclusion of a year-long high school AP class, a student may take an AP exam—for a small fee, of course. The fee for each AP exam is eighty-seven dollars. Individual colleges and universities decide for themselves how much credit they will give to incoming students based on the AP exam score. Remember, in order to take the AP exam, you have to take the AP course first.

Taking the AP or CLEP exams may be worth your student's time to take, but don't just take them for the sake of taking them. Look at the colleges which your student is interested in attending. Find out what their M.O. is regarding these exams. Find out if course credit can be given for ACT or SAT scores in the first place, making the additional testing unnecessary for your student if he already has high enough scores on these tests to opt out of freshman-level classes. In my opinion, unless there is a good reason to take the APs and CLEPs, don't worry about them. In some cases, however, they may be necessary. It all depends upon the policies and academic criteria of the university your student wishes to attend.

Dual Enrollment

Taking classes at a local college as a junior or senior in high school can earn your student high school and college credit at the same time. That is just what dual enrollment is: taking actual college classes as a high school junior or senior. Most often, community colleges offer dual-enrollment options to students; however, some public and private colleges offer the option as well. Dual enrollment is also available online through distance learning programs.

Dual enrollment costs you money. You pay for credit hours just like you would for college because it *is* college. Dual enrollment will help your student begin accumulating college credits while still in high school, but again, make sure there is a good reason to do this. Ensure that the classes your students take in the dual enrollment arena are challenging. However, if they are too challenging, the student's transcript will reflect the struggle.

Distance Learning

Remember correspondence courses? My husband studied cartooning via a correspondence course back in the day. The way correspondence courses worked was you would receive your lesson via the U.S. Mail; you'd do the lesson, and mail back your work. The teacher would correct it, and your work—along with the next lesson—would be sent on to you. It used to take quite a bit of time to learn via correspondence courses.

Enter the computer age, and today correspondence courses are pretty much obsolete. Distance learning has taken its place. Learning in a virtual classroom via the computer is growing by twenty percent each year. It is the wave of the future but available now. If you like the concept of being able to earn your degree from your laptop at home, distance learning is for you!

I've earned several professional certifications through Notre Dame's distance learning program. A lot of the content was presented via online videos followed by online exams. I loved it and look forward to perhaps getting another degree this way in the near future. However, I prefer that my college-age students get the full college experience on campus. There is a richness and depth of experience to brick-and-mortar education that I want my kids to experience for themselves. Not all parents feel this way, and I totally respect that. If you would like your students to have a minimum of college campus experience, distance learning is an excellent option.

Finally, if you are interested in learning more about distance learning, a great book to guide you is entitled, *Accelerated Distance Learning*, by Brad Voeller. Brad's book is an excellent resource guide for both you and your college-bound student.

Summary

AP courses, CLEP exams, dual enrollment, and distance learning options are just that—options. I have not utilized any of the above aside from distance learning, and I am not sorry. That's not to say we won't ever use the others. Every student is different. If there is ever a need to use any of the options we've discussed, by all means I'd use them. But don't stress yourself over them, thinking that you could not home educate through high school because you don't want to mess with figuring all of this out on your own. There's a plethora of resources right at your fingertips via Google when the time comes to think about college prep.

Speaking of college prep, if you have high schoolers and they are college bound, I highly recommend a company called CollegePlus. I know many parents who have used CollegePlus to guide their students in accumulating college credit while in high school. They even assist freshmen and sophomores with a program called CollegePrep. There are probably other cool programs like this in existence, but CollegePlus also has a heart for families, which I think is unparalleled in the industry.

Helping Your Student Uncover His Areas of Interest

Sometimes it will be very clear to a high school student what he would like to do with his future, and that is wonderful. But don't be discouraged if your high school junior or senior does not have a clue as to what he would like to pursue in college.

One of the most important things we can do for our children—beginning when they are in ninth or tenth grade—is to help them identify their interests and areas of giftings. We touched on this a little bit earlier, but it bears repeating. The beauty of home education is that we can expose our kids to a variety of experiences both at home and via field trips. Job shadowing is a great option for students who want to experience an area of interest out in the real world.

Only one of my first three kids knew what he or she wanted to pursue as a major before entering college. The other two took a little while to decide. All had their own particular interests, and talking with them periodically about what they would like to do—or not like to do—was invaluable to them in the decision-making process. Young adults still need a degree of parental perspective to see themselves clearly.

Nicholas was clearly interested in debate and perhaps law, he thought. But in his senior year of high school, he got a guitar, and he developed an interest in music, especially songwriting. He ended up attending Belmont University as a music business major. Now that he has finished that degree, he is currently applying to law schools. He took the LSAT (law school entrance exam) and scored a 174/180, which puts him in the 99th percentile. Now the process of applying to several different law schools begins as he takes a hiatus from schooling.

Lauren, on the other hand, was pretty sure that she was interested in working towards some sort of English degree. She ended up majoring in English with a writing emphasis. She is a senior at the moment, and she is very happy and comfortable in her major. She had written one book and had started a second one before leaving for college. She is an excellent writer, and she has remarkable business acumen. She has her own website, as I mentioned earlier, where she sells beads and other jewelry-making supplies. She is quite the entrepreneur. If you're interested, you can visit her website by going to BeadBoxBargains.com. Tell her I sent you.

Taylor is a sophomore in college, and his major is pre-med at the moment. Remember reading earlier in this chapter that he and I were visiting and re-visiting three different schools, weighing the college options during his junior and senior years in high school? Taylor's talents are quite obviously in logic, science, engineering, and mechanics. He considered studying civil engineering for a while, and then he thought perhaps something in the medical field would suit him. Tim and I totally agreed with that conclusion, as he is very calm under pressure of blood and injuries and all of that. He has had plenty of practice coming to my parental rescue when one of his siblings was sick or injured, or even if one of our animals needed attention. Taylor never seemed to be squeamish or flustered.

Taylor thought he would like to shadow a dentist for a couple of days, so we did that the second semester of his senior year in high school. By this time, he was fairly certain he wanted to look at being a dentist or going into some type of medical field. We re-visited one university in particular to check out their pre-dental and pre-med programs. It was this campus visit—sitting in on an advanced chemistry class and talking with the department chairman—that clinched it in his mind. From that moment on he knew what university he wanted to attend.

By the second semester of his freshman year in college, Taylor ruled out dentistry in favor of pre-med. While he is not sure what kind of medicine he would like to practice, he has narrowed down his options a bit. In the summer of 2012, Taylor will have the opportunity to go to Guatemala to do volunteer work with a medical mission team from his university. What a cool opportunity to look forward to!

When comparing colleges the senior year, make sure you check out all of the fringe benefits of attendance at various schools. As students at Lee University in Cleveland, Tennessee, Lauren and Taylor must complete an intercultural experience before graduating. Lauren had the opportunity to study biology in Australia for three weeks in the summer of 2011, and Taylor, as I said, will be going to Guatemala in 2012. Franklin hopes to study in Finland or Sweden during his college career, so we checked out the Study Abroad program at the University of Tennessee. It offers programs in both Finland and Sweden. Additionally, Nick spent three weeks in Moscow following his junior year via an on-campus club he founded at Belmont. The travel and study options available at many colleges and universities today are phenomenal!

The college experience can be broad and rich. While colleges and universities have their shortcomings, they also offer valuable life experiences for students who want to get the most out of their four years of higher education.

Start at the End, Work Backwards

How does a parent help a high school student figure out what direction to take after high school? One of the best ways to map out a path for post-high-school life is to ask your student what he would like to do if he could do anything. Be prepared for some interesting ideas to be shared.

Our fourth child, Franklin, was the first of our kids to ever ask Tim and me, "Why do I have to go to college?" Yes, that surprised us a bit except for the fact that my husband and I were well acquainted with Franklin's passion. He had been playing hockey for less than two years, and had only been at his position of goalie for a year, yet he truly wanted to play serious hockey and work his way up the chain. His question about college was disturbing to Tim and me at the time, quite honestly. It's not that we didn't think he could reach his hockey goal (no pun intended), but having just played his position for over a year, it would be pretty tough to get to play on a decent college hockey team.

Franklin didn't seem to have any particular career interests other than semi-pro sports, or ideally, pro sports. However, in our educational co-op in the fall of his senior year, Franklin took a *Programming in C* computer class, and he really enjoyed it. He was challenged, yet he reveled in the challenge. This type of programming seemed to come easily for him even though it was a tough course. At last! A career direction!

I think Franklin got a little frustrated with me during his junior and senior years for continually asking him every now and then if he had thought about what college he wanted to visit. Whenever I would ask him, the answer always was, "Not really." Finally I asked him what he would like to do if he could do anything. His answer was not just to play hockey, but it was to play hockey in Sweden. Yikes! Why couldn't he choose something normal? But that was at least something to go on.

I said, "Okay. I can understand that. But how are you going to get there?" I was asking him what steps he thought he could take to reach that goal so we could work backwards. Of course he had to think, and I did some thinking and some research online into colleges in Sweden. I learned that the University of Tennessee in Knoxville has a great cross-cultural program, and one of the study abroad programs was in Sweden! Imagine my surprise when we did a little more research and learned that while they didn't have an SEC hockey team, they did have a serious hockey club. I reported this to Franklin, and he thought it might be worth a trip to Knoxville to check out the school.

So we went. We met with several guys from the hockey club, and we learned that they were intertwined with a semi-pro hockey team that played in Knoxville as well. That meant that if Franklin got into the hockey club and worked really, really hard, he would have a chance to get noticed by the semi-pro club. Incidentally, UT also has a great computer science program, and they are preparing to open a brand new facility for this area of study. We left the UT campus that day feeling very much like Franklin had found a place that had everything he was looking for, and it was still in-state where tuition would be lower than at an out-of-state school.

Can you see how in Franklin's case, we took what he was interested in—where he saw himself down the road—and we took what his passion was, looked around, and prayed for something that would meet the uniqueness of our son? And we found it. (Special note: As of January 2012, Franklin is the starting goalie on the University of Tennessee's hockey team. Not bad for a freshman.)

If you have a high school senior who needs some guidance about interests and future plans, continue to ask your student where he sees himself after high school. How can he get there? How can you help him get there? Setting goals can be an excellent thing if there is a way to reach them. Start with the end in sight first, and then ask yourself, "How can my young adult get to this spot?" Working backwards is the key.

Each one of your children will be different. There is no such thing as a cookie-cutter education in Home Education Land. It's amazing, isn't it, that we have the freedom to be with our children, to enjoy them, and to help them find their way in the world? What a blessing!

It is very important that children move in a direction in which they are comfortable. As parents, we don't want to push our young adults in a particular direction because *we* think it is best. Pushing does not bear good fruit. The decision about where to go to college—or what path to pursue if not college bound—should be a joint effort with the student buying into the final decision. If the student isn't excited about his next step after high school, he will have a difficult time motivating himself when the going gets tough. Remember though, we have raised our children to make good choices. If we have a respectful and close relationship with our young adults, assisting them in determining the next step in their post-high-school journey will be a joy and privilege!

Parent's Corner

1. Do you or your spouse have any reservations about home educating through the high school years? If so, make a list of your reservations. Talk to someone you know who is home educating through high school, or better yet, talk to several people who are home educating their children through high school.

2. There are hundreds, maybe thousands, of websites online that can be of assistance to you in the high school years. If in doubt, find out. Do your own research and by so doing, you'll be demonstrating self-learning skills to your children.

3. When should you begin preparing for college with each of your college-bound students?

4. Just a reminder to keep good records. Know your state's high school graduation requirements by the end of your child's eighth grade year.

CHAPTER 11

CALDERWOOD KIDS SPEAK

*The object of education is to prepare the young
to educate themselves throughout their lives.*
—Robert M. Hutchins

I would love to have you come on over to our house and sit a spell. It would be so lovely to meet you and your family. Wouldn't that be fun? In this chapter I am going to welcome you into the minds of my offspring. That's a scary thing for any parent to do. And after seeing what's inside those minds, you may rethink your plans to visit. Well, hopefully not, but here's to transparency.

I'd like to start off this chapter by sharing with you an excerpt from an interview with my oldest daughter, composed in 2008, when she was a senior in high school. It was first printed in *Home School Enrichment* magazine. I hope you enjoy a little peek into her life as a self-propelled student.

A Student's Take on Self-Teaching

My name is Lauren Lindsay Calderwood. I am 17 years old, a senior in high school, the second oldest of eight siblings, and an aspiring author, avid reader, and entrepreneur. My mom, Joanne Calderwood, is a popular speaker at conferences across the country, where she addresses the topic of self-teaching. I often come along on these trips, during which I am usually asked the same set of questions by quite a number of people wondering just how self-teaching differs from "traditional" home education and what my personal views on this subject are. Even those who have listened to Mom's workshops often come by our booth to get a student's take on this method. I have gathered the questions most often asked, and I present them here along with my answers.

First off, what exactly is self-teaching?

Well, strangely enough, it means I teach myself! My mom gives me the books: for example, my current textbook on psychology. I take the book, read it, follow the instructions, and do all the coursework necessary to learn the material. I proceed at my own pace until I have finished the book. That's pretty much it! My mom knows I am perfectly capable of doing this without her constant supervision; I can learn things on my own, without her needing to look over my shoulder or, say, read my chemistry text aloud to me to make sure I understand it. If I have any questions, or if there's anything I don't understand, I am free to research the issue on my own.

While I know I can always go to my parents for help, I can usually find the answers myself using various resources. My good friend, Google, almost always helps me out. The beauty of self-teaching is that I *can* learn on my own, and it's a much more efficient and motivating way to learn.

I tend to get more work done in a day when I assign the workload than when Mom assigns it to me. No one is telling me how much or how little to do; how quickly or how slowly to do it. I'm learning at my own pace, and this motivates me to do my very best. Surprisingly, I find myself able to go at a much faster pace when I do it voluntarily.

Being forced to do two math lessons in a day isn't fun; deciding to do an extra lesson because you want to finish your book sooner makes that second lesson a lot easier to stand. It's a strange but true element of the human mind, or of my mind, at least.

How long have you been self-teaching?

I have been self-teaching since about the fourth grade when my mom was so busy trying to teach and care for our rapidly growing family that she just didn't have time to constantly supervise all of our schoolwork. Consequently, she focused her attention more on the younger children, allowing the older ones to start doing more and more work on their own. She soon realized we were not only capable of making this transition, but we were also mighty enthusiastic about making it.

Do you prefer self-teaching versus your mom acting as your teacher?

My answer to this question is always a very definite yes! I learn more in less time, and I have a real freedom with my own work schedule. Mom and I sit down at the beginning of each year to plan which courses I need to complete, which subjects I need to study, and which extracurricular activities I should get involved in. I set goals for myself, for example, "Get to Lesson X in Physics by the end of 1st Semester." Then, when I know what I need to get done in a year, I write out weekly work schedules and pace myself appropriately. I often find I exceed the goals that I've set for myself.

The driving force behind this method of education is my own desire to learn and succeed rather than the desire that a parent or teacher has for me to learn and succeed. I believe that this motivation is helped greatly by the fact that I am learning on my own, doing things on my own without someone constantly looking over my shoulder. I am challenging myself, and that's an exciting way to learn!

Do you check your own work? If so, how do your parents know you're really learning the material?

Yes, I check my own work. My parents know my desire to do well, and they trust me to be honest. I'm not adrift by myself in a vast ocean, either; my mom checks up on me at regular intervals, and after each quarter we go over all the work I've accomplished in the last nine weeks.

Another way Mom and Dad know that I'm keeping up to speed and really learning is through my performance on standardized tests like the PSAT, SAT and ACT. Self-teaching helps with these tests, too; through this method of education, you learn to think for yourself, to analyze test questions and to answer them more easily because you are used to working on your own. The exams require a student to reason independently.

Would you recommend the self-teaching method to other students?

If students truly desire to excel in their work and are willing to exercise sufficient diligence and self-discipline then yes, definitely. I love self-teaching because it allows me the freedom to learn independently.

Everyone learns differently; when you teach yourself, you can utilize your learning style to better gain and retain information. For example, when I was doing chemistry, I memorized the table of the elements by making up a very short story that mentioned the name of each element. Alright, so it was a ridiculous story that would never reach the bestseller list, but it helped me learn the elements and pass the tests in my book. I do a lot of things like that, the sort of voluntary assignments I would never do if I learned in a classroom or was taught by anyone but myself.

Self-teaching motivates me to push myself further than I probably would if I had set assignments each day. I don't always love or even enjoy my schoolwork, but I enjoy the feeling I get when it's finished for the day. I also enjoy the feeling of accomplishment when I master a difficult math concept [trigonometry... shudder...] or finish a workbook ahead of schedule.

Do you think self-teaching has helped you prepare for college?

Yes, I do. The ability to think on your own, without having to be spoon-fed knowledge by a parent or teacher, is an invaluable skill useful in high school and in all levels of education beyond that point. Teaching myself has done more than merely enable me to pass high school exams; it has also shown me that if I apply myself, I can learn how to do just about anything I want.

There's a world of information out there, and how much of it ends up in my brain is directly dependent on my effort to get it there.

What are the disadvantages to self-teaching?

Well, the only disadvantage may be the fact that self-teaching requires slightly more effort on the student's part. Maybe it is easier to let your parents arrange your workload and check your work and explain things to you instead of thinking them through by yourself. Maybe it requires less of you as a student to have knowledge tossed at you rather than to pursue it on your own, but in the end, the more "difficult" road almost always produces the better result. You get what you pay for, so to speak. I am convinced that the results of self-teaching are more than worth the effort. I also enjoy learning much more when I'm the one making myself learn. My mom appreciates the load self-teaching takes off her shoulders, and I appreciate the freedom to excel which this method of schooling promotes.

The ability to teach myself has allowed me to do far more than learn math and English skills. For example, I taught myself business skills. I have an online store selling gemstone beads and jewelry-making supplies, which has been successful enough that I quit my fast-food job to work from home, making more money in fewer hours per week.

Self-teaching is an element that carries over from schoolwork into every aspect of my life, giving me a thirst for knowledge, a drive to succeed, and a passion to learn. In this life, you won't always have a teacher to sit you down and explain everything to you. It's nice to know you're able to figure things out for yourself.

Siblings Speak

While writing the *Self-Propelled Advantage*, I asked members of my focus group if they or their children had questions they would like to ask my children about pretty much anything education-related. I received a myriad of responses, some with duplicate questions. I printed out a list of these questions and stuck them on my desk to await the time when all ten of my family members would be present in the same place at the same time. About two months later when everyone was home, I blew the dust off the stack of papers, assembled everyone in the family room, and fired a few rounds of questions at them. Here are answers to the most commonly-asked questions—with one caveat: there may be a tongue-in-cheek response here and there.

Just as a reference, here are the names and ages of my children: Nick (22), Lauren (21), Taylor (20), Franklin (18), Olivia (16), Adrienne (14), Lydia (12), and Lilie (10).

No, I didn't make this stuff up. Here we go.

What do you do if you don't understand the directions in your lesson books (any subject)?

ALL: Read them again.

Lydia: Then ask someone older who has done the book before you.

What leads you to want to actually learn rather than just doing the work to "get it done?"

Franklin: Sometimes you are just following orders.

Lydia: It's just what you do.

ALL: Tests!

How do you balance your work? Do you just work so you can get it out of the way and then you're done?

Franklin: In middle school I would get up and just get all of my work done fast to get it done. But in high school I had fewer subjects. I'd do the hardest ones first.

Lilie: I do my easiest stuff first, and then I can take my time on the hard stuff. I use P.E. as my break from work, and lunch is also one of my breaks.

Taylor: I would alternate the more mentally intensive subjects such as math and physics with the less intense subjects such as history and literature.

Adrienne: I do my harder work first, and I do it all at once.

What motivates you to overcome your weaker areas?

Franklin: I don't try to avoid what I like least. I just do it. I have done tons of things I don't like to do, but it is required, so you have to do it.

Lauren: The fact is that sometimes you are not motivated, and you just suck it up and do it. You have to learn to take pride in doing something well even if it is not something that you enjoy doing.

Nick: I like to be better than everyone else.

Taylor: I am competitive like Nick, and I take pride in my work.

How do you deal with constructive criticism from your parents when they feel you could do something better?

Lauren: Accept it gracefully and process it later.

Adrienne: Suck it up and know they are right.

Have you ever felt overwhelmed by self-teaching?

All: No.

Franklin: Sometimes the material was tough, but not the self-teaching.

Taylor: There is value to having a professor explain things in a college classroom.

What is your motivation for excelling?

Lilie: Everyone doubts me because I am the youngest. I like to stand out.

Lydia: I do my best so that I can move on quickly.

Adrienne: I just kind of do my best. I'm not sure why.

Olivia: My motivation is being the best and earning respect. Another motivation is the satisfaction that I know all of that stuff. If you are well-educated and think well, you can pretty much do anything you want to do.

Franklin: I have to do it; it's required, so I do my best.

Taylor: It has always been assumed that we would do our best, so we do. Accountability.

Lauren: I am a perfectionist. I am dissatisfied with anything but my best effort.

Nick: I like to amaze people.

How many books do you read for fun in a typical month?

Lilie: Three or four big books and lots of smaller books.

Lydia: If it's a month where we get to the library, I probably read five or six because I am a slow reader

Adrienne: Probably around 15 or 16.

Olivia: Six or seven.

Do you plan to homeschool your kids? Why or why not?

Olivia: Yes because the whole environment is so much better; you are free to be learning-oriented, family-oriented, and religion-oriented without dealing with persecution aside from relatives.

Taylor: I would definitely consider it. I can see the value in it. Depending on the circumstances wherever I am living, I would definitely consider it.

Lauren: Yes. I think it provides excellent educational opportunities. Also, I am a control freak, and I don't want other people teaching my kids.

Nick: It depends on where I lived at the time. I would make sure my kids have self-defense training if I don't homeschool them.

What do you like best about being self-taught?

Lilie: It is easy because you don't have to wake up at 5:00 AM. I don't have to be awake early, and I can have my work all done by 1:00 PM. I can take my time if I want to.

Lydia: I can go through as many math books as I want to; nobody stops me. I get to go at my own speed so I can skip a grade if I work hard enough.

Olivia: Mostly, I like going at my own speed and being able to absorb things.

Lauren: Home education gave me the opportunity to follow my interests and my dreams in my free time. I had a lot more free time than if I had gone to a school.

Adrienne: I like what Lauren said.

Questions for the College-Aged Kids

Was it a difficult transition from being at home to being in a classroom situation?

Lauren: Not at all. Lots of students were like, "Oh my goodness, they expect us to do all this stuff outside of class." For me, it was like going from reading the book, to reading the book and having a professor discuss it. Discussion helps retention. For me it was less work than I was used to, and for others it was more.

Taylor: Not really. The ability to learn from a textbook is absolutely invaluable. I used the lectures more as a reinforcement of what I had already read on my own, so I wasn't struggling to absorb it all in a 50-minute classroom session. Unfortunately, sometimes the point of a class is just to certify that you learned the material you were assigned to read.

Nick: No, it was just annoying. If you can't read a freaking book, you should not be in college. Lectures are the biggest, most useless wastes of time in the history of big, useless wastes of time. Discussions are fine; you can get deeper into what you just read.

Do you wish you had dual-enrolled in a community college your senior year?

Nick: Yes.

Lauren: No.

Taylor: It depends. It's a gray area because you never know what credits will transfer.

Franklin: No.

If you could go back and do your homeschooling years over again, what, if anything, would you change? Why?

Lauren: I wouldn't change anything related to academics, but maybe I would have saved up more money.

Taylor: I probably could have thought earlier about what colleges were looking for as far as volunteer hours go, although I didn't need them for scholarships since I had the academic scholarships I needed.

Nick: I would not have slacked off so much my senior year. I probably would have taken physics AP classes or done some dual-enrollment. I had done almost everything academically, so I worked part time my senior year. I would have done something more involved than just working.

My daughter, who will be a senior this year, would like to know how you do so well on the ACTs and SATs. She has taken the ACT three times and still only scored an 18 after studying and preparing a lot using various books.

Nick: A student has to have good basic math skills and reading comprehension skills. You can increase your score by learning to read faster, but having good basic skills is important. Don't do anything test-related twenty-four hours before the exam. Another idea is to try the SAT and see if you test better on it than on the ACT.

Taylor: Know yourself well and your weak areas. If you are not used to thinking early in the morning, then practice getting up early. If you didn't test well, why do you honestly think you didn't do well, and what can you do to remedy the situation before the next exam?

Franklin: You have to know the basics: grammar rules and math, and you have to work well with scientific data. It is always about how fast you can do it.

How did you learn time management?

Lauren: My senior year in high school forced me to learn time management because I was involved in a lot of extracurricular activities. You don't goof off when you have work to do.

Taylor: I watched a video on it.

Nick: It is something you learn as needed. You figure it out as you go.

Was college what you thought it would be?

Lauren: I came to college with the delusion that it is about learning. I found that really it's about earning credit hours and earning a degree. I did my best on everything at first, but you don't have time to do your absolute best on everything; I had to prioritize. I disliked professors giving us busywork: assignments that seemed to have no purpose. It was hard to find other students who shared my values and my faith, but I found a group on campus with kids who did.

Taylor: I overestimated the maturity of my peers (for example, naked Frisbee in the dorm). I believe I was one of the ten percent of guys in the dorm who studied my freshman year. I don't like lectures; I prefer the professor gives me something I can't get from the textbook. Exam review sessions are good.

Franklin: College is not so much about education anymore. It is about job preparation because you have to stand out in a crowd of thousands of people by doing tasks that others refuse to do: homework, and in general just being a good student. Lots of kids aren't willing to be good students.

Nick: Socially speaking college was a more mature environment than I expected, meaning not as cliquish and petty as I thought it might be. Educationally, I found that people pretty much didn't care about classes. But in my honors classes, students took their work seriously. A very small percentage of freshmen actually studied.

I hope you've enjoyed this foray into the hearts and minds of my favorite self-propelled students. If you could be sitting here with us, literally, in our family room, I would send one of the kids out to the kitchen to grab some goodies to pass around. Incidentally, Olivia just handed me a freshly-made oatmeal raisin cookie, my favorite. I'll save you some.

CHAPTER 12

YOUR LEGACY

*If you want to build a ship, don't herd people together to
collect wood and don't assign them tasks and work, but rather
teach them to long for the endless immensity of the sea.*
—Antoine de Saint-Exupéry (1900-1944)

To give our children an advantage, we must do things differently than
most of society does in this day and age when mediocrity is often the
standard of excellence. There absolutely is an alternative to the public-
school mentality so prevalent today which treats each student not as an individual,
but as a test score. I don't know about you, but I am not raising children who are
merely employable. I don't want to raise cogs which fit well into the machine. I
don't want to raise children who think and act just like everybody else. I want
to raise children who think differently and act differently because they have
been raised differently; they have been raised to think independently and work
with excellence.

Our world is getting smaller, but it isn't getting simpler. The United States lags
behind several other countries in areas in which it used to lead, such as science and
mathematics. There is a critical lack of individuals who can come up with complex
solutions to complex problems. Isn't it a good idea to try something fresh and
new, especially when the old and outdated methods of education yield less-than-

spectacular results? Yes, I think so. The self-propelled advantage is definitely fresh, and it definitely yields extraordinary results.

What Are You Seeking?

Beyond providing your children with the best education possible, what do you want for your child or children? Twenty-five years from now, where do you hope your children will be? Literally, do you have a vision for them? Of course we don't know completely because each child will have various decisions to make that, depending on which way they turn, will lead them in one particular direction or another. The decisions they make as young adults are theirs to make, not ours. However, through faithful and careful parenting, we will have developed the kind of relationship where our children actually ask for our advice from time to time.

Your children may be young now, but before you know it, they will be off on their own independent journeys, and the opportunity to spend large blocks of time with them will be a thing of the past. That window of opportunity is only open for about seventeen or eighteen years; then it is not just shut, but it's gone. What will your children take away from their childhood years spent at home?

As parents of young children, it's easy to think that our children will never grow up and move out on their own, but they do. At that point will you, as a parent, become passé in their lives? Unnecessary now? Or will you still be an integral part of their lives despite distance? The answer to that question is up to you. What kind of parent you are right now will—in large part—dictate what kind of relationship you have with your grown children. Will you be proud of the people your children have become, day by day, bit by bit, over time? Will you *like* who they have become?

If you have poured your life into your children, training them well, you will have raised children you not only love but also like. I'm blessed to say that my husband and I don't just love our grown children, we like who they have become. That doesn't mean we approve of everything they do or say, but we enjoy being in their company, and vice versa. Hanging out with my family—including my grown children—is one of the greatest joys of my life! I can only imagine how wonderful it will be to watch my children raise their own children.

What I Would Change

If I could go back to my young-motherhood days, there are a couple of things I would do differently the second time around. The first thing that I would do is laugh more. Much of what I thought was crucial at the time—like having a well-kept house, a pristine yard, a clean car, or simply matching socks—turned out to be inconsequential in the long run and certainly was not worth getting upset about. Children much prefer having a mom who enjoys life instead of one who easily finds things to stress about. Wisdom is recognizing what the small stuff is and not fretting over it. In retrospect, I would give my children the gift of an underwhelmed mom. Of course I cannot go back, but I can walk in what I've learned and go forward. I can choose to be underwhelmed today.

The second thing I would do differently is I would not compare myself with other moms. I wasted a lot of time feeling like I most likely was ruining my children because my husband and I opted to have a lot of them, first of all, and then raising them according to our convictions which meant doing things rather unconventionally. Tim and I spent many hours praying together, asking God for His wisdom in the raising of our family. Nowadays we can see the fruit of our labor, and we're so very thankful that we made the choices that we've made. All that worrying about not looking just like everyone else was wasted time and energy— energy that I wish I could have back for just one hour. Being content, happy, and peaceful in one's particular circumstances is a gift we give to ourselves and to our children. I didn't give this gift often enough.

Now that I'm older and perhaps a little wiser, I see that parents have the power to change the world—one little heart at a time! You don't have to have grown up in a happy home to have a happy home either. If your own family tree is a little droopy and parched, that doesn't mean you can't buck the trend and raise healthy, well-adjusted, smart, caring, responsible, and well-educated children! Give your children the gift of you!

One Final Question

When your children are grown, what will they say you gave them besides food, clothing, and shelter? What would you like their answer to be: love, acceptance, confidence, courage, morals, independence, support, discipline, or tools for success? The answer to this question is your legacy.

This is a very profound question, and I hope that you will take some time to think about what it is you truly want to give your children as a lasting gift that shadows them throughout the course of their lives and affects the way they raise their children.

As for me, I hope my legacy will be that of teaching my children how to fly so that they can soar without me. I hope I have many years ahead to watch them become the people they have been designed by God to be, but whenever I am called Home—be it sooner or later—it is my hope that my children will live each day according to their convictions with faith, hope, and love.

I strongly encourage you to take some time to think about what legacy you want to leave behind in the hearts of your children which they will in turn pass on to their children. When you know what that legacy is, you can live each day instilling your legacy in their hearts—bit by bit, piece by piece.

Our legacy will not be a reflection of what we've done for ourselves. No, a legacy reflects the things we've done for others. While parents often focus their life's work on things outside the home, I urge you to focus your life's work on those inside your home while they are still at home. After eighteen years of faithful planting and pruning and watering, you will reap abundance in many, many forms—not the least of which is lasting relationships with those whom you most cherish.

As a parent, you've been given all the tools you need to raise the particular child or children that you've been given. Think and reflect on your profound role in their lives, and choose the educational course that you know in your heart is best.

Above all, trust your instincts.

BIBLIOGRAPHY

De Posada, Joachim and Ellen Singer. *Don't Eat the Marshmallow...Yet! The Secret to Sweet Success in Work and Life*. New York: Penguin Group, 2005.

Fischgrund, Tom PhD. *SAT Perfect Score: 7Secrets to Raise Your Score*. New York: HarperCollins Publishers, Inc., 2003.

Gibbons, Maurice. *The Self-Directed Learning Handbook: Challenging Adolescent Students to Excel,* San Francisco: Jossey-Bass, 2002.

Hedrick, Joan D. *Harriet Beecher Stowe: A Life*. New York: Oxford University Press, 1994.

Pink, Daniel H. *Drive: The Surprising Truth About What Motivates Us*. New York: Penguin Group, 2009.

ABOUT THE AUTHOR

Born and raised in Summerdale, Pennsylvania, Joanne Calderwood has been working with children for over twenty-five years. She graduated from Geneva College with a degree in elementary education. Since then Joanne has been a youth director, a houseparent at a children's home, a fourth grade teacher, and has borne her own eight children. (Seventy-two months of pregnancy, but who's counting?)

Joanne is the founder of URtheMOM.com, a site designed to encourage and equip parents for the incredibly amazing and taxing job of raising self-propelled children in a couch-potato world. She is a columnist with Home School Enrichment magazine, and is a popular speaker at events across the country. She has been described as a "Mom Magnet" due to her down-to-earth persona and ability to speak to the real issues of parenting in the twenty-first century.

In her spare time Joanne enjoys gardening, drying flowers, and taking naps. Joanne and husband Tim reside in beautiful Normandy, Tennessee, where they educate their crew and try not to disturb the neighbors.

Ways to connect with Joanne:

E-mail her via joanne@joannecalderwood.com.

Friend her on Facebook.

Like URtheMOM.com on Facebook.

Follow her on Twitter @jcalderwood.

FREE AUDIO BONUS

From
Joanne Calderwood entitled:
12 Strategies for College Board Exam Prep NOW!

High test scores on the SAT, PSAT, and ACT don't just happen. Discover the simple things you can begin to do today *with any age student* to prepare for stellar performance on college entrance exams down the road!

Joanne says, "The strategies I reveal on this audio are things I've been doing in my household to prepare my young children for an exciting lifetime of learning, not to specifically prepare them for the SAT. However, the fact that the average of my first four kids' College Board exam scores is in the 97th percentile tells me there is infinite value in the *12 Strategies* that will enhance any child's education for life."

DOWNLOAD YOUR FREE AUDIO AT
www.SelfPropelledAdvantage.com

CPSIA information can be obtained at www.ICGtesting.com
Printed in the USA
LVOW111430130313

324130LV00009B/404/P

9 781614 482963